COLOR IN MY GARDEN

BY LOUISE BEEBE WILDER

My Garden   1916
Colour in My Garden   1918
Adventures in My Garden and Rock Garden   1923
Pleasures and Problems of a Rock Garden   1927
Adventures in a Suburban Garden   1931
The Rock Garden   1933
What Happens in My Garden   1934
Adventures with Hardy Bulbs   1936
The Fragrant Path   1936
The Garden in Color   1937

THE WAY INTO THE GARDEN

*T*HERE *is a gate at the opposite end of the garden and one on each side, but this hallway through the Garden House that we reach by pleasant stages through the Nursery and Herb Garden is the one most commonly used. The fine rose on the Garden House porch is the Lion Rambler. A description of the large bed opposite will be found in Plate No. 16 (July 10).*

THE WAY INTO THE GARDEN
JULY 21ST

PLATE NO. 1   FRONTISPIECE.
SEE PLATE NO. 16.

COLOR
IN
MY GARDEN

LOUISE BEEBE WILDER

COLOR IS THE MOST SACRED ELEMENT
OF ALL THINGS.
—RUSKIN

ILLUSTRATED BY ANNA WINEGAR

FOREWORD BY PENELOPE HOBHOUSE
INTRODUCTION BY LYNDEN B. MILLER

ATLANTIC MONTHLY PRESS
NEW YORK

PUBLISHER'S NOTE

Observant readers will notice (and perhaps be perplexed by) an inconsistency in our edition of Louise Beebe Wilder's classic book. In the early years of this century it was not uncommon in this country to spell the word "color" as "colour," and this certainly was Mrs. Wilder's preference. But since 1918, when *Colour in My Garden* was first published, the standard American spelling has become "color," and the word "colour" is a Britishism, plain and simple. Especially in gardening circles, use of the English spelling says to the American reader: "another English gardening book." That is precisely the impression we wish to avoid regarding Mrs. Wilder, hence our decision to title her book *Color in My Garden* on the dust jacket and title page of this edition.

It was equally our aim, however, to remain faithful to Mrs. Wilder's original text, which we have not altered one iota. Therefore, in the text the word is spelled "colour," as Mrs. Wilder would have had it; only new material conforms to modern usage.

First published in the United States of America in 1918 by Doubleday, Page & Co.
First Atlantic Monthly Press edition, May 1990
Published simultaneously in Canada
Printed in the United States of America

Library of Congress Cataloging-in-Publication Data

Wilder, Louise Beebe, 1878–1938.
[Colour in my garden]
Color in my garden / Louise Beebe Wilder; illustrated by Anna Winegar; with a foreword by
Penelope Hobhouse—1st Atlantic Monthly Press ed.
Reprint. Originally published: Colour in my garden. Garden City, N.Y.: Doubleday,
Page & Co., 1918.
ISBN 0-87113-373-3
1. Color in gardening. I. Title.
SB454.3.C64W55 1990 635.9'68—dc20 89-77939

The Atlantic Monthly Press
19 Union Square West
New York, NY 10003

FIRST PRINTING

Horticulture is, next to music, the most sensitive of the fine arts. Properly allied to Architecture, garden-making is as near as a man may get to the Divine functions.

—MAURICE HEWLETT.

CONTENTS

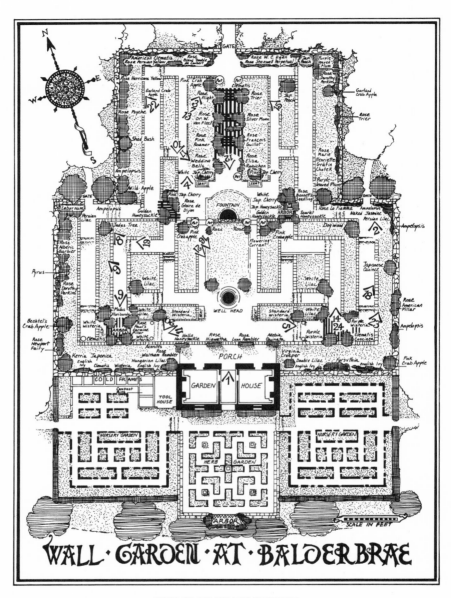

WALL · GARDEN · AT · BALDERBRAE

THE PLAN OF MY GARDEN

The numbers shown on the plan refer to the numbers of the color plates,
and the caret in each case indicates the direction of the view portrayed.
Map drawn by Deborah Dutko after an original by Walter Robb Wilder.

LIST OF COLOR PLATES

FOREWORD TO THE NEW EDITION

PENELOPE HOBHOUSE

I FIRST started reading books by Louise Beebe Wilder in 1986; fortunately, it is never too late to discover a new influence. At the time I much regretted that I had been previously unaware of her contribution to both American gardening and gardening literature (even today, few English gardeners have come across her works). I am glad and excited that this new edition of *Color in My Garden* will make her ideas available to audiences on both sides of the Atlantic.

I would have been grateful for the chance to allow her carefully chosen words and descriptions of garden schemes to sink into my gardening subconscious far, far earlier. I wish I had read her before I attempted to express my own developing thoughts on garden color schemes. Since 1986, her books (I started with *My Garden* and followed up with her masterpiece *Color in My Garden*) have remained on a nearby shelf (beside those of Gertrude Jekyll) for speedy garden-planning reference as well as for writing inspiration. Her work expresses her gardening ideals but is more than an artistic philosophy. She is immensely practical and detailed. It is her intimate descriptions of plant and color associations that remain in the mind, rather than grander overall schemes of bewildering color complexity.

xiii

FOREWORD TO THE NEW EDITION

Louise Beebe Wilder's ideas do not call for slavish copying. Rather, they lead and stimulate; with charming and detailed word pictures they provoke new thoughts. Mrs. Wilder writes only of plants and horticultural practices that she thoroughly understands. Because she grasps and expresses clearly the climatic differences and difficulties involved in translating contemporary English-style gardening for Americans, she has a special value today for the American gardener, the English garden writer who aspires to find readers in America, and for the English home gardener who wants color direction on an intimate scale.

Gertrude Jekyll wrote (mainly between the 1890s and 1930) for an affluent society; it was not uncommon to find twelve or more gardeners employed in gardens of as many acres. Her bed and border schemes, when conceived to cover whole summer seasons, were immensely elaborate — orchestrated masterpieces of color organization that depended on fine gardening skill and many manhours of manipulation daily. For this reason, many of today's gardeners (who have little or no paid help) find her recommendations for individual borders difficult to adapt or indeed even to contemplate. Of course Miss Jekyll also suggested having separate garden "rooms" or areas for each season: a spring garden, an early summer area, the July borders, an August border, Michaelmas daisy borders, and special sections for winter display. This was all very well when gardens were large, but it has little relevance to modern garden spaces.

Mrs. Wilder understood that in the cool English summers many perennials will flower for six weeks; in the hot summers in the United States, flowering periods are fleeting. She catered to these differences and arranged her garden "pictures" so that each was complete in itself. At any one time, some sections of the borders in her walled garden would be temporarily out of bloom although visually sustained by luxuriant and beautiful foliage, while another stretch would be at its peak. She writes, "Often a single section of border may be brought to display three or four pictures" during the summer, but there would be "inset" resting periods. Today, with few gardens — in England or in America — having more than one border area, her seasonal "pictures" are specially relevant on both sides of the Atlantic.

What were Mrs. Wilder's color theories? First, she did not lay down dogmatic principles, but instead worked through the seasons, following in the main nature's own color arrangements: yellow and white early in the year, pink and mauve (rose colors) in June, blues and yellow in midsummer, "which deepen to scarlet, gold, and purple as autumn lavishly spreads the colors." By using these natural schemes, she found much of the work of planning simplified. Sharp primary colors placed side by side cannot mingle harmoniously (she says), yet even that is a question of degree. "A single scarlet poppy will kindle into life a whole sea of dim blue campanulas, whereas an equal mass of scarlet would so outshine the fainter hue as to make it appear poor and dull." How well she expresses herself. Red, scarlet, and yellow are given to us as stimulants, to be enjoyed as vivid experiences, while blue, green, and violet are restful and reparative, to "make up the beautiful commonplace of our daily seeing." Her advice to "be less lavish" with color strikes a chord of sympathy; how frequently such an admonition is ignored to the detriment of good garden effects.

Do read *Color in My Garden* for inspiration and then adapt and even duplicate many of Mrs. Wilder's detailed plant associations. Skilled in horticulture and a real plantswoman, she only recommends plants as neighbors that will grow happily in similar situations. For spring try "bold clumps of gorgeous crown imperials (*Fritillaria imperialis*) standing out against the soft white skirts of...*Spiraea Thunbergii*." Scatter scarlet tulips "crowding between crimson peony shoots" under the boughs of crab apples. A June border is planted with flowers in lavender, mauve, pink, rose, lilac, orchid, violet, and heliotrope — all colors named for flowers — and is exquisite with foundation planting of varieties of lupins. Like Miss Jekyll, she loves to improve a blue border by introducing the orange Herring lily (*Lilium bulbiferum* var. *croceum*) or adding white, cream, or the pale yellow of evening primrose. She suggests growing the hardy American native *Veronica virginica*, with its gray-white tapering flower spikes, next to scarlet phlox and dark blue aconitum for August effects in rich, heavy soil. It would be equally at home behind the double orange day lily (*Hemerocallis fulva* 'Flore Pleno'), which thrives in similar conditions.

These examples are only vignettes of Louise Beebe Wilder's many garden suggestions, glimpses of a true garden artist's sure sense of occasion that remain as fresh and useful today as when they were first formulated.

INTRODUCTION TO THE NEW EDITION

LYNDEN B. MILLER

LOUISE Beebe Wilder's books — written between the end of World War I and her death in 1938 — are as relevant and exciting for today's gardeners as they were for her many contemporary followers. In the early years of this century, a time of extraordinary excitement and invention among American gardeners and garden writers, Louise Beebe Wilder was widely recognized for her inspired writing, her profound horticultural expertise, and the sage yet sensible advice her many books conveyed. Her works are still much admired by those few gardeners fortunate enough to have access to horticultural libraries or book dealers specializing in out-of-print gardening titles. Given today's enormous (and still growing) interest in gardening in this country, it is both fitting and timely that her wonderful writing and knowledge of plants be brought back into print for the enjoyment of everyone who loves gardens.

It is especially appropriate, in light of today's interest in the artful blending of colors in the perennial border, that *Color in My Garden*, originally published in 1918, be made available once again. *Color in My Garden* describes with great delight and detail a year in the life of Balderbrae, Mrs. Wilder's walled garden near Suffern, New York. After reading Mrs. Wilder's suggestions for plant combinations that are practical and hardy in North America, there need be no more sighing for the delicious-sounding perennials possible only in Great Britain's mild climate or the large-scale planting schemes possible only with the aid of fourteen hired gardeners. Best of all, Louise Beebe Wilder's descriptions of her plants and how to grow and combine them are so charmingly vivid and mouth-watering that they will cause a rush of adrenaline in even the laziest of Sunday-afternoon gardeners.

The original edition of *Color in My Garden* was replete with lovely illustrations made under Mrs. Wilder's direction during a single season at Balderbrae, and this new edition reproduces them all. In many instances, several illustrations were made of the same corner of the garden in different months. From them it is easy to see how the garden changed and developed throughout the year, as Mrs. Wilder orchestrated a succession of bloom, with new flowers blossoming as others faded.

Color in My Garden is really a book by an artist whose medium is not paints but plants. Although an extremely knowledgeable and accomplished plantswoman, Mrs. Wilder was interested in far more than collections of plants. "No occupation known to me is so absorbing as the distributing and arranging of flowers in the garden with a view to creating beautiful pictures," she says.

Some things, it seems, change little: in the younger years of this century we Americans looked just as eagerly to England for models for our horticultural aspirations. But Mrs. Wilder, while she was well versed in English gardening ideas and corresponded with her contemporaries there (among them Gertrude Jekyll and William Robinson), recognized just how far

INTRODUCTION TO THE NEW EDITION

English models could be followed in American gardens. She gets right down to business by explaining the chief difference between gardening here and in Great Britain: climate. Partly, we in North America have much colder winters, but we also suffer much hotter summers. Mrs. Wilder points out that flowers do not last in bloom here nearly as long as they do in England, where summers are gentler. The result is that it can be extremely difficult to achieve the blazes of color over long periods that she (and we) read about in English gardening books. Since every gardener at times believes that nature is being unduly unkind to him, it is comforting to learn how well Mrs. Wilder understood (and accounted for) the "brutal eccentricities of our climate." She explains from first-hand experience how perennials and annuals behave in our gardens and how to achieve the spectacular effects for which we long.

After quoting Miss Jekyll, who even in England advocated different gardens for different seasons to achieve best results, Mrs. Wilder points out that this will only work for those with very large places. She advocates instead a "series of pictures to follow each other closely," and this is exactly what *Color in My Garden* describes. Her intention is to "choose and combine plants so that at no time from early March to November shall the garden be without a number of lovely pictures, each complete in itself, and that such sections of the borders as are temporarily out of bloom shall be so constructed that their fullness and freshness shall be maintained by luxuriant and beautiful foliage." Undoubtedly this should be the goal of everyone who wishes to garden well no matter how large or small the plot, but as anyone who has gardened for even one season will know, accomplishing it is no mean task. The great value of this book is that Mrs. Wilder tells us with great energy, enthusiasm, sophistication, and detail exactly how to go about creating a mixed border of beauty and interest from March's first bulb to November's last fallen rose petal.

But best of all, reading *Color in My Garden* would be a pleasure even if you knew nothing about gardening, for Louise Beebe Wilder delights in her work, relishing even the names of her plants, and gets quite carried away by her love for them. So vivid and original are her descriptions that one can visualize the colors she discusses without aid of pictures. She describes the range of colors of certain tulips as "tender dove colors and tobacco brown, bronze and apricot, curious restrained reds with sudden white centers, dull yellow and terra cotta, crushed strawberry and chocolate, rose-mauve and tawny yellow, orange-scarlet and bronze, gray-brown and violet, plum and gray and many more." Aquilegias are listed as coming in a "variety of delicate tints and shades of old rose, pink, lavender, purple, buff, cream yellow, and a sort of skimmed-milk blue." And when she gets to poppies she says, "My thoughts have been alight with them, my paper stained with their gallant colour, my heart vibrating with their waywardness." With an imagination like this, it is no wonder that she planned herbaceous borders as an artist would paint a canvas.

Like all good gardeners, Mrs. Wilder had strong opinions and was quick to express them. She prefers single flowers, loves phlox in all its varieties, is extremely fond of gray-leaved plants, and suggests using them with "a lavish hand, not dotted about among the gayer colours where their quiet sway would scarcely be felt." She gives a list of annuals that should never be used in a good garden, her "taboo list," which includes caladium, coleus, crotons, and echeveria. She describes a certain aquilegia she doesn't fancy as "having the quaint appeal of a pudgy baby." But most of her opinions are passionately in favor of certain plants, such as kniphofias, or red-hot pokers, of which she is "extravagantly fond." She is also mad about Michaelmas daisies, those hardy asters bred by the English from our native *Aster novae-angliae*. And she devotes a chapter to the color magenta, which she claims has been unfairly maligned by garden designers. She goes on to explain how to use it to good effect with "dim blue, pale buff, sky blue, white, mallow pinks, lavender, and gray foliage."

In her own day, Louise Beebe Wilder was widely read, profoundly influencing the way gardens were made, by amateur gardeners and professionals. Mrs. Wilder herself was the quintessential hands-on amateur. Although she wrote ten books between 1916 and 1938 and scores of articles for *House & Garden*, she is known to have designed very few gardens other than her own near Suffern and in Bronxville, New York. She was content to experiment and perfect her own ideas on her home turf. There she observed how perennials behave in every season and condition; then, with a thorough command of her subject and the written word, she invited her readers into an enchanting world of ideas that contains equal measures of underlying principles and practical particulars.

Louise Morris Beebe was born in Baltimore on January 30, 1878, the daughter of Charles Stuart and Mary Harrison McCormick Beebe. As a child she spent many an hour in her parents' garden and, during summer months, at Beebe Farm in Wakefield, Massachusetts, where her paternal grandparents kept a large garden. Her father was a serious enough amateur gardener to have a small lean-to greenhouse off his library. Louise Beebe Wilder is said to have started her first garden at the age of six; one of the pleasantest memories of her childhood was going with her father to visit a commercial greenhouse not far from her home. She recalled that while the adults talked shop, she delighted in comparing the scents, shapes, and patterns of the abundant leaves.

Louise Beebe married Walter Robb Wilder, of New York City, in November 1902. Not long thereafter, the walled garden that is the subject of her first two books, *My Garden* and *Color in My Garden*, was born. It was one small part of Balderbrae, the 220-acre farm for which Mr. Wilder, an architect, had grand designs. Her husband collaborated with Louise in laying out the enclosed country garden, and he designed and made ornaments and built high stone walls, an elaborate wellhead, and other features in much the same way Sir Harold Nicolson would lay out the bones for the garden at Sissinghurst Castle for his wife, Vita Sackville-West, some twenty years later. (Mrs. Wilder describes planting an all-white garden two decades before Vita Sackville-West created her now-famous white garden at Sissinghurst.) A plan of the walled garden at Balderbrae forms the frontispiece of *Color in My Garden*, and the text and paintings by Anna Winegar refer to corners and particular beds in the garden at various seasons.

Balderbrae was no simple backyard. Besides the main residence there was a garden house with latticework and porches and a passageway that led into the walled garden. To reach the walled garden, the visitor passed through nursery beds, an herb garden, and finally an archway through the garden house. On the center axis of the walled garden were a carved stone wellhead, then a fountain with a series of pools planted with iris and hostas, and at the far end a series of pergolas festooned with climbing roses. Surrounding the central axis, a series of paths led through many borders richly filled with bulbs and countless perennials. Flowering shrubs and small trees were arrayed against the enclosing high stone walls. Plants were selected with an eye to their foliage and form as well as for their flowers.

This book describes all that went on in this magical place and how the plants fit together to make a season-long display. It is the only way to know this exceptional garden, for only fragments of it remain, and they are in private hands and not open to the public.

The Wilders also owned a home in Bronxville, just north of New York City, and there they became part of a thriving colony of artists, writers, and architects. Mrs. Wilder made an ambitious rock garden and wrote many magazine articles and books about the plants she collected and grew, including alpine specimens from around the globe. Living across the street from the Wilders' Bronxville home was the artist Anna Winegar, whose paintings of Balderbrae adorn this book.

During a busy life (she also raised two children), Mrs. Wilder contributed monthly columns to *House & Garden* from 1925 until her death in 1938 and wrote ten books, including *My Garden* (1916), *Pleasures and Problems of a Rock Garden* (1928), *Adventures in a Suburban Garden* (1931), *The Fragrant Path* (1932), *What Happens in My Garden* (1935), and *Adventures with Hardy Bulbs* (1936). T. H. Everett, the author of the definitive ten-volume New York Botanical Garden Encyclopedia of Horticulture and for decades the foremost authority on all facets of horticulture, described Mrs. Wilder as "one of the finest horticulturists of her time and one of the best writers of horticultural books." Mrs. Wilder was well-known on both sides of the Atlantic for her books and articles, and she visited Gertrude Jekyll and William Robinson and many of the finest gardens of Great Britain. Most important of all, Louise Beebe Wilder was a working gardener. She wrote from experience on her hands and knees in her own gardens and not from second- or thirdhand dictums of other authorities.

Although her books enjoyed rave reviews and great popularity in the 1920s and 1930s and went through many printings, each eventually went out of print until none was available except through out-of-print bookstores. Even then, her reputation remained so high that it was difficult to obtain copies.

A word is in order about the nature of this reissue of *Color in My Garden*. Most important, we have not tampered with Mrs. Wilder's text; any mistakes she or her original publisher may have made stand, and plant names (that most ephemeral of all gardening matters) are therefore in some instances out-of-date. But to tamper at all with the original text would be to transgress, and *Color in My Garden* is first and foremost a book to read and absorb, not analyze.

There is more to the original edition than the text. We have, as I mentioned, reproduced all twenty-four original oil paintings commissioned by Mrs. Wilder and executed by her neighbor Anna Winegar. Mrs. Wilder's extensive and fascinating captions are also reprinted verbatim.

INTRODUCTION TO THE NEW EDITION

Ever inventive and cognizant of what would be most useful to the aspiring gardener, Mrs. Wilder also included an appendix in chart form recording, week by week, all the flowers blooming at Balderbrae, listed by color. This chart is invaluable, for at a glance one can learn which plants in which colors bloom concurrently.

Plant names were nearly as interesting to Mrs. Wilder as plants themselves, and in another appendix she lists all the plants mentioned in the text, including not only Latin and common names, but also the charming names her children invented. We have revised this list, for it provided the perfect opportunity to bring the nomenclature of 1918 up to the standards of 1990, so that readers can learn exactly what plants they should ask for at the garden center or send away for from their favorite mail-order nurseries. Hostas, to take one example, used to be called funkias, and many specific names have been changed or modified by botanists deeply concerned with such matters. Even genus names used by Mrs. Wilder have come and gone out of fashion. By looking up in this appendix the names Mrs. Wilder uses in her text, readers can find the names that the plants go by today.

In recent years, many Americans have been able to visit the great gardens of Europe, particularly those of England. Our bookstores are brimming with popular and beautiful books depicting luscious gardens that inspire American gardeners to dizzying heights. Yet I believe that many Americans have a slight inferiority complex about what we can accomplish, thanks in part to learning what is possible in England's gentler climate. With the reissue of her great book, with its original illustrations, fascinating list of plant names, and detailed charts, Louise Beebe Wilder will influence new generations of American gardeners to experiment with the lovely plants she describes so well and to dare to use them to "create beautiful pictures" in their own gardens.

FOREWORD

FOREWORD

The quality of charm in colour is like the human attribute known as fascination, "whereof," says old Cotton Mather, "men have more experience than comprehension." —ALICE MORSE EARL.

IN HIS garden every man may be his own artist without apology or explanation. Here is one spot where each may experience the "romance of possibility," may give free rein to his fancy, and gather his living materials into compositions as gay, as splendid, or as wan as his individual enjoyment of colour dictates. "Parterres embroidered like a petticoat" are for some; gardens tricked out in all the tints and shades of a single colour are for others; still others find their pleasure in a throng of many-hued flowers smiling with the naïveté of an old-fashioned bouquet in defiance of criticism. And there are many like myself who know the delight of seeking to fashion, from the myriad shades and diverse forms laid to our hand, a series of lovely pictures to rejoice the eyes throughout the growing year. No phase of gardening is to me so fascinating as this scheming with flower colours, the more so perhaps that no arbitrary laws may be laid down for our following. Each within his green inclosure is a creator, and no two shall reach the same conclusion; nor shall we, any more than other creative workers, be ever wholly satisfied with our accomplishment.

FOREWORD

Ever a season ahead of us floats the vision of perfection and herein lies its perennial charm.

> "A man's reach should exceed his grasp
> Or what's Heaven for?"

In offering this second book of My Garden to those who held out so warm a hand of welcome to the first, my desire is merely to be suggestive. It is my hope that in these loitering peregrinations up and down my garden paths, following the chancy flight of young Spring along the langourous road of Summer to Autumn's shining house, each may find something that to him is beauty, some happy assortment of flashing hues, an old flower-friend newly companioned, a pleasant use of vine or shrub that gives impetus to his own contriving.

A pen is a poor instrument to chronicle the beauties of a garden, a brush is a better, and Miss Winegar has sympathetically set down part of the pageant of the long season spent within my garden walls. All the paintings were made within the garden in the same year. The fleeing days carried many a charming mood beyond our grasp before it could be recorded, but surely there is enough to show with what simple, friendly flowers a glad garden may be maintained for many months of the year.

LOUISE BEEBE WILDER.

"Balderbrae" Pomona, N. Y.

CHAPTER I
COLOUR IN THE GARDEN

COLOUR IN MY GARDEN

CHAPTER I

COLOUR IN THE GARDEN

Flowers first broke up the prism and made the most subtle portion of our sight.　　　　　　　　　　　—MAETERLINCK.

THE chief concern of the gardeners of old was simply to make things grow. They prized each flower for itself, chose for it the most suited location, and called it by quaint and charming names, but they were not disturbed that its colour failed to harmonize with that of its neighbour. Crimson Peonies elbowed magenta Foxgloves unrebuked, and Tiger Lilies and "purple" Phlox consorted comfortably without censure. Under the care of our green-fingered grandmothers gardens throve and were full of hearty, wholesome colour and searching fragrance; and they breathed subtly the gentle personality of those whose rare leisure was spent in digging and pruning, weeding and dreaming among the plants they loved so well.

We may learn much of patience and tenderness, sincerity and thoroughness from these gardeners of other days and may well seek to endow our gardens with the restful charm of theirs, but we may fairly claim for our own day the great

3

advance that has been made in the decorative employment of flowers—their arrangement and relation in the garden so as to bring about beautiful pictures. Never has the planting of gardens been so effective as a whole; never before have their owners endeavoured to bring to bear upon their work, not only the skill and knowledge of the horticulturist, but the inspiration and taste of the artist.

In our own earliest attempts at gardening we in turn are satisfied with the interest and delight of simply seeing things grow, but there very soon comes a time when a new desire crosses our green threshold. We become obsessed by what John Sedding calls the "malady of the ideal," we are haunted by visions of exquisite colours in perfect harmony, and our aim is henceforth to make the garden a place for broad survey as well as for minute scrutiny; to enjoy, not only the individual flower, but to make the most of it in relation to other flowers.

Of course, as is often the case with artistic pursuits, this new gardening with a view to colour arrangement is by some enthusiasts sadly overdone and degenerates through its extreme exactness of finish into something not far from the mosaic gardening of the Victorian era. A few years ago in England I saw some handsome modern gardens wherein the colour arrangements were so obviously planned and executed according to a pattern that one had no realization of groups of living flowers but looked admiringly upon what seemed a huge and clever scheme of decoration. Such a garden is wonderful as a spectacle but lacks entirely the gay and changeful spirit that is so lovable a characteristic of less-studied gardens. We miss the challenge of the unexpected.

COLOUR IN MY GARDEN

To know that blue is indelibly stained upon this spot and scarlet upon the next, that only devastating frost will dull the yellow glow of another, and that to gather a Rose is to leave a rent in the tapestry, is surely at variance with our most cherished garden ideals.

It is perhaps fortunate that our climatic conditions render this sort of gardening almost an impossibility, so that we must of necessity be satisfied with something much more simple and approachable. On account of the extreme heat and dryness of the American summers, flowers here enjoy a far shorter individual life tenure than in the damper atmosphere of the British Isles. No sooner is a fine display of colour unfolded before our delighted gaze than it is gone, and unless we have planned so that other groups shall at once follow, a flowerless garden is our dour portion. Even in the favoured climate of Great Britain it is not so simple a matter to keep the garden abloom for months at a time. In the introduction to Miss Jekyll's fine book on garden colour she says: "I believe the only way it can be done is to devote certain borders to certain times of year; each border or garden region to be bright for from one to three months."

The reasonableness of this method is of course obvious, yet it seems to me fitted for adoption only in very large places, where a "spring walk" or a "June border" might be contrived in some portion of the grounds that need be visited only at the season of its festival. In a large majority of American gardens there is not space to give up any one part to a single season; that is, without seriously lessening the fine effect of the garden as a whole. When the owner is regularly away from his garden during a certain portion of

the season it is, of course, sensible to make use of plants
that bloom during the period when he is at home to enjoy
them. It would be short-sighted to give space to spring
and autumn flowers if the owner occupies his country home
only during the summer months, or to plant summer
flowers when the family is at home only during the spring
and autumn. But for the average American gardener who
aims to enjoy his garden for six months of the year, or more,
the only feasible practice, it seems to me, is to arrange a
series of pictures to follow each other closely, the number
of these pictures in bloom at one time to be governed by the
size of the garden.

My personal endeavour is so to choose and combine my
plants that at no time from early March to November shall
the garden be without a number of lovely pictures, each complete in itself, and that such sections of the borders as are
temporarily out of bloom shall be so constructed that their
fullness and freshness shall be maintained by luxuriant and
beautiful foliage.

Often a single section of border may be brought to
display three or four pictures, but of course to accomplish
this end one must needs have a fairly exact knowledge of
the appearance, habits, and possibilities of a good many
plants. It is my hope that the explanations accompanying
the pictures may serve to illustrate my own simple method
of procedure and also to show of what easily grown and
familiar flowers very lovely pictures may be created.

The "one-colour" gardens that are at present enjoying
a good deal of favour seem to me satisfactory mainly as
achievements. They are apt to be monotonous in effect,

SPRING CANDLELIGHT
MARCH 28TH

THIS venturesome little climber so bravely flowering in the teeth of March gales is the Naked Jasmine (Jasminum nudiflorum). Too venturesome has it been this year, however, for when a few melting days triumphed over the ice and snow of February the ready Jasmine opened wide many of its buds in grateful acknowledgment of the genial warmth, thus dimming the brightness of the present display.

Below in the border are purple Crocuses and Arabis, where yesterday gleamed Snowdrops and Winter Aconites.

Very soon the crimson points of Tulips will be seen forcing their way up behind the fresh green of a clump of Iris. In the angle of the wall is a Persian Lilac bush with which the bright yellow Tulip Mrs. Moon and the soft buff Intermediate Iris Halfdan create a pleasant group in mid-May.

In late June a few scarlet Lilies (Lilium elegans) appear here; and in early autumn the long branches of sky-blue Salvia uliginosa and pure yellow Helenium autumnale, that are planted behind the Irises, against the wall, again bring this southeast corner to our notice.

PLATE NO. 2

A CHARMING OFFERING OF THE SPRING
APRIL 28TH

*T*HIS *flowery little tree is Pyrus pulcherrima Scheideckeri, a near relation of the more brilliant Pyrus (or Malus) floribunda. On account of its sheltered situation near the warm south wall of the garden it is blossoming a little earlier than is its usual habit. The erect gray foliage in front of it belongs to Iris Queen of May, which is shown in bloom a month later in Plate No 7 (May 21st).*

On the other side of the tree and beyond the vision of the artist mats of lavender Aubrietia and gatherings of pale Star Narcissus ornament the path in lovely harmony with the delicate colouring of the Crabapple blossoms.

For later flower groups vouchsafed by this same bit of earth, see Plates Nos. 7 and 13 (May 21st and July 1st).

PLATE NO. 3
SEE PLATES NOS. 7 AND 13

are seldom truly harmonious, and fail to give the pleasure generally derived from gardens where all colours are blended and contrasted finely and where no lovely flower is shut out because it fails to offer a blue or a pink variety.

It is true that in the natural progress of the seasons we have certain colours predominating at certain periods. The earliest colour scheme of the garden, as of the world beyond its walls, is yellow and white; this is followed by the rose colour of late spring and early summer when fruit blossoms and then Roses adorn the world. Next come the blue and yellow of midsummer which deepen to scarlet, gold, and purple as autumn lavishly spreads the colours. This natural scheme of colour we may modify or accentuate as much as we like, but to choose it as a sort of underlying theme much simplifies our work, since there are always plenty of good and willing flowers decked in the prevailing colours of the season.

No occupation known to me is so absorbing as the distributing and arranging of flowers in the garden with a view to creating beautiful pictures, but each gardener will have his own way of going about it. The enjoyment of colour is, in the garden as elsewhere, entirely a matter of individual feeling and, whatever the result, it is mete that every garden should be a personal manifestation. Whether our desire be toward a whole garden full of vibrant, stirring hues, or whether we turn from all save wistful violets and tender blues, is not nearly so important as that each of us should feel free to express himself—his most extravagant, whimsical, ardent, honest self; to work out his own theories and bring his bit of earth to what seems to him its finest and fittest expression.

In the following pages my desire is simply to be suggestive, and perhaps to show that even in little gardens, by this simple method of picture making, beauty may be enjoyed continuously throughout the season. From the time when a sheaf of golden Willow stems, thrust through crowding Snowdrops, portrays for us the first sweet consciousness of the awakening world, to the last days of the garden's life when, from a sunny crevice in the garden wall, a flashing Snapdragon defies the silver sword and stirs us by its passionate protest there need be no dirth of colour.

A garden writer has recently advanced the theory "that nearly all colours go well together in a garden if only they are thoroughly mixed up." This, of course, is true in that we are conscious of no particularly resounding discords, but I think we desire, and may easily have, more than this negative satisfaction, more than the mere absence of inharmony.

My own feeling in the matter of flower colours is that none is bad if given a happy association, and that few associations are unpleasing if the elements are used in happy proportion. A single scarlet Poppy will kindle into life a whole sea of dim blue Campanulas, whereas an equal mass of scarlet would so outshine the fainter hue as to make it appear poor and dull. Again, white used in broad masses has dignity and a serene beauty, but spotted all about the garden is simply a stirrer-up of factions, setting the flowers against one another instead of drawing them into happy relationships. The strong red, blue, and yellow of the spectrum are the colours most difficult to manage in the garden. These

8

colours are typified in scarlet Lychnis, Coreopsis, and Delphinium King. When these plants are placed side by side there is no hint of harmonious mingling. Each stands too clearly defined. They create the sharpest contrasts possible and to me are not pleasant in association.

The Japanese are very daring in their use of flower colours but there will always be a mediating tone used with the strong ones. Miss Averill* gives us an example of flaming Maple branches and yellow Chrysanthemums "subdued and brought together by the use of autumn grasses that have turned to soft browns and yellow." Without the harmonizing grasses the association of scarlet and yellow would be garish to a degree. The strongest colours may be grouped together to produce great richness of effect if there be some intermediate tone or tones to draw them into agreement.

Frequently different tints and shades of the same colour are delightful in association. The picture facing page 202 shows an ascending scale of pink beginning with the soft pink of Phlox Selma, deepening in the Roses, and reaching a good deal of depth in the Hollyhocks. Tones of yellow, from cream to orange, are effective when brought together, and a touch of scarlet added to such a group gives great brilliance but entire harmony.

I have recently heard it advocated as a short cut to harmony that all red and scarlet flowers be banished from the garden. This, I think, would be sad indeed, for much of warmth and strength, of flash and spirit would depart with them, and our garden would be in grave danger of showing a wearisome suavity. But our effort must be to

*"Japanese Flower Art."

keep these stirring hues from overpowering the weak and from flaunting too obtrusively in certain places.

In Nature, broadly speaking, we find that red and scarlet and yellow are rare, given to us as stimulants, as vivid experiences. They are confined to sunset and sunrise skies, to autumn foliage and to flowers; while the "restful and reparative colours"—blue, green, and violet, as revealed in the sky, the sea, the distance, and the great green setting of grass and trees—make up the beautiful commonplace of our daily seeing. Surely there is a lesson here. The constant perception of broad masses of emphatic, exciting colour would prove severely taxing, yet do we most surely need them here and there to bring out the quality of neutral colour, and to arouse the immobile beauty of the garden to glowing life.

Yellow, orange, and scarlet flowers show to greatest advantage in full sunshine. In shadow they seem to lose much of their flash and vigour; while the reverse is true of lavender, violet, and blue flowers. These in shadow assume a piercing distinctness, while in sunshine much of their colour seems to be scattered among the sunbeams and their outlines blurred. One of the most striking flower colours for shaded places is that worn by the "old purple" Phlox—a rather weak magenta. I have seen great masses of this despised flower growing along the shady roadside in the neighbourhood of some old garden, the mellow soil of which it has shaken from its straying roots, that glowed and shone with a soft radiance almost startling to behold. White flowers are always more pure and beautiful in shadow, and it is one of Nature's beneficent dispositions that there should be many white, lavender, violet, and blue flowers that flourish in shaded places.

Deep purple and dusky violet-blue flowers are of significant value to the creator of garden pictures. Their character is almost that of shadow, and shadow is as important in the garden as upon the canvas or the façade to define the quality of light and to give variety and interest to the composition. All dark-coloured flowers have something of this value, as have dark-leaved shrubs and evergreens and may well be considered with trees and architectural features in the distribution of light and shade in the garden picture.

Someone has said that gardening is an art of observation and though it be true that

"Nature hath meal and bran, contempt and grace,"

no stretch of roadside or meadow, wild hedgerow or breadth of marsh but has some lesson to convey to us of beauty or usefulness. One of these that we in our anxiety for a frost-to-frost display of colour are apt to overlook is the boon of simple green—the intrinsic beauty and value of foliage. The arrangement of our gardens so that there will always be a sufficient amount of luxuriant foliage as a setting and foil for the many-hued flowers is most important yet seldom considered. Fine foliage gives to the garden an expression of freshness and vigour and against it the blossoming groups stand out with power and distinction.

It is said that green is the last colour to be appreciated even by the most aesthetic, and it is significant that the Japanese, who are more sensitive to colour than any other people and unequalled in their flower art, plant whole green gardens wherein few flowers unfold to stir the cool tranquillity. In crowding our colour groups one against the other we do not give ourselves opportunity to appreciate the full beauty of any. "Be less lavish" is often good advice to the gardener.

Some years ago Sir Edwin Arnold, in comparing the flower art of the West and of the East, wrote: "We crowd our blooms and sprays together until they are like the faces of people in the pit of a theatre—each lost in the press; a mass, a medley, a tumultuary throng. The Japanese treat each gracious beauty or splendour of the garden or the pool as an individual to be honoured, studied, and separately enjoyed. Each suggests and shall provide for his eyes a special luxury of line, sufficing even with one branch, one colour, one species, to glorify his apartment and make the heart glad with the wonder and the grace of nature."

CHAPTER II
THE PROBLEM OF THE BARE PLACES

CHAPTER II

THE PROBLEM OF THE BARE PLACES

A gardener is a master of what a French writer calls the charming art of touching up the truth. —JOHN SEDDING.

THE usual garden border is very unequal in its display. There is its budding loveliness in spring, its satisfying June opulence, a sad falling off in July, partial recovery by means of the reliable Phloxes in August, and much general dishevelment in September. This inequality is not caused so much by the failure of flowers as by the failure of foliage. Wherever the foliage is fresh and luxuriant, there the border appears full and well furnished and conveys to the mind a gratifying impression of promise, though there may be no flowers actually in bloom. It is usual, however, after the all-pervading richness of June is past, to find great blank spaces in the borders where spring bulbs, biennials, Lilies, and even some perennials have accomplished their allotted task and taken themselves off; or where plantations of Delphiniums and Hollyhocks, large because we so delight in them, have flowered and been cut to the ground, leaving sorry patches of torn and untidy foliage and yellowing stalks. Many perennials that are very charming while in flower lose all pride in their appearance as soon as flowering is accomplished. They go to seed most untidily, quite lose their figures, and make no effort at all to grow old with dignity and grace, so that theirs is another case to be looked to in achieving our ideal of a garden border fine and full and freshly luxuriant throughout the season.

These bare and unkempt places are very distressing and mar the fine effect of the plants still in the prime of their blossoming. To prevent their occurrence is the most embarrassing problem with which the gardener is confronted. Each of us, however, who goes daily about his beds and borders, bestowing upon his flower tenantry the sort of loving inspection that enables him to foresee and understand their shortcomings, weaknesses, and defections, cannot fail to find out for himself many ways of meeting and solving this problem. My own little artifices are very simple and obvious but withal effective and may help some beginning gardener past those disheartening stages when the blank spaces seem so much more numerous than the full and luxuriant ones.

To attack these difficulties in the order of their occurrence we have first, the desertion of spring bulbs after they have flowered. Ordinarily we plant these in irregular groups near the front of the borders. If, in our enthusiasm, we want the joy of a dozen or so Daffodils in one assemblage or a broad space showing the incomparable colour of the little Grape Hyacinth, so well named Heavenly Blue, we must prepare ourselves for a subsequent bareness of the same dimensions, as grievously afflicting to our gardening souls as the earlier flowering was sweet. But all bulbs submit cheerfully to a ground cover of some lightly rooting trailer or tufted plant; many, indeed, the little ones like Snowdrops and Scillas especially, are benefited and protected by such a provision, for it keeps the delicate blossoms from being spoiled by spattering mud. Planted in the grass they are naturally shielded, but in the borders few of these small things complete their brief span of existence in unsullied beauty.

To plant above small bulbs, I have found very comforting and becoming the Woolly-leaved Thyme (Thymus lanuginosus), with a soft gray surface that makes a delightful setting, and Veronica repens with very small leaves and pale lavender flowers. These two are the most satisfactory, but good also are Sedum album, Gypsophila repens, Mentha Requieni for moist shade, Lotus corniculatus, Herniaria glabra and Kennelworth Ivy (Linaria Cymbalaria).

For large bulbs (Daffodils, Tulips, and Crown Imperials) there are the Aubrietias, Arabis, Gypsophila repens, Creeping Phloxes, Arenaria montana, Stachys lanata, Veronica prostrata, Saponaria ocymoides, Cerastium, all of more or less creeping habit; or we may plant the bulbs closely among tufts of Myosotis, Thrift, Corydalis, Tunica Saxifraga, Primroses, Nepeta Mussini, Silenes, Hardy Candytuft, Viola cornuta, Pinks of all kinds, Heucheras, and dwarf Campanulas. These all maintain a steady show of good foliage throughout the summer, and contribute much to the thrifty and well-furnished appearance of the border verges. Some bloom with the bulbs, others flower later, giving us two displays of colour upon the same spot.

Many of the most decorative plants at our disposal are biennial in habit, that is, they grow from seed one year,

17

flower and die the next. Of these the most important are
Foxgloves, Canterbury Bells, Anchusas, Clary, Honesty,
Mulleins, Chimney Bellflowers, and some Evening Primroses.
All these we desire to plant with a lavish hand, but we are
again faced by the problem of what to do with the broad
spaces they leave bereft when their day is past.

I plant biennials in two ways. Perhaps the more satisfactory is in long narrow drifts, running between groups of plants
of permanently fine foliage or later flowering, so that when
the Foxgloves or Canterbury Bells are past, the broadening
out of the plants behind and before them will fill the space and
we are not aware of our loss.

This, too, in the main, is the way in which we meet the
defection of Delphiniums, Hollyhocks, Globe Thistles, and
others that grow up tall and beautiful but must be igno-
miniously cut to the ground after flowering.

Some plants of fine and lasting foliage that may be used
in screening biennials and others of the disappearing habit
are:

Baptisia australis	Ruta graveolens
Baptisia tinctoria	Elymus arenarius
Lythrum Salicaria	Funkia subcordata
Galega officinalis	Funkia Fortunei
Michaelmas Daisies	Achillea filipendulina
Flag Irises in variety	Hemerocallis in variety
Artemisia abrotanum	Thalictrum in variety
Helenium autumnale	Phlox paniculata
Helianthus multiflorus fl. pl.	Eupatorium coelestinum
Dictamnus albus	Cimicifuga simplex

Another way is to set them in broad groups and *interplant*
with plants of spreading habit and long flowering. Many

annuals are good for this purpose—Cornflowers, Sweet Sultans, Snapdragons, Zinnias, Marigolds, Anchusa, Marvel of Peru, and such perennials as Gypsophila, Sea Lavender, Michaelmas Daisies of the ericoides section, Linaria dalmatica, Anthemis, and others of a like habit of growth.

Oriental Poppies leave terrible blanks in the wake of their brief brilliance, but we meet the difficulty by planting Gypsophila between the Poppies and Michaelmas Daisies behind, and the wandlike branches of the latter may be drawn down to flower when the other two are passed. It is astonishing how close together plants will grow and not suffer any appreciable inconvenience. An examination of the several paintings that were made in exactly the same spot a month apart will show how completely a section of the garden is rehabilitated in a short period, and one wonders what has become of the plants that seemed to fill the entire space a few weeks before. Late-flowering plants with long, wandlike branches may be planted at the back of the border and drawn over and through the plants of earlier flowering as their beauty fades. Some of these are:

Boltonias	Vernonia arkansana
Michaelmas Daisies	Aconitum Wilsoni
Heleniums	Eupatorium ageratoides
Salvia azurea	Campanula pyramidalis
Salvia uliginosa	Helianthus

All Lilies have the disconcerting habit of taking themselves off after flowering. Interplanting is the best course to be pursued with them, and as their own foliage is scanty and they enjoy the slight protection of cover plants, a double purpose is happily served.

19

COLOUR IN MY GARDEN

A few good arrangements for Lilies are the following:

Lilium candidum with Papaver rupifragum *
Lilium croceum   "   Linum perenne album
Lilium elegans   "   Heuchera sanguinea alba
Lilium tigrinum   "   Aconitum Napellus
Lilium Hansoni   "   self-sown Cornflowers
Lilium speciosum   "   Statice latifolia
Lilium Browni   "   Linum perenne
Lilium canadense   "   Gypsophila paniculata
Lilium Henryi   "   Corydalis cheilanthifolia

Of course thoughtful staking has much to do with the well-furnished appearance of the borders. No plant should have its slender branches gathered into a stiff bunch and tied tightly to a stake. A flower stem should never be fastened more than half way up its length. In this way the natural curve of the stem will not be diverted.

In staking plants of many slender stems, several thin pieces of raffia should fasten them lightly to a strong central stake, allowing the whole plant to assume its natural direction. For plants of the type of Michaelmas Daisy, spreading pea brush provides the best means for staking as the stems may be spread out naturally over the stiff branches and fastened wherever it is desirable that they should remain.

It is the proper custom in well-ordered gardens to keep them pretty well cleaned up, not only of weeds but of the gypsy seedlings of authorized dwellers as well. This, of course, in the main, is as it should be. Phlox seedlings and many others become a pest, for they firmly resist eradication and are nearly always inferior to the parent; many Cam-

*The surest way to get this little Poppy established is to sow the seeds among the Lily tufts early in the spring, letting them come up in patches at will. This is the best course to follow with the Flax also.

panulas may not be allowed their own way, nor Dame's
Rocket for all its sweetness. Hollyhocks are too large to
admit of their taking up quarters anywhere the notion
strikes them, but Mulleins, for all their great stature, I
have seen tucked into a cranny of an old wall, rearing
their gilded stalks against the sky with incomparable
effect. In England I saw a broad, high flight of stone steps
that led up to the entrance of a fine old Tudor mansion
literally spouting Chimney Bellflowers, five feet tall, from
the joints along the sides. Doubtless the seedlings that had
started life in the central portion of the flight had been
pulled out that the chief end of steps be not entirely dis-
regarded, but certainly the gardener who left the rest to
raise and flourish their blue and white banners against the
gray old building was gifted with imagination and foresight.

Of course wise selection must be practised among the
many seedlings of the garden's largess; none should be
allowed in the middle of the paths or where they would
overpower lesser subjects, but I am very sure that in our
passion for tidying up we deprive ourselves of many a
charming picture. My own garden, built on several levels,
is rich in low retaining walls, dry built, and low flights of
stone steps, the joints of which are filled with inviting
sandy loam in the hope of attracting some little green
home-seeker. Of course, many times I must evict the
would-be tenant. Dandelions are always very pressing,
and Hollyhocks can squeeze themselves into the tightest
quarters, but it is surprising how often the right ones come
to fill me with delight at their bright unexpectedness and
entire fitness for the position. One flight of steps is almost

covered by mats of Cerastium, that, beginning a frail thread of life in the top joint, has gradually felt its way, tumbling over the treads and running its little green fingers along the transverse joints and on, until the hard lines of the steps are quite lost beneath the soft gray covering that does not suffer in the least from being walked upon. One would think that the Cerastium would be about all the soil in the narrow joints could sustain, but more than one lusty Columbine breaks through the thick mats, and here and there, on the shaded side, are little irrepressible bursts of Yellow Fumatory (Corydalis lutea) wresting a comfortable living from the most barren-appearing crannies.

In our country, where time is slow to bestow its softening touch of moss and lichen, stonework in the garden is apt to have an alien, unconnected look. But by encouraging suitable plant life in the chinks and joints and, where it is possible, building the walls and steps and pavements with this end in view, a more harmonious *ensemble* is created of the widely differing elements that go to make up the garden.

Tiny Ferns will grow in shaded places in chinks and crevices, and Arenaria balearica from a comfortably cool cranny will creep mosslike over the surface of stones, and few plants are prettier for such positions than the fluffy Yellow Fumatory. For sunny places, besides the many garden plants that will of their own volition seek out these narrow quarters, are numerous small things just suited for the purpose. Some that I have established are Campanula pusilla, some Acaenas, Viola gracilis, Sedum album, Sedum acre, Cerastiums, Veronica prostrata and V. repens, Armeria juncea, Thymus lanuginosus, Campanula rotundifolia, Sempervivums, Achillea tomentosa, Tunica Saxifraga, Lychnis alpina, Alpine Pinks in wide variety, Arabis, Alyssum montanum, Lavender, Sedum Sieboldi, Antennarias, Linum salsoloides, Gypsophila repens, Linaria Cymbalaria, and L. hepaticaefolia, Aubrietias, Aethionemas, dwarf Phloxes, Silene acaulis, Stachys corsica, and Mazus rugosus.

When my garden was first laid out the paths appeared too wide, but as changing them would have meant expense and delay they were not altered. Now, all along at the foot of the stone border verges are mats and tufts and trails of gray and green leafage—dwarf plants that have self-sown from the border above into the path, thriving there amazingly and creating the most delightful associations of colour and form, while they narrow my paths to more pleasing dimensions. These have not an untidy or haphazard appearance at all, but seem a quite intended and happy ordering of the garden's scheme, and of course we sharply check any sally designed to take a venturesome seedling toward the centre of the path.

As the seasons pass these small green squatters make their floral offerings with the prettiest grace imaginable and put forth as great a claim to admiration as do any of the dwellers in more official circles. Here may be found fountains of sky-blue Flax and rich stores of spicy Pinks; trails of yellow Flax and tufts of rosy Thrift; spreads of silvery Cerastium, velvet Woundwort, and brilliant gatherings of fluttering Spanish Poppies with alert Johnny-jump-ups prying between. It is amazing what carefully nurtured plants will elect to lead a gypsy existence in this apparently barren no-man's-land of the garden and will there thrive when elsewhere in more favoured spots they pine. Anchusa myosotidiflora is one of these—a harrowing uncertainty in the prepared borders but of a most gratifying dependability after it took up its residence in the path. That favourite of my Irises, too, Iris tectorum, has planted a colony at the edge of the path and here faces every untoward climatic condition with entire serenity.

Of course the explanation of this seeming anomaly is perfectly simple. Sufficient rich earth and humus have drained down from the borders to nourish the plants, and while providing perfect drainage there is always plenty of moisture to be found by thirsty roots among the gravel stones and sand of the path. It is the same principle upon which we build our rock gardens. Many a mountain plant finds in such a position the conditions of its natural habitat comfortingly reproduced, and any plant which fears the winter damp is far safer at the path edge than in the heavier soil of the borders.

As the season advances unsuspected annuals make their appearance among their free-thinking sisters—California Poppies and scarlet field Poppies; Snapdragons and little clouds of Alyssum and Ageratum, Pansies, annual Anchusa, and this year an ingratiating outlaw Morning Glory, coming from no one knows where, wound its slender way upward into the brown meshes of spent Gypsophila causing it to flush warmly with the lovely alien bloom.

These self-appointed border verges are ever a delight to me. They give me many a gay surprise and accomplish far more than I, with my heavier touch and anxious planning, could ever hope to toward making the garden sweet and approachable, full of charm and change and winsome perversity, a spot where every mood meets quick response.

24

CHAPTER III
THE COLOUR OF THE YOUNG YEAR

CHAPTER III
THE COLOUR OF THE YOUNG YEAR

My spring appears, Oh see what here doth grow.
—SIDNEY.

EVEN a careless observer cannot but be aware that in the floral world certain colours predominate at certain seasons. In the early spring a distinct majority of the flowers are yellow and even the young leafage is instinct with yellow principle. Thoreau says that "the spring yellows are faint, cool, innocent as the saffron morning as compared with the blaze of noon," and most of these spring yellows have an ascid cast like the colour of the Winter Aconite, though there is no hint of this sharpness in the radiant, light-suggesting petals of Daffodils. These radiant and ascid yellows are in wonderful harmony with the pale young leafage, while the delicately enveloping spring light seems to draw them all into a soft illumination to honour the season of renewals and fresh hope.

Several trees and shrubs give their flowers before winter has quite gone from the world. Folk so fortunate as to be in the country in very early spring know the shapely Spice Bush (Benzoin aestivale), and welcome it as a friend. Harriet Keeler writes that it "begins and ends its sylvan year in yellow." The little greenish-yellow flowers, so typical of the underlying spring colour tone, are "borne in umbel-like clusters in the axils of last year's leaves." It is graceful in form and even its slender branches embody a pleasant colour scheme—"at first, bright green, smooth; later, olive green, sometimes pearly gray; finally grayish-brown." The whole plant is deliciously aromatic, and what a boon is the rich spicy scent at this season of delicate manifestations!

Earlier even than the Spice Bush comes the blossoming of certain of the Witch Hazels. As the wistful flowering of our native Witch Hazel (Hamamelis virginica) is our farewell to flowers, so the Japanese and Chinese species are our welcome to the new order, often before the snows are gone. Hamamelis japonica forms "a large bush twelve to fifteen feet high, with many stiff, ascending branches and twiggy shoots and smooth leaves like those of the native H. virginica. The star-shaped flowers, each with five long, straplike, canary-yellow petals, surrounded by a calyx wine coloured on the outside, are fragrant and thickly stud the shoots and branches." H. arborea is another good Japanese sort and Mr. E. H. Wilson, whose article in the *Garden Magazine* for February, 1916, is quoted above, says that H. mollis, a Chinese species with larger flowers, is the finest of the genus.

Surely these shrubs that flower during the bereft season of winter should be given a place where those who spend the winter in the country may enjoy them, even though they must forego a few treasures of the opulent later year. Ever eagerly greeted is the Pussy Willow with its gay yellow-tipped stamens, that, hawked about the city streets, causes many a pang to homesick country hearts.

COLOUR IN MY GARDEN

In the garden the naked Jasmine (Jasminum nudiflorum) contributes a rich star harvest to this earliest festival of the year. Sometimes a warm spell in January will spoil the display, but ordinarily we may expect some time during the strident month of March a dainty picture in a sheltered corner of the garden; a shower of Jasmine stars upon the garden wall, the ground carpeted with Winter Aconites (Eranthis hyemalis), Snowdrops, and early Crocuses, and near by the quaint flowering of the Spice Bush. How intensely welcome are these flowers that come to us when there are so few signs that winter has relaxed his clutch and when our snow-bound imaginations are so eagerly seeking a sign.

The Jasmine needs to be persuaded to the wall top by some such decided hint as chicken wire spread upon the wall face. Its preference is to scramble about over rough ground or rocks—and very charming it is following its own whim—but it also makes a handsome wall covering and its dark green leafage is a fine background for gay flowers. Its waywardness may be brought to serve a more conventional purpose also if the long branches are kept cut back, thus forming a little shrub, very useful for underplanting shrubs of greater stature or tucked about where our flower-hungry eyes may catch its yellow glint at the earliest possible moment.

Both Snowdrop and Winter Aconite enjoy the light shade of spreading Spice Bush and overhanging Jasmine and spread and flower freely. The Winter Aconite is a modest, old-fashioned flower, which, in the extravagance of the later year, might pass unnoticed but at this season of our eagerness seems a rare and precious blossom. It grows from four to six inches in height, and carries its greenish-yellow cup above a widely spreading whorl of shining, deeply cut leaves. It is one of the plants good to naturalize upon grassy banks and beneath lightly shadowing trees where the roots will not be disturbed by the continuous digging and cultivating that must needs be carried on in the borders. Old books call it the Winter's Wolfsbane and like other members of its family group—the Ranunculaceae —it is poisonous, though not so deadly as the beautiful Monkshood of the midsummer garden.

Still another member of this family that wears its yellow garb jauntily is the Spring Adonis (Adonis vernalis), that bears large yellow flowers—a little sharp in colour but quite in harmony with the scheme of the season—upon stems a foot tall above the whorls of anemone-like leaves. And before March is very far under way comes the first Crocus.

> A little candlelight at a gray wall,
> One dauntless moment snatched from the March brawl
>   And, like the candlelight, to be forgot.

This, in my garden, is Crocus Imperati but it is closely followed by C. biflorus (the little Scotch Crocus sometimes called Cloth of Silver), C. vernus, and the splashes of molten gold—the hottest colour in the whole spring garden—that proclaim the Cloth-of-Gold Crocus (C. susianus), and then the great vase-shaped Dutch Crocuses. The earliest Crocuses we tuck in about the feet of the hardy little Mezereum that sometimes gives a hurried flowering in February, that they may not be alone and may form a little spring picture. Daphne Mezereum is a curious lilac-pink in colour and there is a sort whose blossoms are white. I am very fond of the strong purple Dutch Crocuses. Thickly planted about the scarlet Japanese Quince they create a gorgeous breadth in the pale spring garden.

By now there are many shrubs come to flowering that we should be taking advantage of in creating charming pictures. There is the snow-white Magnolia stellata so pretty with a ground cover of the common Grape Hyacinth, Muscari botryoides. There are long lines of radiant Forsythias which droop their laden branches upon a floor jewelled with sky-blue Chionodoxa and yellow and white Crocus; there is the Twin-flowered Honeysuckle scenting all the world, and the fluffy little Spiraea Thunbergi with bold clumps of gorgeous Crown Imperials standing out against its soft white skirts. The shrubbery border is a haven for spring bulbs. Here they may ripen their foliage and increase their kind without the constant prying and digging and making over that go on in the haunts of perennials; and here we may have picture after picture, from the first flowering of Jasmine and Snowdrop until the last heavy-headed Darwin Tulips group about the creamy Mock Orange bushes; and again in autumn, when the autumn Crocuses gleam before the reddening foliage of the shrubs.

Yellow and sky blue is ever a gay and sprightly association. We may have it sweetly of Primroses and Forget-me-nots along the edges of a damp north border.

It is a pity we do not make more use of Primroses in our country. Given the proper soil conditions, and divided yearly, the every-day sorts are charmingly responsive. I mean the true English Primrose (Primula vulgaris), which has a number of soft-coloured varieties, the Cowslip (P.

31

veris), the Oxlip (P. elatior), and the gay red and yellow Polyanthus, which I think is a variety of the last. All these are closely related but there are differences both in treatment and in appearance. The true Primrose is a plant of moist woods—a dry soil is fatal to it—and it requires plenty of good food. "Good loam, leafmould, and old hot-bed manure with a liberal proportion of sand" suits them well if there is also some shade.

The Oxlip and the Cowslip are very similar; both have the fresh cream-and-butter colour scheme, but the Oxlip has a shorter stem and a broader corolla and is thus a bit more showy. Both belong to sunny pastures of rich, moist soil. They will endure partial shade; indeed such protection is safest for them in our sunny climate. Dryness at the root causes them great suffering.

"The Polyanthus of unnumbered dyes" is easier pleased and increases and thrives in any position where the soil is deep and rich. These make a charming spring border edge planted among Forget-me-nots.

A sweep of streamside or pond shore may be made the scene of a most lovely spring picture. On the opposite bank to that upon which we are accustomed to walk we may plant groups of such shrubs as have highly coloured bark: Cornus alba with scarlet stems; C. stolonifera with purplish twigs; and for rich orange C. stolonifera, var. flaviramea, and the beautiful Golden Willow (Salix vitellina aurea). Thickly planted between and beneath may be Primroses and all sorts of white and checkered Fritillaries, Adder's Tongues, Crowfoot Violets, and Poet's Daffodils. If not allowed to be overpowered by coarse-growing meadow weeds these plants and bulbs will spread into great jewel-like patches, and if the bank is so situated that the sun shines through the gay twigs and stems upon the gayer flowers casting their reflections upon the water, we shall have a spring picture rare even at this season when all is glorified.

As the spring advances yellow flowers become even more numerous. Tulips have sprung into being; Corydalis lutea from chinks in the wall and C. cheilanthifolia from the edge of a shady border send up spikes of yellow flowers amidst waving, fernlike foliage. Groups of tall Doronicums open their round yellow blooms among clumps of early purple Iris; yellow Alyssum edges a long border with the sky-blue Anchusa myosotidiflora and hardy white Candy-tuft.

Often the common Golden Alyssum is a bit too prominent in the spring garden. It seeds itself so generously that there is usually a good deal of it and it wears a most aggressive hue, too raw and harsh. Kept in the soothing neighbour-hood of light blue or lavender flowers or freely mingled with white, it is amiable enough but it is out of harmony with the rosy blossoming boughs of its season, and here, where it wrapt the scarlet skirts of the Japanese Quince with a fiercely yellow scarf, it was like a strident voice transcending the delicate harmonies of the spring world. It is too bright and useful to be eliminated entirely, but it should be carefully placed and restricted, and more use might well be made of the pale variety called sulphureum which is of a delicate sulphur colour and quite lacks the harshness inherent in the type. This plant is in most happy accord

with all its contemporaries, especially with the bright
purple and lavender Phloxes and Aubrietias. Alyssum
Silver Queen is said to wear the same soft colour, and seed
of this kind is to be had in this country, but, while I have a
sturdy colony of seedlings in the nursery, I have not yet
seen it in flower.

The little Hedge Mustard or Fairy Wallflower (Erysimum
rupestre, syn. pulchellum) provides us with more yellow
treasure for this season. It, too, is a trifle ascid in its colour,
but it is so small and pretty and has so wild and sweet a
fragrance that we would not be without it, and are pleased
indeed when it takes possession of a vacant cranny in the
steps or walls and spreads its fine dark mat of foliage. It
enjoys a stone or two to trail over but it will thrive willingly
in the ordinary sunny border if the soil is not too heavy. It
is a nice companion for the silvery lavender Phlox called
G. F. Wilson, or if thickly set about with the bulbs of Grape
Hyacinth it creates as pretty an edging as one would wish
to see.

This spring there is a delightful bit of blue and gold
planting in my garden—a blue and gold carpet that spreads
back beneath the Lilac bushes in the angle of the high wall,
woven of the Grape Hyacinth called Heavenly Blue and
the little wild yellow Tulip, T. sylvestris, so full of grace
and gracious sweetness. The small bulbs are closely
planted, but here and there among them are set tufts of the
baby Meadow Rue (Thalictrum minor) that grows only six
inches tall, and spreads about its delicate greenery after
the spring blossoms are past. In another angle of the garden
a pretty composition in yellow and lavender bespeaks

34

admiration. Here a well-shaped bush of old-fashioned yellow-flowering Currant stands like a great fragrant bouquet above a close ground cover of Canadian Phlox (Phlox divaricata).

But all this is but by way of preamble. The sweetest and fairest of spring's yellow blossoms has been for many weeks sending up its slender water-green spears and opening a radiant blossom here and there—"a sudden flame of gold and sweet"—until they are assembled army strong and one seems to hear the challenge:

> King Trumpeter to Flora Queen,
> Hey, ho, daffodil!
> Blow, and the golden jousts begin!

Begin indeed with such a burst of fluttering, soft-coloured confusion as never was and never will be until Daffodil time is again upon the land.

There they go streaming the length of one border—pale, starlike hosts with a ribbon of purple Aubrietia wound among them; there they stand, long golden trumpets, in a flutter above a cloud of silver-lilac Phlox, and again how they pick their way among the fallen Cherry blossoms.

Why plan colour harmonies for those to whom inharmony is impossible—why even choose varieties when every separate flower is a spring poem? May we not just go "dancing with the Daffodils" where ignorance is bliss? But the wise ones tell us that if we have not knowledge of how to choose our partners the dance may prove a dirge. All Daffodils do not thrive equally well in all gardens nor in all situations. The white trumpets (like N. albicans) ask

35

for shade; the poeticus group enjoys a heavier soil and are happiest with some moisture; the dwarfs, like N. nanus and the Hoop Petticoats, should have the sharp drainage and sandy loam of the rock garden. But while these rules generally hold, it is best to experiment a little to find out which Daffodils our garden will entertain most successfully.

For naturalizing along the banks of streams none is better than the various forms of Narcissus poeticus. The old Pheasant's Eye is so inexpensive that it may be put in by the thousand and looks lovely gleaming among the young fern fronds in the short grass. The variety ornatus is also very inexpensive and blooms quite a little earlier than the Pheasant's Eye.

Daffodils belong to the radiant yellows and run the gamut from the pale, creamy N. albicans to the pure sunshine of such as Golden Spur. Their personal colour scheme is of a loveliness to be noted quite apart from their possibilities in combination with other flowers. More than any other flower they express supreme and exquisite freshness. The leaves are of that cool blue-green shade strongly suggestive of water, and the flowers themselves, radiant, crisp, vital as are no other blossoms of the year, seem their perfect accompaniment.

Daffodils are in bloom with many flowering trees and shrubs and more use should be made of these in association. Narcissus Golden Spur and N. obvallaris come early enough to bloom in the wraith shadow of the Shad Bush, or in the rosy glow of the Double-flowered Peach-trees. In my garden is a gay picture where a Peach-tree spreads its pink-clothed branches against the garden wall; beneath it are mats of silver-gray Phlox subulata G. F. Wilson and groups of yellow Daffodils.

I have found the various Star Daffodils the best for naturalizing in grass. Minnie Hume, Mrs. Langtry, Grandee, and Queen Bess are inexpensive sorts that are timed to the flowering of the orchard Cherries and with them seem to express the very fulness of the spring. I remember that the meadows about the beautiful old colonial mansion of Homewood, near Baltimore, used to be a sea of yellow Daffodils in spring—a rare treasure trove for flower-loving children. These were the fat old double sort with crumpled green-gold petals and the smell of moist earth. The poeticus varieties bloom with the Apple blossoms and may easily be naturalized in orchards where the grass need not be cut until after the Narcissus foliage has died naturally.

To-day, May 8th, a pink-flowered Japanese Cherry is in full flower, the ground beneath it carpeted with pale Star Daffodils and the edge of the bed hidden under alternate mounds of purple Aubrietia Dr. Mules and sky-blue Iris pumila caerulea. A week later Malus floribunda will shed its pink petals upon the pale gold trumpets of Narcissus beauty. Old-fashioned Bleeding Heart consorts gaily with pretty Narcissus stella superba and nodding white Checker Lilies, and to-morrow the band of purple Viola cornuta and Forget-me-not about the pool will be starred with the fragrant double blossoms of the Gardenia-flowered Narcissus,

A poet could not but be gay
In such a jocund company.

37

DOWN THE PATH OF SPRING
MAY 1ST

*T*HIS *gay little tree is a Japanese Cherry named Mt. Fuji, which at the time of its flowering dominates the garden as does its great namesake the blossomy island of Japan. In its shadow bloom Aubrietia, Golden Alyssum, Iris pumila caerulea, and the pretty pale Star Daffodil Minnie Hume.*

Later in the summer the tall stalks and feathery flower spikes of the Japanese Snakeroot (Cimicifuga japonica) reach up among the low branches of the tree, and on still further into the fall frail Japanese Anemones flower here.

In the border at the left, which is the same as that shown in Plate No. 10 (June 10th), we see Golden Alyssum, Hardy Candytuft, Anchusa myosotidiflora, and the bright orange-scarlet Tulip Thomas Moore. The little pink-flowered shrub at the end of the border is the Rosette Plum (Prunus triloba).

PLATE NO. 4
SEE PLATE NO. 10

A BIT OF BIZARRERIE
MAY 14TH

*T*HIS gay detail is part of a procession of Wistarias and scarlet and white Tulips that follows the broad transverse path in front of the Garden House. The Tulips are the Cottage variety White Swan and the sweet-scented, glowing T. Gesneriana spathulata major.

Earlier in the year Crocuses in purple and lavender tones outlined the border edges. The Tulips and Crocuses are planted between tufts of Heuchera in coral and pale pink and thrifty plants of the Carpathian Hairbell (Campanula carpatica). These keep the border edge gay until frost.

Behind these are German Irises aurea and Celeste, for June flowering; Delphiniums for early July; and for the late summer and early autumn a striking planting of the brilliant Phlox Coquelicot and Campanula lactiflora E. Molineaux, with its wedge-shaped heads of lovely blue-lavender bells.

PLATE NO. 5

CHAPTER IV
TULIPS AND BLOSSOMS

CHAPTER IV

TULIPS AND BLOSSOMS

Tall tulips lift in scarlet tire
Brimming the April dusk with fire.
—Lizette Woodworth Reese.

MY GARDENING life began with a prejudice against Tulips. My experience of them was confined to what I had seen of their geometrical array in the parks and squares of the city of Baltimore—stiff and flamboyant precursors of the Cannas and Coleus to come— and I had no desire to repeat these scenes in my first little garden that was destined to be the home of only the most gracious and beauteous flowers.

But late one April afternoon, when taking a walk, I paused to peer over a white picket fence into an old and neglected garden. The tangled area, swept neat by winter's fiercely tidying regime, was presided over by an ancient Apple-tree that seemed, with every twig wreathed in fragrant bloom, to stand lost in an ecstatic dream of its departed youth. Beneath it in the fresh grass, crowding between the crimson Peony shoots, were swaying hosts of little scarlet Tulips.

"Brimming the April dusk with fire."

41

COLOUR IN MY GARDEN

Thus carelessly disposed beneath the radiant boughs they showed such matchless grace, such piquant vivacity, that I was loath to go, and lingered, full of delight at this choice bit of April's fancy, until the tender spring gloom came out and wrapped the picture round, sending me on my way.

I could hardly wait for summer to wear away to the time when I might add to my little garden the "awkward grace" of a Crabapple tree and plant the ground beneath it with glowing Tulips. Since then it has been my happy lot to plant many Tulips beneath many flowering trees, and I feel that no arrangement is so felicitous for both. My feeling for Tulips has quite changed—few flowers are of so fine a quality—but as I have met recently some people who confess to a prejudice against them, the object of this chapter is not so much to give lists of the best varieties, as to go up and down the garden paths this fair May day, enjoying the Tulip pictures in all their beauty and variety.

The early or Dutch Tulips, that flower in the latter days of April, we use as quaintly stiff and conventional garden decorations. They line the beds and paths with demure severity, exactly spaced and one in height, and fill the garden pots and jars with even surfaces of bloom. Their stems are short and sturdy, their colours frank and bright, with a thin almost transparent quality to their petals that gives them a shining look, as of an inner light. These are the Tulips most often used for bedding and they are the best for forcing indoors. Those belonging to the "Duc" group have very small flowers and bright, pure colours. They are the earliest to bloom out of doors, and may be had in flower indoors by Christmas. Many of these early Tulips are most graciously inexpensive and I love to use them lavishly, picking out the design of the garden with their delightful colour and planting Japanese Cherry and Peach-trees to flower at the same time.

For pink ones we have Cottage Maid, La Reine des Reines, Rose Luisante, Pink Beauty, and Flamingo.

For white: White Hawk, L'Immaculée, and La Reine.

For yellow: Chrysolora, Golden Queen, Yellow Prince, Primrose Queen, and Leopold II.

For orange: Thomas Moore, Prince of Austria, Leonardo da Vinci, Couleur Cardinal, and De Wet.

For Scarlet: Belle Alliance, Rembrandt, Sir Thomas Lipton, and Crimson King.

We enjoy the pretty primness of these Dutch Tulips in the April scheme of things, but none the less do we welcome the willowy grace and æsthetic colours of the Tulips that bloom in May. These we plant beneath the flowering trees in groups of six or a dozen and all about the borders among the many charming flowers that with them adorn the season.

Directly in front of the garden house, along the straight path that crosses the garden, is my favourite Tulip picture. At either end a Cedar arbour hung with Wistaria spans the path and in between standard Wistarias decorate its length. All along beneath the low-drooping ropes of pendent purple blooms flutter troops of scarlet-and-white Tulips. Perhaps this picture will seem a trifle bizarre to some decorous imaginations, but to me it is so fresh and unaffected—so entirely "chic," that no offering of the garden the season through gives me quite the same thrill of pleasure. The Tulips used are Gesneriana spathulata, a great, thin-petalled flower with a rich blue base, and White Swan, a particularly choice white Tulip.

Thoreau reminds us that we cannot make a hue of words, that they are not to be compounded like colours, and when we stand before the radiant groups of the spring garden, so desirous of conveying to others the loveliness that we see so plainly, we are baffled by the impotence of our means of expression.

Here is a full-flowered Crabapple tree, Pyrus ioensis (Bechtel's Double-flowering Crab), like a great bouquet against the gray garden wall. Beneath the spread of its wreathed branches are groups of May Iris—the old purple Flag and the French gray florentina; and scattered all about are pink and cherry-coloured Tulips—Pride of Haarlem, Loveliness, and Clara Butt—all Darwins.

At the other side of the garden is another Crabapple spreading its branches above a group of delicately flushed Tulips— La Candeur—that rise from a waving sea of Forget-me-nots. All my Crabapple trees have their attendant gatherings of Tulips, but none is fresher and more delicately lovely than the one that Miss Winegar has so finely reproduced on plate 6. Here the white Wistaria blossoms mingle delightfully with the crowding pink flowers of Pyrus floribunda, and the gay colour scheme is repeated lower down where early cream-coloured Iris and bright pink Tulips stand.

My next Tulip and blossom planting is to be of mauve-coloured Tulips like Nora Ware or Euterpe against the low-sweeping boughs of Malus Scheideckeri—a little tree that is so delicate and filmy in its close-set rosy bloom that it always makes me think of the dainty trappings of a baby. Mauve Tulips stream away beneath the crooked branches of the Judas Tree repeating its singular colour among patches of silvery creeping Phlox and the sober ornamentation of Velvet Stachys (S. lanata).

The Tulips belonging to this colour scale are a most fascinating group. They run from pearl-gray with a slight flush to warm plum and dusky prune colour, some inclining toward the pinkish tones, others having more blue or slate in their composition. There are two old colour names, now quite laid aside but to me richly suggestive, that I always think of when looking at these deep-hued Darwin Tulips; they are puce and murrey. They still have a place between the pages of the dictionary but we do not hear or see them used and Dr. Ridgeway has not made use of them in his Colour Chart. What could be more descriptive of such a Tulip as Zulu than "murrey velvet"? or more expressive of the pinky-brown and purple richness of Frans Hals than "puce"?

Very pale Tulips in this class are: Electra, Pearl, and Mauve Clair; deeper in tone are Euterpe, Nora Ware, Rev. H. Eubank, Crépuscule, Bleu Céleste, and Lantern. Melicette has a decided pink flush, as has Ed. André. Erguste is a fine deep heliotrope, Bleu Aimable is bluish heliotrope and very late, and La Tristesse is a tall slaty-blue sort with a gray rim.

In darker shades that incline toward blue we have Bleu Céleste, Sir Trevor Lawrence, Sweet Lavender, and Valentine. Reddish sorts are Morales and Frans Hals.

COLOUR IN MY GARDEN

Of those very dark kinds with blackish lights are Faust, Zulu, La Tulipe Noire, Black Knight, and Philippe de Comines.

I should like to plant a spring walk in these æsthetic colours. It should lead to some pleasant spot; and, following its length on either side, but irregularly spaced, would come white Dogwood trees, mauve-pink Judas Trees, and groups of white and purple Persian Lilacs. At their feet would stream the mauve and heliotrope and plum-coloured Tulips interrupted by stretches of silvery Phlox G. F. Wilson and P. canadensis, Pink Thrift, white and lavender Horned Violets (Viola cornuta), White Flax, Linum perenne alba, silvery Cerastium, Stachys lanata, and Nepeta Mussini. To this spring walk for an earlier display one might add a few Japanese Cherries and double-flowering Peaches and plant the ground beneath them with Daffodils, Polyanthus Primroses, and Forget-me-nots.

Sometimes I think yellow Tulips are the best of all, their colours are so pure and shining and they are so charming planted in front of the white-flowered shrubs of their season—Lilacs, Weigela candida, and the many lovely

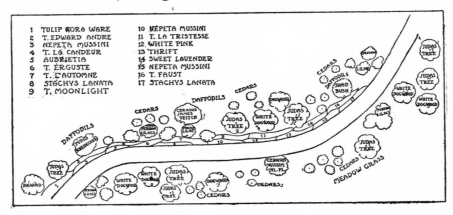

1	TULIP MORA WARE	10	NEPETA MUSSINI
2	T. EDWARD ANDRE	11	T. LA TRISTESSE
3	NEPETA MUSSINI	12	WHITE PINK
4	T. LA CANDEUR	13	THRIFT
5	AUBRIETIA	14	SWEET LAVENDER
6	T. ERGUSTE	15	NEPETA MUSSINI
7	T. L'AUTOMNE	16	T. FAUST
8	STACHYS LANATA	17	STACHYS LANATA
9	T. MOONLIGHT		

new Mock-oranges—and interspersed with patches of soft lavender and deep purple Aubrietia, Arenaria montana, Iberis sempervirens, and goodly clumps of such May Iris as Kharput and Amas.

My favourite yellow Tulips are the following—all Cottage varieties:

Avis Kennicott—tall; a lovely long flower of deepest yellow.
Bouton d'Or—a small flower of warm tone.
Ellen Willmott—pale yellow pointed flower; tall.
Mrs. Kneightly—pale yellow; fine.   Medium.
Inglescomb yellow—pure butter yellow.
Leghorn Bonnet—creamy yellow.
Moonlight—long pale flower; tall and early.
Mrs. Moon—splendid pointed flower; full yellow.
Retroflexa—reflexing petals.   My favourite tulip.
Walter T. Ware—deep golden yellow.
Vitellina—cream coloured.

The warm, tawny-coloured Tulips like La Merveille, Golden Spire (syn. elegans maxima lutea), and Orange Globe are striking planted among sky-blue and white Flax, or behind little spreads of silvery Nepeta Mussini with its clouds of lavender flowers.   These orange-coloured Tulips are pretty for filling the beds or borders of Tea Roses.   The coppery shoots of the Rose bushes are in fine harmony with the warm-toned Tulips.   Later the beds might be carpeted with Pansies or Viola cornuta, or sown with the two pretty little annuals Ionopsidium acaule and Gypsophila muralis.

There are three old-fashioned looking Tulips that seem to breathe the atmosphere of the old gardens where their ancestors sought shelter during the period when the gardening world was in pursuit of other gods. When we wearied of the stiffness and artificiality of "bedding out" and again turned to simple, graceful things, these long-stemmed willowy Tulips, found tucked away in old-fashioned gardens, seemed a boon indeed. They are Sweet Nancy (syn. Gesneriana albo-marginata), Picotee, and Blushing Bride (syn. Isabella, Shandon Bells). They are white with a narrow cherry-coloured edge that gradually expands until the petals are deeply flushed. Carnation is said to be an improved Picotee. These belong among Florentine Iris, Southernwood, and other old-fashioned looking things.

Besides the Irises of the Germanica group, those known as Intermediate flower with the May Tulips. Many of these are in tones of buff and pearl-gray. I always enjoy greatly a flashing group in my garden composed of Intermediate Iris Empress and the sweet-scented Tulip macrospeila, glowing rose-scarlet in colour.

My favourite pink Tulips are Flamingo, Mrs. Cleveland, and Suzon for delicate tints; Clara Butt, Edmée, Inglescomb Pink, Loveliness, and Mrs. Krelage for deeper tones; and for cherry and cerise, Pride of Haarlem, Nauticus, Mr. Farncomb Sanders, and Prince of the Netherlands.

And then there are the old Dutch "Breeders," an old-fashioned race, long neglected, that is being again caught up in the unstable web of popular fancy. I do not know these flowers as yet in my own garden but stand before them in other gardens astonished at their unusual colours and combinations. There are tender dove colours and tobacco browns, bronze and apricot, curious restrained reds with sudden white centres, dull yellow and terra cotta,

48

crushed strawberry and chocolate, rose-mauve and tawny yellow, orange-scarlet and bronze, gray-brown and violet, plum and gray, and many more.

No early garden literature is so interesting and amusing as that concerned with Tulips. They were the florists' flower *par excellence* of the seventeenth and early eighteenth centuries. The old writers, in a fever to do justice to this flower of their hearts—and pocketbooks—recklessly mixed fancy with fact in their disquisitions upon the Tulip and its culture. I have a little old brown volume published in 1711 called the "Dutch Gardener or the Curious Florist" written by Henry Van Osten, "the Leyden Gardener," wherein are pages and pages of almost impassioned writing about Tulips and of curious theories concerning the influence of the moon and the wind upon their welfare. In Van Osten's day the Gillyflower was the Tulip's rival. Early works devote equal space and equally elegant language to the two, but the Leyden gardener leaves no doubt in the minds of his readers as to his personal preference. In those days as now the charge of scentlessness was made against Tulips and the eloquent Dutchman was moved to the following defence:

"Those that value the July Flowers [Jilly Flowers] above the Tulips because of their pleasant smell, their lasting longer, and their bearing of more Flowers, would do well to consider that flowers ought chiefly to please the Sight, and that the Smell gives them no Beauty and indeed affords but little pleasure before the Flower is pulled and removed from its place. Those, therefore, that delight in Flowers, are willing to be without the Smell, if their Eye be but satisfied:

And they who value Flowers chiefly for their Smell, may supply themselves with Perfumes, and not upbraid this Queen of Flowers for want of that Quality, which abrogates not in the least from her Beauty nor renders her less pleasing in a Florist's Eye. Let them consider, besides, that what seems to some a pleasant Smell, stinks in the Nostrils of others, nay, many cannot endure the most fragrant Perfumes without a great Alteration in their Bodies, as infinite Examples and daily Experience convince us. The Lovers therefore of sweet Scents ought not to reproach the Tulip with this as with a Defect, seeing Nature has been so lavishly bountiful to her in other Respects and given her wherewithal to satisfy a far more noble Sense, and to make us admire in her the exceeding Power of the Donor."

Nevertheless, in spite of Van Osten's brave plea the lack of sweetness is the Tulip's one defect. A few, however, are endowed with a peculiarly fresh and uncloying fragrance, and whenever I come across one of these I feel that I have received a gift.

Darwin Tulips, as far as my knowledge of them goes, are quite without scent. The old English Cottage Tulips, however, from which so many handsome forms have been developed, were once praised for their fine, sweet scent, but alas, in the work of "improvement" this quality, with their simpler garment, has to a large degree fallen from them. Some that retain their fragrance are: La Merveille, Primrose Beauty, Orange King, Gala Beauty, Ellen Willmott, Emerald Gem, Lion d'Orange, Macrospeila, Mrs. Moon, Mrs. Kneightly, and others of the Gesneriana group.

COLOUR IN MY GARDEN

Among the fragrant Dutch or early Tulips are Thomas Moore, Prince of Austria, Proserpine, Ophir d'Or, Yellow Prince, Gold Finch, De Wet, Hector, Yellow Rose, and Duc Van Tholl.

Many of the wild Tulip species are fragrant, and these are most fascinating to grow. Some of the sweetest are: the wild British Tulip, T. sylvestris (that has a scent like hot-house Violets), vitellna, with the bouquet of oranges; Didieri with a fragrance of Sweet Peas; and australis (syn. Celsiana), Billietina, persica (syn. Breyniana), primulina, and fragrans (syn. sylvestris major).

CHAPTER V
FLOWERS O' GRACE

CHAPTER V

FLOWERS O' GRACE

We cannot fathom the mystery of a single flower, nor is it intended that we should; but that the pursuit of science should constantly be betrayed by the love of beauty, and accuracy of knowledge by tenderness of emotion.   —RUSKIN.

THERE is a class of plants in the garden toward which we feel a peculiar tenderness. Most of them are too light in build and too fugitive to be of great value in our colour arrangements; they are the butterflies of the flower world, careless, gay, full of whimsical charm; and without their fluttering life the garden would be bereft indeed. There is room for many of these flowers of grace in even small gardens, for they occupy little space and they will, if allowed a bit of freedom in the matter of their own bestowal, redeem the garden from the stiffness which is apt to be the result of our heavier touch. It is their special mission to add the touch of laughter to the serene; to lift our thoughts from the gravity of gardening to the witchery of gardens.

The fairy Flax is one of these. It is an unstable, whimsical thing; opening its wide eyes with the pleading sun, closing them at its noon insistence, and the little plant cannot be said to be reliably perennial in our climate and yet, once

55

admitted, it is not long before "indent with azure is many a fold" of the garden, for the Flax is a hardy and persistent self-sower. The flowering of the Flax continues long, and all the while the work of seeding and distribution is going on at a great rate, and each year we are enchanted by its latest whims of association. This spring I found the feathery seedlings springing up all through a stretch of Iris Innocenza and when the two flowered late in May—the fluttering sky-blue blossoms among the thick-petalled, pure white Iris—I thought I had never seen anything so fresh and pretty.

Sometimes there will be a gay colony in the garden path at the foot of a retaining wall where Flax and California Poppies have foregathered in blithe haphazardy; next summer this will not be, but over the way a blue haze will underlie the sunshine of the Lemon Lilies, or my garden steps will tremble into blue from every joint and crevice.

One of the prettiest associations that came about by accident but is now permanently established is where Flax grows among the jaunty Spanish Poppy (P. rupifragum). They both have a grand blossoming for nearly two months in the spring and early summer and then for the rest of the season give little snatches of gay colour now and then. The Spanish Poppy is especially persistent, opening an occasional frail blossom right up to freezing weather.

The Narbon Flax (Linum narbonense) is perhaps a little more delightful even than Linum perenne. It is a trifle more substantial in appearance, a shade bluer, and its wide eyes face the sun all day long, not closing in the provoking way of the other in the middle of the day, but unfortunately it is somewhat less reliable. It is not quite hardy and while some winters our promising batch of seedlings comes safely through, we may not count upon them. In sunny, sheltered places, in well-drained rather gravelly soil or among rocks it is fairly persistent.

The common white Flax (Linum perenne album) also is a charming plant. There is a beautiful group in my garden that came without my assistance, where Gypsophila paniculata tumbles over the top of a low retaining wall and at the wall foot, growing lustily in the path, is a patch of white Flax. The intermingled gray-white and porcelain-white with the delicate greenery of both creates a charming effect.

Linum monogynum* is another white-flowered Flax; an elegant, sprightly little plant with myriads of round white blossoms continued over a long period. The luminous yellow colour and more substantial appearance of Linum flavum are well known. There are few more striking plants for the border edge in well-drained soil with a sunny aspect. It blooms practically all summer, and if one plants with it Campanula carpatica, both the blue and the white sorts, one has a persistently flowering border edge in very pretty colours.

Linum alpinum and L. salsolides are little sprawling Alpines, blue and pale pink respectively, only suited for a chink between two stones, but the beautiful annual grandiflorum, the colour of. red wine held up to the light, should have a place in every garden. All these Flax flowers are easily raised from seed and all self-sow freely and may safely be left to the wind and their own caprice in the matter of their associations.

---

*This plant is not reliably hardy and should be carried over in a frame.

COLOUR IN MY GARDEN

Coral Bells (Heuchera) next occurs to me as a flower of grace. The slender stems set with tiny flowers—pink, blush, cream, coral, scarlet, flame—rise from a tuft of beautiful leafage, ornamental enough in itself and often flushed with deeper colour. The flower spikes continue to develop for weeks during the late spring and summer, and wherever the groups of Heuchera are set a light and graceful effect is secured. There are many fine sorts of recent introduction, all superior to the old sanguinia—an uncertain bloomer—that flower for several months. Of these are: Mignonette, deep rose; Pluie de Feu, flame scarlet; Rosamund, coral pink; Pink Beauty, a charming shade; Mousquetaire, rose-scarlet; Virginale, cream; and Flambeau, scarlet. The varieties Cascade and Richardsonii have richly flushed foliage that makes them useful for border edges or for planting at the foot of low shrubs with Saxifraga cordifolia. Heucheras* do not seed themselves in my garden but come readily from hand-sown seed and spread rapidly from the root. They are almost as ever-harmonious as the Flax flowers and should be used freely about the borders wherever a light and graceful effect is desired. White ones planted among the stout elegans Lilies relieve their heaviness and soften their scarlet glare; pink ones reflect delightfully the glow of Evening Primroses; scarlet ones are pretty behind mats of trailing white and gray Cerastium, or standing among clumps of slim Siberian Irises, themselves veritable plants of grace.

Another plant giving this airy and graceful effect is the old-fashioned Garden Heliotrope (Valeriana officinalis). It

*Heucheras should be divided every year or to keep them in good blossoming form.

carries its flat pink and gray lace flower heads upon slender stems four feet tall, waving them above the scarlet Oriental Poppies, the soft-toned Irises, the rows of smart Sweet Williams, enhancing the special quality of beauty in all. Many speak against it because it spreads with such ardent enthusiasm, but its mats of roots are so easily pulled out that this is no drawback and if one leaves a bit here and there to survive and expand its lace like flower head we are sure to give it a welcome.

Later in the season Gypsophila lends its gossamer blossoming to the same end, and later still the great Sea Lavender (Statice latifolia), with its mistlike lavender flower heads, gives a touch of lightness to the robust physiognomy of August. Statice incana and S. eximia are white-flowered Sea Lavenders with the same airy inflorescence. These plants should be left long in one place without disturbance as it is only after several years that they become fully effective.

Columbines, with their poised blossoms and streaming spurs, are charmingly buoyant in effect. They are the most enchanting of flowers. Even the debonair little red-and-yellow native sort that we are so glad to meet upon our April walks, rollicking over a great brooding rock, is fit to be brought into the garden to shine among the best. It seems pleased to come for it seeds itself about most graciously, setting up little colonies here and there and flowering gaily among the Arabis and Aubrietias—its jaunty colour scheme only rivalled in the spring garden by Crown Imperials and scarlet Tulips.

Two other fine Columbines are native to the United

States: Aquilegia chrysantha, a late-blooming sort with small leafage and light yellow, long-spurred blossoms, that is one of the best of hardy plants; and A. caerulea, the beautiful Rocky Mountain Columbine. This latter plant is so innately a wild thing that it is with difficulty brought to the conditions and conventions of garden life. The best place for it is on the north side of a wall among Ferns and Bloodroot, where these flowers, perhaps by their likeness to the friends of its mountain home, may insure its contentment. Even thus considered it will often pine away and we must be constantly raising it from seed if we desire to enjoy continuously the lovely lavender-blue and white blossoms. But A. caerulea has given us some fine varieties of sturdier habit: White Lady is one that I am hoping will prove more generously persistent than the type; Mrs. Nicholls is said to recall the clean lavender and white colouring of the parent; and Rose Queen gives many charming pink blossoms. This plant is decidedly more dependable than the type, is taller and the blossoms have longer spurs.

White Columbines are particularly pure and lovely. There is a dwarf one very fine and free in its flowering called flabellata nana and a good semi-double one known as nivea grandiflora. The wild British Columbine (A. vulgaris) has a good white form called grandiflora alba. The short-spurred Columbines, while lacking the peculiar airy grace of the long-spurred sorts, are yet pretty enough, and even the double ones have a quaint appeal like that of a pudgy baby.

The wild Columbines, Skinneri, glandulosa, the blue Siberian Columbine, alpina, and Stewarti are only fit for careful treatment on rock work. They are exquisite but too shy and wild to give any sort of effect in the ordinary flower garden. The best for this purpose are the various strains of "long-spurred hybrids" offered by most seedsmen. These have been carefully selected and grow tall and strong and wear a great variety of delicate tints and shades: old rose, pink, lavender, purple, buff, cream, yellow, a sort of skimmed-milk blue, and many in combinations of two colours.

It is interesting to raise our own Columbines from seed gathered from the best-coloured and strongest of our plants. We get some most delightful results and even the gypsy seedlings springing up here and everywhere about the garden are often of great beauty. To be seen at their best these exquisitely modelled blossoms should shine against a background that throws them into relief. They are splendid massed against evergreens, or tall plants of a good green. In a huddle of other flowers the modelling of the blossoms is lost sight of. The persistently fine foliage of Aquilegias makes them particularly valuable in the borders. We may plant them in broad masses without fear of ensuing bare places, and they may also be used charmingly in association with other flowers of their day. Yellow Columbines (A. chrysantha) are gay among the soft blue Peach-leaved Campanulas; white ones with the Forget-me-not Anchusa (A. myosotidiflora); pink ones among the stiff spikes of mauve Camassia, and so on. Among Ferns they are always happy and at home.

But preëminent among flowers of grace are Poppies. Like the children, I like to save the best for the last, but all this while my thoughts have been alight with them, my paper stained with their gallant colour, my heart vibrating with their waywardness. Surely they are the acme of grace, the best of laughter, the rarest embodiment of all that is delightsome, careless, touchingly fugitive.

> Joys too exquisite to last
> And yet more exquisite when past.

Many flowers have given their names to colours. The wonder is that some brave hue does not challenge our admiration as "poppy colour." But after all, which of this flower's daring or tender revelations would be chosen? To me poppy colour would mean that peculiar, sparkling rose-red found among the Shirleys—one of the most telling and distinctive hues in the floral world—but perhaps the thin scarlet glare of the English Field Poppy is the most typical. I shall never forget the wonder of a high meadow afloat with these vibrant flowers I once saw against the setting sun in England. Ruskin says: "The poppy is the most transparent and delicate of all the blossoms of the field. The rest, nearly all of them, depend on the texture of their surface for colour. But the poppy is painted glass; it never glows so brightly as when the sun shines through it. Wherever it is seen against the light or with the light, it is a flame, and warms the mind like a blown ruby."

It is a pity that Poppies are in such haste to shed their silken petals and display their crowned seed pods, for there are few flowers that we would rather have in masses in the garden borders. Few exhibit such entrancing shades and tints and none displays the exquisite poised grace of the great Poppy flower swaying upon its delicately slender but quite adequate stem. It is not the part of wisdom to sow annual Poppies in broad stretches in the borders. Their days are too few and they leave such sad blanks when they are gone. But of course one must have them, and a good way is to sow a few seeds here and there among perennials that will broaden out and cover the annual's subsequent defection. Joan-silver-pin is its quaint early English name, which means, I believe, a bit of finery, and as such we must regard them.

The English Field Poppy exists in my garden of its own whim. Years ago a few seeds were scattered to fill a blank space and ever since they have been as the proverbial mustard seed. Each year I am constrained to pull out hundreds of fresh young tufts, for one place is as good as another to them and often a path will be solid with complaisant seedlings, the beds all threaded with them, and peace and harmony in dire jeopardy. But I leave a few and often these haphazard elect supply the needed touch of brilliance to some too-neutral group. Where I sit on the Garden House porch I can see a stretch of lavender Nepeta and slightly bluer Campanulas that would be lifeless in effect were it not for the flashing trail of self-sown Poppies that brings out all their delicate quality.

Shirley Poppies are of a delightful pinkness not to be found elsewhere in or out of Nature. They run the enchanting scale from faintest blush to the dazzling rose-scarlet that seems to me to be the true poppy colour, and the diaphanous, silken blossoms are poised on stems so frail that they seem to be ever balancing to keep from tipping over.

Other annual Poppies, the Carnation-flowered and Peony-flowered types, have even a wider colour range, embracing the soft wine tints, venous purple, pinky mauve, silver-gray, smoky lavender sometimes touched with scarlet, or flushed with heliotrope; and now, from the secret places of the hybridists, comes the exciting rumour of a race of *blue* Poppies—can it be true? Surely they will be the cool, shadowy, changeful blues like those shown by Campanulas. These would not seem strange, but a Poppy with the colour of an Anchusa would somehow affect one as unpleasantly abnormal, like a green Carnation or the black Tulip. Few flowers are more chaste and lovely than single white Poppies; the Bride is a fine one, and Virginia is white with a delicate pink edge. Poppies and Cornflowers make a good association, for when the Poppies are spent they may be pulled out and the Cornflowers left to continue on their quaint blue way until frost. I once saw a bed of silvery-lavender Poppies and Cornflowers that was very pretty.

The crepe-petalled Iceland Poppy (Papaver nudicaule) that sows itself about my garden, springing up in the most unlikely nooks and crevices, has much of the airy charm of the annual sorts and decks itself in the loveliest colours: apricot and orange, buff, scarlet and white. I had from an English seedsman this spring a kind not too whimsically named Pearls of Dawn, for a rosy glow underlies the soft buffs and creams of its fragile petals.

My favourite among perennial Poppies is P. rupifragum, that in lieu of any proper English name I call the Spanish Poppy.* It has all the whimsical appeal of its delicately bold race and hoists its little snatches of gay colour on stems

---

* P. rupifragum is a native of Spain.

as thin as wire. But there is nothing frail about the solid tuft of leaves or the mighty tap root that, when you essay to get it out of the ground intact, seems to reach to China. This plant, too, is as hardy as iron and unmindful of drought continues to send aloft its colours until frozen to inactivity.

It is easily raised from seed and grows freely in the border of well-drained soil or in the rock garden where it is particularly valuable on account of its late blooming.

I can never quite feel that Papaver orientale is a Poppy for all it boasts the simple form and silken characteristics of its fellows. It lacks all the spiritual qualities and is too coarse of texture, too stout of figure, too altogether insistent. It brings to mind Chaucer's portrait of the "Wife of Bath," "Bold was hire face, and faire and red of hew," and yet there is some magic appeal in this great Poppy, too, and one wants to splash it about the garden regardless of consequences.

CHAPTER VI

IMPRESSIONS OF A JUNE MORNING

CHAPTER VI

IMPRESSIONS OF A JUNE MORNING

Soon will the high Midsummer pomps come on,
　Soon will the musk carnations break and swell,
Soon shall we have gold-dusted snapdragons;
　Sweet-William with his homely cottage-smell,
And stocks in fragrant blow;
　Roses that down the alleys shine afar,
And open, jasmine-muffled lattices,
And groups under the dreaming garden-trees,
　And the full moon and the white evening-star.
　　　　　　　　　　　　　—MATTHEW ARNOLD.

WHAT a chaos of beauty there is upon a June morning! Standing in the midst of the garden one experiences a sort of breathlessness of soul, and sends forth little subconscious pleas to the powers that govern our limitations for more capacity to enjoy the bounty of this glowing, exuberant month. June is so prodigal, so extravagant of all that makes the world beautiful, so kind to gardeners. We should be thankful for even one of the great flower families that grace this month—for the Roses, the Lupines, the Peonies, the Iris—but June comes to us with a green apron recklessly overflowing, spreading her largess upon every hand, until it is small wonder that we stand bewildered.

69

COLOUR IN MY GARDEN

In whatever direction we choose to turn our steps, this fifth day of June, beauty awaits. Down this long, straight path to the left Oriental Poppies are creating a high-pitched fanfare of colour. We may not allow them in all parts of the garden, on account of their emphatic colour. But there, among the cool lavender Irises (pallida dalmatica, Céleste, Albert Victor, Blue Jay), with an interplanting of lacelike Garden Heliotrope (Valeriana officinalis), they may trumpet unrebuked. I love them in great masses so that one may revel in their thrilling colour, but thus planted we must have a thought for the great blank spaces that follow when the Poppies are spent, and place intelligently the clumps of Gypsophila and Michaelmas Daisies that will later rehabilitate the border.

Some of the finest of the strong-coloured Oriental Poppies are bracteatum and beauty of Livermore, red; and Prince of Orange and Royal Scarlet, orange-scarlet. These are too strong in colour to be scattered broadcast over the garden. It is best to give up to them certain portions, furnishing them the milder companionship of lavender Irises and Canterbury Bells, blue and white Peach-leaved Campanulas, patches of soft-toned Nepeta and fluffy white Pinks, tall creamy Foxgloves, with now and then a yellow Lemon Lily or a group of scarlet Geums to rival their own brilliance. Nothing so softens the outlines of these intense colour masses as do the little spreads of gray-pink Valerian or Garden Heliotrope carried well above the Poppies. I am not fond of the mahogany-coloured Poppies like Mahony, but the salmon and shrimp-pink and flesh-coloured sorts are extremely beautiful. Planted in groups with Lyme Grass and Nepeta,

MAY IN THE GARDEN
MAY 15TH

THIS happy mingling of blossoming boughs and exuberant, flowery climber is created by the lovely Crabapple (*Pyrus* or *Malus floribunda*) growing beside an arbour over which trail the long branches of a white Wistaria. The Tulips in the border below are the Darwin Nauticus, the Iris is the Intermediate Empress, seen also in Plate No. 9 (*May 28th*) which is painted from a little further along this same border.

Arabis, Daffodils, and lavender creeping Phlox flower here a month earlier.

In June a fine group of Delphinium belladonna flowers with a foreground of coral-coloured Heuchera, and by the time the Delphinium is spent and has been cut down a strong plant of Gypsophila paniculata has spread out and covered its defection flowering delicately and making a striking picture with the orange Day Lilies (*Hemerocallis fulva*) that grow thickly beneath the tree, and some clumps of Blue-spiked Veronica (*Veronica spicata*).

Often blue annual Cornflowers are added to this group, and, if the frost spares them, are pretty enough with the small yellow Chrysanthemums that bloom here late in the season.

PLATE NO. 6
SEE PLATE NO. 9

IRIS AND LEMON LILY

MAY 21ST

*T*HIS is exactly the same portion of the garden as is shown in Plate No. 3 (April 28th). The little Crabapple then filling the picture with its delicate flowering is now quite secondary, yet creates with the fresh green of the Baptisia bushes on the left a pleasant background for the soft-coloured Iris Queen of May in the foreground. The gray foliage of Lyme Grass is now added to the group; and a little back, against the garden wall, the white rugosa Rose Madame Georges Bruant with its companion groups of Lemon Lilies and pale yellow Iris Canary Bird comes agreeably within the same vision-scope.

Still another grouping upon this same spot is shown in Plate No. 13 (July 1st).

PLATE NO. 7
SEE PLATES NOS. 3 AND 13

Stachys lanata and Valerian they are among the loveliest of early June's pictures.

The scarlet Geums, Mrs. Bradshaw and Glory of Stuttgart, are as brilliant as the Poppies in colour and may have their feet carpeted with purple and lavender Horned Violets (Viola cornuta), and be set about with sky-blue Flax, Nepeta, white and lavender Iris, or Peach-leaved Bellflowers with which they will live amicably. As the Geums flower nearly all summer, thought must be taken of their later companions. I grow them in a neighbourhood where cool blues generally prevail. Geum Heldreichii is dwarfer and flowers in May. It creates a gay picture set among groups of white Tulips and patches of lavender Creeping Phlox.

A turn of the way brings us to a border tricked out in those delightful colours that Mrs. Earl notes are all named for flowers: lavender, mauve (Mallow) pink, rose, lilac, orchid, violet, and heliotrope. This is an exquisite bit of border. Its foundation is of the newer Lupines—Blue Cloud, Eastern Queen, Enchantress, Beauty, Rosy Gem, Brightness, Excelsior— that show such fine blendings of the colours before mentioned, and few plants of June are so beautiful as these. With them in this border are patches of Rose-pink Pyrethrums, Iris Blue King, deep purple Columbines, Fraxinella, the charming lavender-flowered Meadow Rue (Thalictrum aquilegifolium); pink and lavender Canterbury Bells, and German Irises in the pinky-mauve shades; along the edges of the border, in patches and trails of soft colour, are Nepeta Mussini, Dicentra eximia, Stachys lanata, and Saponaria ocymoides, with an occasional tuft of the bright little Mule

Pink Fürst Bismarck. A few shafts of silver foliage pierce the rose and lavender colouring of the border and at the back some purple-leaved Plums throw the whole into fine relief.

To carry on this particularly soft and lovely colour scheme through the remaining months of the garden's life use is made of the following plants: Salvia pratensis, Salvia virgata nemorosa, Lythrum Salicaria, Veronica spicata, Lychnis (or Agrostemma) Coronaria, Astilbe Davidi, Erigeron speciosus Quakeress, blue Campanula carpatica, blue Campanula pyramidalis, Phloxes Wanardis and Crepuscle, Pink Hollyhocks, Campanula latifolia Brantwood, lavender and violet Michaelmas Daisies, Phloxes Von Hochberg and Madame Paul Dutrie, Rosy Musk-Mallows (Malva moschata), Eupatorium coelestinum, the pretty Blue Spiraea (Caryopteris mastacanthus) hardy anywhere south of New York City, and Gladiolus in the "pansy-flowered" shades. It is my feeling that white flowers would spoil this colour scheme.

As we continue our way, little thickets of tall creamy Foxgloves and pink Canterbury Bells—such a "peaches-and-cream" association—challenge us for praise; there is friend Sweet William, too, in his splendid new rôle of Scarlet Beauty, winding his way the entire length of one border, like a brilliant ribbon through a haze of lavender Nepeta. The older Pink Beauty is a choice thing, too, and has her place among lavender Canterbury Bells and the charming white Iris Innocenza.

I am extremely fond of the very dark red Sweet William with blackish stems, and it is a splendid balance for

high-pitched scarlet Geums and for Lychnis chalcedon-
ica. Sweet Williams, I think, are best treated as biennials, the young plants started in a nursery bed, set in
the garden in autumn, and pulled up after flowering.
The second flowering is always a poor affair and Sweet
Williams are so easily raised from seed that there is no
reason why we should not enjoy the solid blocks of fine
colour given by their first flowering. Young plants of
Ageratum, French Marigolds, Petunias—the pretty white-
throated Rosy Morn or the new and very fine violet sort
Velchenblau—a revelation in Petunias—may be set about
the patches of Sweet William, to expand and flower after
the last mentioned have been cast out.

And then we come to a corner of the garden where an
apple blossom of a Rose—Empress of China—trails its
bloom-laden branches from a corner of the pergola over a
group of rich crimson Peonies and great clumps of rich-
toned purple Campanula latifolia macrantha. Here too are
very tall white Foxgloves, the seed of which was acquired
of an English seed house under the name of Ayreshire
White. They are exceptionally tall and graceful, but some
of them lack the enticing brown freckles that make the
Foxglove flowers look like the noses of little country children. The Yellow Foxglove (Digitalis ambigua) is a fine,
soft-toned thing, seldom growing taller than three feet, but a
true perennial and one that blooms off and on throughout
the season. I often find the pretty yellow blossom spikes
after several hard frosts.

How any one can tolerate the monstrosity known as
Digitalis purpurea monstrosa, that has a great saucer at the

73

apex of its diminishing stalk, I cannot understand. As well crown the spire of a cathedral with a cartwheel and ask for praise! The Cup-and-saucer Canterbury Bell is another lauded development far inferior to the normal type. The simple bell form is always beautiful; to turn it into a cup and saucer is to degrade it.

And then we come to the borders where free-growing June Roses hold their gracious court. I do not know why these are not more often used in wide borders among hardy plants. They accept such a position with entire equanimity, lending a certain stability of appearance to the borders and in the season of their flowering creating pictures of transcendent loveliness. Stanwell's Perpetual Scotch Brier is exquisite, with faintly scented brier foliage and clouds of small, delicately flushed double Roses. The two yellow-flowering Roses, Harison's and the Persian, the latter more golden and more full petalled than the former, are splendid in the borders grouped with soft lavender Irises and white Lupines. Madame Plantier is a lovely free-growing white sort and the rugosa hybrids Madame Georges Bruant, Blanc Double de Coubert, Conrad F. Meyer, and the brilliant Souvenir de Pierre Leperdrieux are fine and suitable for such a purpose. Even the gay red-and-white striped Damask Roses like York and Lancaster and Village Maid are quaintly charming with an edge of white Pinks and mauve Horned Violets and some companion groups of soft blue Lupines.

If I had plenty of space I should certainly have a border given up entirely to early June. I should arrange it in some inconspicuous place where it need not be visited save at the time of its fulness and beauty. There should be white and purple Persian Lilacs, all these gracious free-growing Roses, masses of soft-coloured Lupines and Irises, spreads of mediating gray foliage and trails of spicy Pinks, soft-coloured Nepeta and Stachys. The accompanying plan is for a border long dreamed of and desired.

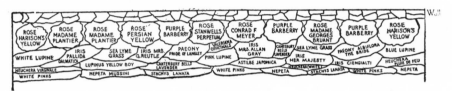

The free-growing Roses require no pruning beyond the thinning out of old or dead wood and the shortening of frost-nipped branches. The briers, Harison's Yellow, Persian Yellow, and Stanwell's Perpetual, are most effective when planted rather close together in groups of three, as their growth is rather straggling. I have a beautiful garden Rose whose name I do not know. It was here growing in the tangle of the old-fashioned dooryard when we came. Its branches are long and wandlike and laden with loosely double bright pink Roses—the base of each petal being white. The illustration Plate 11 shows it blooming, about the middle of the month, in a north border among Delphiniums, white Goat's Rue, Galega, and Anchusas.

Pinks are a delicious garnish for the June borders. Besides the Grass and Scotch Pinks there are delightful developments of the plumarius type. Better, I believe, than either Mrs. Sinkins or Her Majesty for a double white Pink are Perpetual Snow and White Reserve. They are less likely, in the stout doubling of their scented petals, to rend their strained calyxes. Cyclops is a lovely clear rose-coloured single Pink with a crimson inner circle and Delicata is a pretty flushed sort. After the first prodigal flowering these Pinks should be well cut over, all the faded flowers removed, and the old shoots shortened. This done, there will be a second more delicate flowering and the plants will retain their tidy forms and tender gray colour until well into the winter. There are few more brilliant plants than the hybrid Pink, or Mule Pink, Napoleon III. It produces its double blossoms on stiff stems with the utmost generosity, but unfortunately its generosity often means its death. More easily managed Mules are Fettes Mount and Fuerst Bismarck, both lovely shades of pure pink and very fragrant. The latter has proved so truly perpetual flowering in my garden that it formed, this autumn, with a few purple Horned Violets, the very last posy to be brought into the house. Many of the wild Pinks grow freely in the ordinary garden, but these were treated somewhat at length in "My Garden." No garden is too small for many Pinks. The plants require little room and will flower freely in any sunny corner. I tuck them all about in nooks and corners, allowing them to seed themselves into all sorts of places where I would not dare to put them. They grow in crevices of the stone steps, in the retaining walls, in little patches in the gravel walks. I can seldom bear to disturb them, unless they are actually in a way to obstruct traffic. An edging of double white or single white fringed Pinks, Nepeta Mussini and gay pink Thrift, is the very prettiest thing I know. The best Thrift for this association is plantaginea, a variety of Armeria cephalotes (syn. formosa), that bears its rosy globes on naked scapes well above the rosettes of dark green foliage.

Of course the June pictures having Irises as the basis of their beauty are many, for the so-called "German" Iris is the flower *par excellence* for our American gardens and gains steadily in favour. No other so staunchly braves the brutal eccentricities of our climate, giving us unblemished foliage and flawless petals though summer drought and deluge beset it; though in winter a temperature plying violently between the zero point and summer heat harry its needed rest. The temptation is to fill our gardens with this sturdy, beautiful flower, to enjoy to the full the resplendent period of its festival, and to rest content for the remainder of the season in the gracious memory of those June days. We are, moreover, being encouraged in this course, for from out the Green Work Shops of the world issues a bewildering procession of new Irises in the most enchanting furbishings and all the wondrous colours that can be imagined.

In the English *Country Life* for June 24, 1917, Mr. Eden Phillpotts writes, "Man has availed himself of the great laws of evolution in mightier matters than the Iris, but in no theatre of his unsleeping efforts has he created purer beauty or wakened for flower lovers a truer joy than among the bearded Irises of June." Truly this is the great day of the Flower-de-luce, of which John Parkinson, thorough-going gardener and devout flower-worshipper, wrote three hundred years ago "for his excellent beautie and rarietie deserveth first place." So the German Iris is after all an old friend, but what would John Parkinson say could he see to what grand estate it is risen?

77

COLOUR IN MY GARDEN

No modest gardener can hope to keep abreast with the triumphal procession of the Iris to-day; few gardens are large enough to hold a tithe of the radiant throng, and many of the newest varieties are held at prices whose equivalent is not to be drawn from the toe of a modest stocking. It is, however, one of the many compensations that attends the path of the gardener that though he possess but a patch of the common Purple Flag or a stalk or two of the gray-cowled Florentine he has for his portion perfect beauty, dignity, and sweetness.

My own garden boasts few of the fine new varieties, but we are very gay indeed this bright June day and full of diversity. Here against a full-flowered Scarlet Thorn (Paul's) is a great splash of the pure lavender colour of the great Dalmatian Iris. The Thorn is not scarlet, but a full crimson pink that accords perfectly with the colour of this finest of German Irises. Again the tall lavender Iris Celeste consorts charmingly with a troupe of pink Canterbury Bells. Surely no Irises are finer than these of the pallida group, whether of lavender or of the enchanting pink shades; Albert Victor is superb among the older sorts, nearly resembling the Dalmatian variety, and Celeste, Australis, La Tendresse, and Khedive are equally lovely and as modestly priced as one could wish. Yet there seems no end to desire; one has no rest for thinking of that fair Isoline, whose price the tiny root is a dollar and a quarter; of Shelford Chieftain and that fine group of lavender-blue Irises brought to life by Mr. Farr—Chester J. Hunt, Massasoit, Mary Gray, Glory of Reading, Juniata, and many others. Mr. Farr's pink seedlings also fill the soul with beatitude. How truly beautiful are these that range from tender rose-mauve to deep rose and claret—Wyomissing, Windham, Pauline, Mt. Penn, and Hugo. Beautiful, too, among the so-called pink Irises are Ed. Michel with very large flowers of warm wine-red; Lohengrin, uniform soft rose-mauve; and Mrs. Alan Gray, very tender in its colouring. All these are still rather costly but one is easily consoled with the older sorts, Queen of May, Her Majesty, Leonidas, and Madame Pacquitte, which, were it not for those intriguing eulogies in the catalogues, would satisfy one's every desire.

No flowers offer a lovelier accompaniment for Irises than do the new Lupines. Their beautiful spreading foliage is just the right foil for the svelte leaves of the Iris, their classic flower spike the perfect antithesis of the heavier Flag flower. Here we have mauve-pink Iris Her Majesty with creamy Lupines, the paler Queen of May with some of the delicately opalescent lavender sorts, deep blue Lupines with the fine chrome-yellow Iris aurea (variegata section), and pink Lupines in lovely association with the pure white Iris Innocenza.

Canterbury Bells and Foxgloves are good company for Irises, the latter furnishing tactful companionship for the strange harmonies to be found in the variegata and squalens sections; gold and smoke colour and purple; crimson, brown, and dull yellow; gray and russet and white; fawn and maroon and amaranth and many more that give one pause when it comes to finding their proper niche among the less complex of the garden's children.

Single Peonies in soft pink and old rose are delightful among the lavender Irises of the pallida group. They do not overpower the more frailly fashioned flowers as do the heavy-headed double sorts. Single flowers are to me nearly always more beautiful, and while I would not part with one of my dear apoplectic—the adjective is Maeterlinck's—double Peonies, I am glad to see the chaste singles and loose-petalled semi-doubles coming into favour.

Other flowers that find a happy companionship among the Irises in my garden are Valerian, Oriental Poppies, Nepeta Mussini, Baptisia australis, Meadow Sage—its dull blue flower spikes are lovely with the mauve-pink Irises—Meadow Rue, old-fashioned Fraxinella, both the white and the pink sorts, and the simple border Roses.

We have not seen half the garland in which June frames her laughing face; and many a sweet and lovely flower has been passed unnoted in our colour-bewildered progress. Truly it is not good to have too much at once; how grateful should we be for a single hour of this bountiful June day in white December!

CHAPTER VII
ROSE COLOUR

CHAPTER VII

ROSE COLOUR

Oho, my love, oho, my love, and ho, the bough that shows,
Against the grayness of mid-Lent the colour of the rose!
—LIZETTE REESE.

IT SEEMS to me that few words register so pleasant an
impression as rose colour. It reminds us of all sorts
of pleasant things and circumstances and yet, like
many other words we use freely, its meaning is vague. When
we consider Roses themselves, we have them,

> Red as the wine of forgotten ages,
> Yellow as gold of the sunbeams spun;
> Pink as the gowns of Aurora's pages,
> White as the robe of the sinless one.

And besides, flame and saffron and blush, cherry and cream
and buff, crimson and scarlet—and which of these is "Rose"
colour?

If one orders a plant catalogued as "rose coloured," it is
sure to arrive that dear besmirched hue—magenta. I have
no quarrel with magenta, but I do not want it when my
heart is set upon a delightful pink, and some spot in my
garden is especially designed to hold it. Magenta is the
skeleton in the closet of nurserymen and seedsmen and "rose

83

colour" is the cloak they use to hide what they deem an unfortunate fact concerning certain of their offerings. It is partly this practice of sending out magenta for rose colour that has given the former a bad name. We order a rose-coloured Peony. It arrives a deep amaranth; and, while the Peony may be very beautiful, the mind cannot so quickly release its rosy vision and switch to appreciation of the more subtle hue. To me rose colour is that lovely colour tone worn by the wild Rose, those shy and exquisite creatures of the tangled wayside and high meadow, whose festal season Thoreau thought should have some preëminence, perhaps such special viewings as are accorded the Cherry blossoms in Japan. This pink of the wild Rose is at once the most luscious and delicate colour in all the kingdom of flowers, and it is all too rare. The fine climbing Rose, American Pillar, comes very near to being pure rose colour and there is a new one now, another gift by an American grower, which has all the grace and charm of the wild Rose combined with the climbing habit and vigorous constitution of the Rambler. Its name is America.

The reign of pink is inaugurated in the garden with the festival of the blossoms. We have the full-costumed Peach-trees, the twisted, rose-wrapped branches of the Crabapples, the many exquisite forms of pink double-flowered Japanese Cherries and Plums, and around about their enchanting skirts in jaunty array are ranks and ranks of pink Tulips. But June is the season supreme for rose colour. Then we have the great mass of Roses, Peonies, Pinks, Poppies, Sweet Williams, and Pyrethrums; and while, in the later summer, there are Phlox and Hollyhocks and some good pink annuals, by autumn pink has practically vanished from the garden, leaving us but a memory of the rose-coloured days of June.

In all our dealings with the garden it seems to me the part of wisdom to go along with Nature as far as we can. She is a rarely sympathetic collaborator, but to go against her means useless effort and often poor or indifferent results. Let us not try to have a blue garden or a yellow garden in late May and early June; let us revel in a pink one, seeking out all the best and loveliest of pink flowers and making them the foundation for our display, with the dim blues, the tender buffs and creams, the rich purples, fluffy whites, and silvery foliage plants used merely as foils to heighten or subdue our gracious breadths and trails of rose colour.

None of the climbing Roses are so entirely charming as the pink ones, and there are some fine newcomers that should be added to the collection of older favourites. I have spoken before of the beautiful America; Coquina is another lovely single pink Rose with a white heart and a brush of golden stamens. Its foliage is thick and shining and almost evergreen. Lucile is a double-flowered Rose of the Rambler type with salmon-pink blossoms carried in large loose clusters. The little single Rose, Paradise, is most gay and sprightly in effect. The petals are rather narrow, widely flaring, and each is quaintly notched. The colour is pink and white and the blossoms are borne in great lax clusters.

Of the other pink Roses none is more beautiful than Dr. Van Fleet, the blossoms of which are very large and the buds particularly fine. Wm. C. Egan is a good fully double pink Rose of the Rambler type, and Mrs. Flight is another of great merit. Dorothy Perkins blooms later in my garden than the other Ramblers and is lovely with the warm purple blossoms of Clematis Jackmanii unfolding among the fluffy pink draperies. Of single-flowered pink Roses there are a great many. My own favourites are Newport Fairy, that has the delicate beauty of a sea shell; Tausendschoen, very floriferous and softly tinted; Waltham Rambler and Empress of China, that looks like an Apple Blossom; and the beautiful American Pillar, a full, frank rose colour.

To use these Roses freely means a brave garden for at least a month, and if we mass Delphiniums against them we have accomplished enough beauty for one season.

Quite as important as anything else in the realm of garden colour is the wise choice of Roses in reference to what they are to climb upon. The beauty of many a full pink Rose is lost because it must lay its satin cheek against a crude brick wall. New red brick is utterly unsuitable as a background for pink or red Roses. The soft vinaceous purple or pinky-drab tones that time's transmuting touch bestows upon brick makes it a happy background for any colour; but new red brick is a problem. Pale blush and creamy Roses and vines of fluffy white flowers, like Clematis paniculata and the fine Knotweed, Polygonum baldschuanicum, are the best for it. Again, buildings of that aggressive pumpkin colour that is popular in some districts should be hung only with white or creamy flowering vines.

A white building offers the most delightful possibilities as a background for gay-flowered climbers. What is prettier than a white house smothered beneath pink and scarlet Roses of all shades, with the starlike flowering in May of Clematis montana, with ropes of purple Wistaria and some space left for the scarlet autumn hangings of Virginia Creeper.

Stone, of course, furnishes as fine a background, and stucco, gray or white, is nearly as good. For pergolas and arbours white woodwork is the most effective though in my garden the long central arbour is stained so dark a green as to be almost black and takes its place in the garden pictures with force and beauty. In England I saw a circular Rose arbour painted very light apple green. Upon it grew white and pale lemon coloured Roses with now and then a great splash of purple Clematis, and in the narrow beds at the base of the posts were crowding purple and lavender Violas, delicate Ferns, and white Stocks. It was most unusually fresh and pretty.

Some fine Roses and other climbers suited to pumpkin-coloured and red walls and to chocolate-coloured ones are: Roses Silver Moon, Alberic Barbier, Gardenia, Trier, Bennett's Seedling, and Rene Andre; White Wistaria, Clematis Jackmanii, Henryii, montana and paniculata; Polygonum baldschuanicum; Honeysuckles of all sorts including the yellow-leaved variety; and Actinidia arguta.

In the pink garden Peonies are next in importance to Roses. To-day the May-flowering Peony is neglected. In peaceful old gardens that remain unfretted by changing fashions and modern introductions we are apt to find huge bushes of the old May-flowering Peony or "Piny" as it is called in country neighbourhoods, Paeonia officinalis. In the Maryland garden where I grew up I remember that there were many clumps of these massed against the evergreens that formed a windbreak for my mother's Rose garden. There was the "old crimson," which is yet one of my favourite Peonies and exhibits almost the richest colour that I know. There was a full pink sort that we children called the "strawberry-ice-cream Peony," and there was a loose-petalled white one, probably some garden form of the old double albiflora.

When, after an interval of many years, this old garden in New York State became my home, I was happy to find those sweet and wholesome friends of my childhood growing in the tangled dooryard—that is the crimson and the "strawberry-ice-cream" were here, but not the white one. There are improvements upon these primitive sorts now offered us, but I have not had the opportunity to see them. Paeonia tenuifolia is a very fine warm-toned crimson Peony with deeply imbricated petals that blooms in May; it has a double form. Wittmanniana, obovata and albiflora Whitleyi are exquisite Paeonia species to be grown by those who care for the chaste beauty of a shell-like flower with golden stamens. I believe they are not more difficult than other Peonies to grow, only requiring a rich, deep soil, light shade, and to be left quite alone.

The Chinese Tree Peony (P. Moutan) flowers in early May. This is shrubby in character, though Mr. Reginald Farrer* says it "is less a shrub indeed, than incarnate beauty itself." After reading Mr. Farrer's description of the Tree Peony, I would not venture to attempt an account of its charms myself, so I will take the liberty of giving his: "The Tree Peony of the East is a loose, arrogant splendour;

*"Alpines and Bogplants."

the flowers are vast, satin in texture and sheen, sometimes torn and fringed at the edges, sometimes double, sometimes single—but always of the most imperious yet well-bred loveliness, in every pure shade of colour from the white snows of Fuji at dawn, through faintest shades of pearl and pale rose to the growing ardours of coral, salmon, scarlet, vermilion, sanguine; and so on, into the deep tones of crimson, claret, and a maroon that deepens almost to black." I do not know who, after reading this, can resist adding these flowers to his garden and it is well also to heed Mr. Farrer's warning that the European grown Tree Peony is far inferior to those raised in China.

Mrs. Basil Taylor* tells us that the Peony is too flamboyant in its dyes to appeal to the sensitive Japanese, who, unlike the colour-loving Chinese, "revel in the pearly half-tints, the mauves and dove colours of their Irises and Wistarias, the pale rosy clouds of their masses of Plum and Cherry." But of late the Japanese has turned the magic of his art toward the Peony and has given us a new race distinct and æsthetic in type, dyed with the tender and illusive colours so dear to the people who send them forth, and exhibiting many charming irregularities of form, double, semi-double, and of the most delicate satiny texture.

After contemplation of these fraily fashioned and gracious blossoms the June Peony seems somewhat coarse and heavy, yet it has its place and we should miss its opulent beauty that seems to typify the fulness of its birth month. Their name is legion and I do not know a great many, personally,

---

*"Japanese Garden."

but as this is a chapter to rose colour, I will give a list of the best pink ones that I have found. Madame Emile Galle is a French Peony of rare beauty. Its colour scheme is opalescent, delicate rose-lilac as to its outer petals, but paling to milk-white at the heart. It is a large, full flower of the flat rose type. Madame Calot wears the peculiarly charming silvery pink of the Hydrangea. This is also of the rose type, a tall, strong grower and very fragrant. Eugenie Verdier wears the same Hydrangea pink, but is attractively flecked with deeper colour. Madame Coste, Milton Hill, Madame Herve, Madame Forel, M. Jules Elie, are all fine pink Peonies.

Lavender Irises of the pallida section are good to grow with these heavy-headed June Peonies. Some of the finest are pallida dalmatica, Albert Victor, Australis, Violacea, Chester J. Hunt, and Blue Jay.

Peony culture is most gratifyingly simple; the requisites being only rich, deep soil and neglect. If they are planted in partial shade the blossoms will last longer in perfection, and some of the deep-toned sorts will be less apt to fade.

Pyrethrums offer many shades of pink and rose colour for the May garden. For once I am fonder of the double form of a flower and find much charm in the compact many-petalled Pyrethrums, which are as yet rather rare in this country. The single sorts that are so good for cutting come easily from seed and form heavy clumps that last for many years. The single white Pyrethrum is too much like our own field Daisy to seem to belong to the garden.

Potentilla formosa and the improved Miss Willmott give salmon-pink flowers over a long period, but while their foliage is good, they are a bit lax in habit to make good subjects for the borders. For other pink flowers at this season we have Sweet Williams and the shining Canterbury Bell, the pretty trailing Soapwort (Saponaria ocymoides), Heucheras, Oriental Poppies, Lupines such as Rosy Gem and Nelly, Dicentra spectabilis and D. eximia, Aquilegias, Pinks, and Thrifts.

As the summer progresses we have Hollyhocks representing pink in the garden. Where single Hollyhocks seed themselves there are many attractive forms developed, none prettier than those in which pink and amber blend, soft yellow Hollyhocks with warmly flushed centres like those in Plate 15. This pink and yellow association takes place charmingly in many flowers. It is particularly well accomplished in various China and Tea Roses, in Snapdragons, Lupines, and Sweet Peas, and while we may not manage it as cleverly as does Nature, still we may bring about some very attractive arrangements. Pink Lupines and yellow Foxgloves are good, groups of Tulips in soft shades of pink and yellow, pale Mulleins with such a Phlox as Peachblow.

Fine pink annuals are numerous; the ashen pink and salmon pink Zinnias are good perpetual flowering plants for filling in the blanks left by biennials, or for planting among the clumps of steel-blue Sea Hollies, with which they are in pleasant accord. Clarkias and Godetias and of course Poppies have many rosy offerings. Many and beautiful pink varieties have Snapdragons, China Asters, and Stocks and there is a dainty pink annual flower well known to frequenters of the Paris flower markets called

Saponaria Vaccaria. It is most graceful in effect and delightful for bouquets.

At the end of the season we must look closely to find a pink flower save where annuals continue or a Hollyhock still keeps a blossom or two. There may be a few groups of speciosum Lilies, but it is to the frail but hardy Windflower (Anemone japonica) that we are indebted for our last glimpse of rose colour, and to the little hardy Chrysanthemum, whose special quality of pinkness might not pass the standards of June but which at this season of departures and farewells wins from us no criticism, but only gratitude and affection.

CHAPTER VIII
MIDSUMMER BLUE

CHAPTER VIII

MIDSUMMER BLUE

Blue! gentle cousin of the forest green,
Married to green in all the sweetest flowers.

—KEATS.

WHEN I say blue I hope not to be taken too literally, for it is difficult not to drift into bluish violet or toward that cool company of lavender-blues to which so many of the so-called blue flowers of garden books and catalogues belong. No colours are so confused as to nomenclature, and I think we should be grateful to Dr. Ridgeway, who, in his splendid "Colour Standards and Colour Nomenclature" gives us the opportunity to be definite if we so choose.

There are comparatively few truly blue flowers; that is, blue after the cerulean manner of the Anchusa, or in the baby way of the Forget-me-not. But with the long blue days of summer comes a tide of colour to the garden, blue in feeling and in effect and grateful to the eyes because of its coolness of aspect in the trying heat and amidst the ever-increasing riot of gay colours.

These blues are of many tones. The Campanulas manifest a range that may be characterized as "dim." They

95

lean toward violet and have sometimes a sort of undertone of gray, and they are particularly cool and suave in effect. Early writers prefix the word "bleak" to such blues as these and I think it finely descriptive as were so many of their terms. Aconites, Veronicas, Platycodons, and the Globe Thistles (Eryngium and Echinops) belong in this class and they are perhaps the most easily harmonized of all flower colours. They seem to have no edges, but a melting colour quality like the blue of the distance. With them scarlet, orange, strong Tyrian pink, or magenta may be placed without fear of discord or too sharp contrast, often with strikingly beautiful effect. The pure red and pure blue of the spectrum used together give a very harsh contrast, but placed with one of the cool blues spectrum red loses much of its truculence and becomes a softened thing.

The colour of the wild Chicory is about the coldest blue. E. V. B. has well described it as "colour so cold, so pure, so spirit blue." It is a charming shade and Chicory would be invaluable in the garden, for it continues to expand its pretty round blossoms right up to the frost line were it not for its thin, tatterdemalion foliage that never will look anything but common. I enjoy Chicory in the sensible democracy of the herb garden and in sumptuous breadths in my neighbour's neglected fields and hope that some day a public-spirited hybridist will take this charming vagabond in hand and fit her for the select world within the garden walls. Some Hyacinths display this peculiar cold blue and make very pretty spring beds when edged with Arabis.

Then we have the rich full blue of the Anchusa type, an exquisite scale, pure and uninfluenced, from the lovely

Neapolitan and Venetian blues, and even paler, to almost the depth of ultramarine, and approaching in some flowers the strength of what are called in the colour chart Smalt and Helvetia blues. For these pure blues—to which belong, of course, the loveliest of blue flowers, the Delphiniums—the happiest associations are flowers wearing soft shades of yellow and cream and buff, apricot and pink.

There is something particularly appealing about a blue flower. This seems always to have been the case, for there is hardly a flower of this hue but has won for itself several intimate and affectionate pet names, showing the closeness of its life, whether in the garden or in the open, with the lives of flower-loving humanity. To-day this affection shows itself in a different manner; there is something like a craze for blue borders and even for whole blue gardens. Yellow and pink and white gardens there are occasionally, but in no such numbers as one sees and hears of blue ones. This in itself is well, for it shows appreciation of and draws attention to these best-beloved flowers; but it seems to me that from an æsthetic standpoint the segregation of blue flowers is a mistake. They, more than any others, need the flash of scarlet, the cloud of white, the drift of apricot or buff to kindle them into life and bring out their full quality.

I have seen a good many blue borders very consistently worked out, but the more successful they were as achievements the less pleasing they seemed as garden pictures. The prettiest blue border I ever saw was one wherein a few Nasturtium seeds had been accidently dropped, and between the elegantly aspiring stalks of Larkspur and Anchusa one got little sparkles of flame and saffron and buff that endowed the blue flowers with a shimmering spirit that would certainly not have been theirs without those unbidden companions.

There is some blue in the garden from the earliest spring. It begins with the Chionodoxas, Scillas, Grape Hyacinths, and Forget-me-nots that precede the Lungworts, creeping Veronicas, and Flax flowers; but perhaps the Italian Anchusa, with its several varieties, may be said to head the tide of midsummer blue, and right royally it holds its position. It belongs to the same family as do the potent Borage of the Herb Garden and the Viper's Bugloss that stains whole stretches of wasteland in certain sections with inimitable colour, to the wrath of the farmer and the delight of the idle wayfarer.

It may be said that the Anchusa has "taken the eye" of the gardening public, and bids fair to be as popular as the Phlox or the Delphinium. This is not surprising, for though we are puzzled by its capricious biennial-perennial tricks, the Anchusa faces our drought-ridden climate with supreme complaisance, for which alone we owe it a debt of gratitude. It is as indifferent to cold, too (though in heavy, damp soils it occasionally winter kills), and has a long period of cerulean flowering. There is about it, however, a certain indifference to garden standards that keeps it out of the ranks of the exquisites; a laxness of carriage, a tendency to flop on its neighbours, and its foliage is undeniably coarse. But there can be no fault found with the tints in which it decks itself. The old parent Alkanet, Anchusa italica, is satisfying enough as to blueness, but each successive introduction—Dropmore, Perry's, Lissadel, Opal—seems to attain a more perfect hue. The Italian Alkanet has more the colour of the Gentian, while Opal is many shades lighter. We have Anchusas in splendid association with the old crimson Peony whose colour is so rich and deep; rising like an Italian sky behind a riotous pink garden Rose, in great felicity in front of a mauve-pink Clematis Ville de Lyon, among free-growing white Roses and gleaming Lemon Lilies, and in many another happy combination.

Not long after the appearance of the Anchusa the Delphinium comes to outshine it in colour and form. Of all blue flowers these are the most lovely. There is no period of the year when the garden is so exuberantly beautiful as that when there are climbing, tumbling, reaching Roses in all directions and spires and spires of Delphiniums gleaming against them or shooting upward like jets of blue flame to touch the fragrant sprays above. Every year there are many named varieties put forth by various nurseries. A modest gardener could not hope to keep up with them and it matters little, for a single packet of seed purchased of a reliable house will fill one's every desire for blueness. Those of the Belladonna type seem to me the loveliest. Cliveden Beauty is particularly conspicuous for its exquisite sky-blue colour and its grace of stalk, and others as lovely are Mrs. Thomson, Persimmon, Capri, and Mrs. J. S. Boonton, all with the satisfying colour and graceful habit of Belladonna. Other fine sorts are Lize van Veen (Cambridge blue), Queen Wilhelmina (pure sky blue), Mrs. Creighten, The Alaak (violet blue), and Somerset.

I have never seen Delphiniums poorly placed, they seem so to grace every situation as to make inharmony impossible, and yet there are degrees of effectiveness in the arrangement even of these ever-satisfying flowers. Two Delphinium pictures in my own garden please me particularly just now. A pale Larkspur is massed against the dark framework of the pergola over which showers a fluffy white Rose (Trier). In front of the Delphiniums are some spikes of Yellow Foxglove (Digitalis ambigua), and to the right a group of single buff-coloured Hollyhocks with pink hearts. Again sky-blue Delphiniums rise from a mist of feathery yellow Meadow Rue (Thalictrum glaucum), one of the most delightful of plants, against a background of pink climbing Roses and with a foreground of Baptisia bushes with their fine metallic leafage.

Of the beauty of Larkspurs and white Lilies much has been written; I have spoken elsewhere of their splendid effect with Herring Lilies (Lilium croceum), and there are two other Lilies that grow freely under ordinary garden conditions with which they are delightful. One is L. Hansoni, of waxen texture and pure orange colour lightly flecked, and the other is L. Brownii, warm ivory with pale chocolate exterior and bright orange stigmata.

More use might well be made of the pretty hybrids of Delphinium grandiflorum. These are charming, fluttering things of but eight or ten inches in height that wear the loveliest shades of blue. As they bloom early the first summer from seed they may be treated as annuals, and the pretty blossoms enjoyed until frost. Azure Fairy and Blue Butterfly are well named. Cineraria marks a new type. Its flowers are a darker blue with a white inner circle and they are quite flat and spurless.

COLOUR IN MY GARDEN

Some flowers fine in association with Delphiniums are yellow and creamy Mulleins, buff and pink Hollyhocks, Anthemis tinctoria, the Evening Primroses, Lemon Lilies— late flowering—Papaver rupifragum with the dwarf Larkspurs, buff and flame coloured Snapdragons and Calendulas. And of course it is always to be remembered that preparation must be made for the time when the Delphiniums shall be cut down by planting Phlox, Baptisia, or some other reliably permanent plant in front of them.

Blue and yellow is always a pleasant combination. To-day, June 28th, in my garden the following are very pretty: Bluish-violet Canterbury Bells and yellow Foxgloves; Evening Primrose (Oenothera fruticosa) and Veronica incana; California Poppies and Salvia Bluebeard; Peach-leaved Campanulas and Linaria dalmatica; Nigella Miss Jekyl and yellow Snapdragons, self-sown.

I have before spoken of the cool beauty of the Campanulas. Theirs is an indispensable family in the midsummer garden. Beginning with the wee C. pusilla, that in lieu of a rock garden we grow in the joints of the steps, up to the towering C. pyramidalis, I enjoy all that I know in one sort of position or another. Even the rather weedy sorts like C. trachelium, C. grandis, and C. rapunculoides when grown in semi-wild places create fine stretches of clean, cool colour.

The Carpathian Hairbell (Campanula carpatica) is a pretty and useful plant for the front of the border, blooming from July until October. There are several very good forms of this; White Star is an improvement upon the ordinary sort, having saucer-shaped blossoms. C. carpatica coelestina wears a peculiarly soft shade of blue.

101

Perhaps the prettiest Bellflower is C. persicifolia, with its many stems of fragile bells. It has the usual violet-blue and white forms and if these are allowed to sow themselves about the garden we shall get intermediate shades all the way from the deepest blue to the curious skimmed-milk hue so often displayed by these inter-marrying Campanulas. C. lactiflora,* with its two fine varieties, E. Molineux (blue) and alba magnifica (white), is one of the most useful. The plants grow often six feet tall and have handsome foliage. They should be left without division as long as they are doing well. C. lactiflora blooms in August, just before the handsome biennial C. pyramidalis, and continues to develop blossoms for a long period if the old ones are cut off. The latter grows six feet tall and carries its splendid flowering well into September.

Of the more strongly purple Bellflowers, C. latifolia macrantha is a fine sort. It does not require division save every five or six years, and grows into splendid, strong clumps sending up many stalks of deep purple bells. This plant is effective with the feathery Spiraea Aruncus (or Aruncus sylvester) and masses of pink Sweet Williams. Campanula glomerata is also a good purple sort and among the Canterbury Bells are several lavender and purple shades. All these Bell-flowers have white forms, but Canterbury Bell is the only one known to me that offers a luscious pink one. C. alliarifolia is a white Bellflower of much beauty, though a bit rampageous for the select circle of the flower garden. It is a delightful wild garden plant.

Platycodons are of these cool coloured midsummer

---

* In heavy soil this plant sometimes winter kills.

ORIENTAL POPPIES AND VALERIAN
MAY 28TH

*B*EHIND this brilliant group are strong clumps of Gypsophila paniculata which, by the time the Poppies are ready for a rather disorderly retreat underground and the yellowing stalks of the Valerian are cut down, has spread a rejuvenating web of wiry branches and delicate gray-green foliage above their heads and rescued the border from dire forlornity.

Again the long branches of the Michaelmas Daisy Top Sawyer, planted between clumps of pink Phlox, in turn are drawn forward to hide the gentle passing of the Gypsophila.

The August aspect of this bit of raised border is shown in plate No. 21 (August 10th).

The spring display here is composed of Cottage Tulip Leghorn Bonnet, Phlox subulata G. F. Wilson, and dwarf purple Irises.

PLATE NO. 8
SEE PLATE NO. 21

THE FULLNESS OF THE SPRING
MAY 28TH

*T*HIS *warm-toned picture shows upon the upper terrace, against the southwest wall, a gold-hung Laburnum tree (L. vulgare), a bush of Persian Lilac, and a group of the Darwin Tulip Gretchen. The purple Iris in the lower border is the common I. germanica, the cream-coloured one is the Intermediate Iris Empress. The Tulips are Mrs. Moon and the patches of white are from Sweet Rocket (Hesperis matronalis) and still lingering Arabis.*

In April the Arabis is in full beauty and with it, along the edge of this border, are clumps of deep purple Iris pumila, festoons of pale lavender Phlox subulata G. F. Wilson, and groups of the bright yellow Daffodil Katherine Spurrell.

Early in June a clump of purple Meadow-rue (Thalictrum aquilegifolium) bursts into feathery bloom. In July a group of pink and buff Hollyhocks and early Phlox Miss Lingard is the offering; and for August a lovely group composed of the tall, soft pink Phlox Tower of Eiffel, Silver Thistle (Echinops sphaerocephalus), and Chimney Bellflower (Campanula pyramidalis).

All this; and yet in October the border is once more rendered demurely festive by a group of cold blue Aconites (Aconitum autumnale) and the Shrubby Ox-eye Daisy (Chrysanthemum nipponicum).

The other end of this border is to be seen in Plate No. 6 (May 15th.)

PLATE NO. 9
SEE PLATE NO. 6

flowers and exhibit also the attractive bell form. The soft gray-blue ones are particularly effective massed in front of groups of such a scarlet Phlox as Coquelicot. The best of the blue Veronicas is spicata, with long spikes of deep blue flowers lasting in good condition for many weeks. It is an invaluable hardy plant; better in most ways than V. sub-sessilis which does not thrive in all gardens. V. spicata may be allowed to go without division for three or four years and is splendid among clumps of late-flowering Lemon Lilies, the July Phloxes Nettie Stuart and Miss Lingard, or creating a soft and lovely effect between hazy breadths of Gypsophila. Veronica incana presents a quaint gray and blue ensemble. It is dwarf in stature and consorts pleasantly with scarlet Geums or bright elegans Lilies near the front of the border. The pretty trailing Veronicas—repens and prostrata—belong to May.

There is a modest little blue flower of which I am fond that seems not to be very often grown. This is Cupid's Dart (Catanache coerulea). Unfortunately it is not reliably hardy in the vicinity of New York, but may be safely carried over in a frame and is well worth the slight trouble, for it blooms all summer, sending up from a tidy tuft of leaves many slender stems in quick succession bearing little Cornflower-like blooms of a fine shade of blue. Two Irises that are very blue in feeling are Iris orientalis Blue King and the great Monspur. Miss Jekyll gives Iris Cengialti as the bluest Iris. The old-fashioned Greek Valerian (Polemonium Richardsonii, P. humulus, P. reptans, P. caeruleum) is a blue flower of midsummer; also Spiderwort (Tradescantia virginica), with its strange three-cornered blossoms; and Baptisia australis, which is one of the very best of hardy plants.

Good blue annuals are quite numerous. One of the prettiest is the Cape Forget-me-not (Anchusa capensis). Not one of its cerulean family boasts a purer blue and its summer-long period of bloom and indifference to drought make it a really valuable annual. It has also a sturdy habit of growth and sowing its hardy seeds freely it does its best to become a permanent resident. Another beautiful blue flower and one rarely seen is Phacelia campanularia that bears its gentian-blue flowers with conspicuous white anthers about eight inches above the foliage. The seed is hardy, so may be sown early, and little patches of its pure blue flowers are very pretty mingled with buff Phlox Drummondi along the border edge. One might search far and not find a more appealing blue flower than the little Cornflower—Centaurea cyanus Emperor William. It is another generous self-sower, so generous that I am often under the sad necessity of rooting out the trusting green tufts from the walks. I let them stay wherever it is possible for they are among the flowers for which we have a special tenderness and nothing is prettier for cutting and placing in old blue and white china jars for indoor enjoyment. There are some very dwarf forms that make pretty edgings.

Miss Jekyll's Love-in-a-mist (Nigella) is a choice blue annual too well known to require description, but Nemesia Blue Gem, a graceful foot-tall plant with slender stems and sky-blue flowers, is less familiar. Anagalis caerulea, six inches tall, and Nemophila insignis or Love Grove, four inches, are pretty for edges, the latter thriving best in damp shade. Borage is a lovely blue-flowered plant with gray foliage and quaintly shaped blossoms once much used as a pattern in ladies' needlework and often to be seen woven into the garlands of old samplers or tapestry work. And still we have the violet-blue of Browallia, the lavender-blue of the little blue Woodruff, that creates a delicate film of pale colour unsolicited in many parts of the garden; the blue and yellow and white of the wide-eyed Convolvulus tricolor, the dark violet-blue of Salvia horminium Blue Beard, the various blues of Lobelias, and the inimitable blue of Salvia patens. This plant is, in fact, a perennial, but in our climate must be treated as a tender annual and started indoors in March.

Other blue flowers of the year are: Lupines, Aconites, Clematis Davidiana, Hyssop, Salvia azurea and S. uliginosa, Plumbago Larpentae, Lithospermum prostratum, Echinops Ritro, Eryngium planum, and E. Oliverianum, Pentstemon heterophyllus and P. glabra, Centaurea montana, and Veronica amethystina.

And while I should most certainly gather all these dear blue flowers into one garden or even into one border, I should plant with them scarlet and buff Tulips, yellow and white Iris, patches of the Spanish Poppy (Papaver rupifragum), groups of pale Mulleins and yellow Fig-leaved Hollyhocks, the delicate yellow Meadow Rue (Thalictrum glaucum), Geums, a few orange and scarlet Lilies, Gypsophila, Valerian, Orange King Snapdragons, pale Calendulas, Torch Lilies, Montbretias, and other plants of like brave colouring.

CHAPTER IX
FLOWERS OF LIGHT

CHAPTER IX

FLOWERS OF LIGHT

There is gold for you.—CYMBELINE.

AS I have said many times I am not fond of gardens or borders devoted to one colour; but if ever I were tempted to make one it would be yellow in all the frank and pleasant tones from cream and buff and the bright butter yellows through apricot to the tawny ochreous shades, reaching now and then to flame. Not all blue flowers may be safely used in each other's company and but few pinks unless they are of the same scale; but all yellow flowers, like the light of which they seem to be fashioned, blend and combine or flash back at each other with never a jar to the most sensitive eye. They are the sunshine of the garden, and it is a pleasant fact that yellow flowers are more plentiful than any others and that from the time of the delicate radiances of spring to the flaring up of autumn's beacons their illumination is un-dimmed.

I like yellow flowers grown in full sunshine. They seem to gather glow from the great luminary and seldom bleach or shrivel before its warmth as do so many blue and scarlet flowers. As a matter of fact, the brightest yellow flowers nearly all grow naturally in full sunshine; those found in shaded places show usually a quite greenish tint as in the Yellow Aconite (Aconitum pyrenaicum) and the Winter Aconite (Eranthis hyemalis).

As I have said, there are yellow flowers in plenty for all the gardening season, but in this chapter I wish to speak of a few that bloom at midsummer—that is from late June through July—a period which is a difficult one.

Among the most lovely and useful of yellow flowers are the Day Lilies (Hemerocallis). Their colour is very pure and fine, and runs the scale from mild lemon colour to strong fuscous orange. The flowering season of the different varieties covers a period of nearly three months, and few plants grow with such hearty good will in all sorts of positions, while none, known to me, are so free from disabilities of any kind, or the attacks of insects. Yet I seldom see any save the common Lemon Lily (Hemerocallis flava) made any great use of in gardens, and this, though truly lovely, is usually relegated to out-of-the-way places where more capricious things have scorned to grow. The Orange Day Lily (Hemerocallis fulva) we commonly see decorating the roadside near to some old garden, but its colour is magnificent and it is well worth a place within the garden.

These Day Lilies are particularly effective used as a base planting for spring-flowering shrubs. Their blossoming does not begin until that of the shrubs is past, when, if the different varieties have been used, they will keep the border bright until well into August. Among the Hemerocallis I should plant a few clumps of Campanula lactiflora and C. latifolia, Salvia Sclaria or Clary (an old-fashioned biennial plant with full spikes of lavender flowers) a few Michaelmas Daisies, and Tritomas. These give a pleasant mingling of lavender, orange, and yellow that is effective against the background of shrubs, and the Michaelmas Daisies and Tritomas tone in finely with the reddening foliage as autumn advances.

Some fine varieties of Hemerocallis with their periods of bloom are these:

Pale Yellow. H. citrina, August; H. ochroleuca, July; H. graminea, early June.

Full Yellow. H. Florham, late June; H. Sovereign, late June; H. flava major, early June; H. Thunbergii, late July; H. Gold Dust, June.

Apricot Yellow. H. Apricot, June; H. Dr. Regel, early August.

Orange. H. aurantica major, July; H. Middendorffii, May and June; H. Queen of May, June and July; H. fulva, July and August; H. luteola, July; H. fulva Kwanso, August.

Orange with Bronze Exterior. H. Dumortieri, May and June; H. Aureole, July.

The double orange Kwanso Day Lily is very striking and useful and flowers longer and later than any of the others, playing an important part in the rich-hued groups of the late summer.

The Dalmatian Toadflax (Linaria dalmatica) is a good yellow-flowered plant of midsummer. It is diffuse and spreading in habit and displays a pretty colour scheme of pale yellow and gray. Knowing only too well its hardy relative, the gay Butter-and-eggs of the roadside—and I am constrained to add, of the garden—one is not prepared for the unreliable behaviour of the Dalmatian. Some seasons it thrives well, spreading out into fine masses of glaucous foliage stuck all over with pretty lemon-yellow flower spikes for many weeks, but again it barely raises itself from the ground, sulking unaccountably. It comes easily from seed but is difficult to transplant so should not be disturbed without good reason.

Two other plants of the season that show the pretty gray and yellow colour arrangement that is most cool and attractive looking in the midsummer garden are the yellow Meadow Rue (Thalictrum glaucum) and the Horned Poppy (Glaucium luteum). The former is a tall plant with clusters of small gray rue-like leaves spread out horizontally, and puffs of feathery citron-yellow bloom which appear in late June. The whole plant is charming and is particularly well placed among pale azure Delphiniums. Its foliage remains in good condition after the Delphiniums have been cut down. It is one of the plants having permanent value.

The Horned Poppy is a bit of an enigma. It is certainly not reliably perennial, nor is it consistently biennial. It is probably a free spirit among flowers—tarrying where it is happy and taking itself off without notice when conditions are not just to its mind. While it stays it is a delightful revelation in silver and gold—very light gray leaves and fragile golden "Poppies" that open only to flutter away but blooming again before we have suffered from its inconstancy.

In my garden is a bit of border the colour scheme of which is very grateful to the eye this warm Independence day. It lies against the dark arbour that is draped with Roses now past their prime and fading to soft ashen tints. The groundwork of the group is gray—Lyme Grass, Thalictrum glaucum, Lychnis Coronaria alba, and Echinops sphaecrocephalus put in with a broad brush. In this quiet setting may be seen the yellow thistle-like heads of Centaurea macrocephala, the citron-yellow puffs of Thalictrum, Baptisia tinctoria with its creamy papilionaceous flowers and pallid leafage, tall white and yellow Mulleins (Verbascum Miss Willmott and V. phlomoides), lemon-coloured single Hollyhocks, and masses of the early white Phlox Miss Lingard. All gray and yellow and white save where a single pale spire of Delphinium rises through the Thalictrums and where at the back some clumps of Lythrum Salicaria bring their lovely colour within the same vision scope. This group lasts long in beauty. The Hollyhocks, Mulleins, and Thistles tarry to mingle with the earliest Fall Asters that are set among them, until the cool yellow and white tones give way before the amethysts and purples of the later Michaelmas Daisies and the silver setting has new jewels in its keeping.

Yellow and white flowers assembled together unfailingly give me pleasure. There is a fresh simplicity in their association that invigorates and refreshes the mind. The white Musk Mallow (Malva moschata alba) is a charming flower with a long period of bloom that I have in association with the yellow Aconite (Aconitum lycoctonum) and the early pink Phlox Nettie Stewart. The dainty white Cranesbill (Geranium sanguineum alba) is lovely also among the lower growing Evening Primroses and California Poppies with a background of lavender Erigeron speciosus Quakeress. Other fine white flowers of the season for use among the yellow ones are Gypsophila paniculata, Galega officinalis alba, Phlox Miss Lingard, White Hollyhocks, Veronica virginica, Campanula lactiflora alba and C. latifolia alba, Verbascum Chaixii alba and Verbascum Miss Willmott, Lychnis Coronaria alba and the many varieties of Chrysanthemum maximum.

Of all the yellow flowers of midsummer none are so indispensable as the Evening Primroses and the Mulleins. They have a long period of blossoming—fully two months; they are particularly adapted to our climate; and they are singularly radiant and shining in effect. The round blossoms of the Evening Primroses wear a full warm tone of yellow. A few, like the wild species of the roadsides, open at night only, and nearly all are more beautiful and striking as the shadows lengthen. Oenothera fruticosa and its variety Youngii form dense clumps of strong stems clothed with lustrous foliage and bear in greatest profusion shining, bright yellow flowers. O. glauca Fraseri is dwarfer, only a foot in height and flowers later in the season—sometimes well into September. The common O. Lamarckiana, that sometimes reaches a height of six feet, is well worth growing, though it is a furious seeder and is best planted in half-wild places where its persistent colonizing will be a delight to the eye and not a menace to one's choicest treasures. I have a handsome tall Evening Primrose, a form of Lamarckiana called Afterglow, that bloomed lavishly the first year from seed and continued right up to the arrival of frost. It is said to be perennial and hardy.*

There are some trailing Evening Primroses with which one may make a bank gay, or plant along the edges of the borders. Two of these are O. riparia and O. missouriensis

* A longer acquaintance with this plant proves that the roots are not hardy in the vicinity of New York, but the seeds are entirely winter proof and as they are freely produced, there are always plenty of young plants to be had each spring.

(syn. macrocarpa). The Evening Primroses are all native Americans and well suited to our climatic conditions. They love heat and sunshine, our burning droughts affect them little, and they adapt themselves easily in dry soil where little moisture reaches them.

The appreciation of Mulleins has but recently begun in this country. Our native Mullein (Verbascum Thapsus) is considered a very troublesome weed but its noble outline is one of the beauties of our country roadsides, where it often takes possession of raw banks, tufting them all over with its velvet leafage and rearing its yellow stalk—Witches Candles as they are sometimes called—with the finest decorative effects.

Most of the Mulleins are of biennial duration, but like the Foxglove, when they are once established, they may be depended upon to sow their hardy seeds so that there will be plenty of young plants to carry on the midsummer illumination both in our own and in our neighbour's gardens.

V. Chaixii is a perennial species that grows very tall—often eight or nine feet—with bright green leaves that appear early and yellow flowers rather larger than is the rule with Mulleins, that are decorated with purple filaments. V. Chaixii has a white variety which is very handsome.

V. olympicum is a magnificent plant with bright yellow flowers and woolly leaves. It is a biennial, or perhaps one should say triennial, for it flowers the *third* year from seed. It grows from six to ten feet tall.

V. phlomoides is perhaps the best of all the species. Its yellow flowers have a warm tone and last for many weeks. It blooms fully two weeks before V. olympicum.

Of hybrid Mulleins there are a number in various fine
colours. One of the best is Miss Willmott, soft ivory
white; A. M. Burnie is a charming shade of yellowish
apricot; Harkness Hybrid is bronze and yellow; and New
Departure is reddish bronze.

For small gardens there are no prettier hardy plants than
the varieties of Verbascum phoeniceum that grow only
three feet tall and show many pretty tones of rose and
violet, lilac and white in the flowers.

No plants of the whole summer through are more pic-
turesque than the Mulleins. They are suited to formal or
natural planting, giving a strong fine line wherever they are
used. In the garden they are best at the back of the
borders, but in waste places they may stand boldly in the
open to shine against the sky. Their flowering season lasts
fully two months and in partial shade the individual blossoms last long in perfection. The first time I saw the
Greek Mullein it was grown in irregular groups along a
ferny bank that flanked a woodland walk, and the tender
green gloom seemed alight with its radiance.

There are many other fine yellow-flowered perennials of
midsummer, among them Aquilegia chrysantha, Digitalis
ambigua, Rudbeckia speciosa or Newmanni, Achillea fili-
pendulina, Thermopsis carolina, Althaea ficifolia, and the
yellow varieties of Lilium elegans.

For sunny effects use should be made of the many lovely
yellow Gladiolis, the charming "primulinus hybrids" that
are so light and graceful in effect and now and then exhibit
lovely rose and copper tones that are in no way out of
place among the soft yellow shades, and such other good

sorts as Isaac Buchanan, Sunrise, Golden King, Schwaben, Klondyke, and Easter Bells. These are particularly fine among flowers of deep blue colouring—Veronica spicata, Aconite, Salvia pratensis.

Good yellow annuals are many. Besides the Marigolds, lemon yellow and burnt orange Zinnias, gay California Poppies, the Calendula—so truly gorgeous in its new forms—there are a few that are not so well known. Of these the yellow Bartonia aurea (or correctly, I believe, Mentzelia Lindleyi) with its glowing cup-shaped flowers so enjoyed by bees. The Mexican Prickly Poppy, too, Argemone mexicana, is a lovely thing with its crinkled yellow "Poppies" and gray foliage. It is a troublesome weed in its own country and might become so here—but both this and the white variety are charming for half-waste places.

The two annual Erysimums (E. Perofskianum and E. asperum arkansanum) are pretty enough for the best of gardens. They are bright orange and mustard yellow respectively in colour, are very like Wallflowers in form, are sweet scented, and self-sow freely.

The California Lupine (Lupinus Menziesii) forms a handsome bush with spikes of soft yellow flowers. Two other very pretty Californians are Layia elegans and Limnanthus Douglasi. The former is a delightful sprawling little plant about eight inches in height that bears the quaint name of Tidy Tips. Its yellow flowers are slightly fringed. Limnanthus has little fine-petalled yellow flowers that are delicately scented and much sought by bees. It makes a pretty edging in poor soils and should be sown twice for a succession.

CHAPTER X
COLOUR BY THE WATERSIDE

CHAPTER X

COLOUR BY THE WATERSIDE

There is a willow grows aslant the brook,
That shows his hoar leaves in the glassy stream.
—SHAKESPEARE.

IT IS simply as a lover of colour that I approach this subject; not along the path of the landscape architect, no branch of whose art, it seems to me, requires at once so deft a touch, such power of imagery, or such sensitiveness to proportion as does the effort to bring to its finest expression the union of shore and water. I venture only to advance the suggestions that the planting of lake or stream margin be after the manner of Nature at her best; that the disposal of trees and shrubs and plants be upon a broad and gracious plan without petty repetitions at regular intervals; that land extending into the water should be planted high to invest the shoreline with some sense of mystery, and that there should be ample stretches where the water, with its enamelled reflections, is plainly to be seen.

No variegated or purple-leaved shrubs or oddities of any sort are suitable for such situations, and only those species should be chosen that grow naturally by the waterside.

It has been my good fortune to dwell where I could observe throughout the year the beauty and fitness of Nature's chance planting by stream and lake margin and in broad stretches of marsh, and while one wants to cut away her too rank thickets of Alder and Viburnum, and extend the sweep of burning Cardinal Flower, there is grace and meaning in her choice of material and even in her limitations and excesses. Daily in winter I pass a bit of marshy stream margin that fills me with a sense of deepest satisfaction. Here, among the warm brown and yellow grasses, spring tall and closely massed the bright orange stems of Willows; in front are the rich red stems of the Red Osier Dogwood, and stretching away against the cold blue sky of winter the warm brown wood of Viburnums. When snow covers the neutralizing grasses my picture shines with arresting brilliance.

No trees or shrubs are so well adapted for use by the waterside as the various Willows. It is their natural abiding place and here only are their special qualities of soft colour and delicate line brought to their best development. Salix vitellina aurea, the Golden Willow, has bark of a warm orange tone that deepens to brilliance in expectation of the young leaves in early spring. It has a red-twigged form that appears very like Cornus alba in the winter landscape, the variety Britzensis, and there is, I believe, a variety with soft bluish stems called colorado. The beautiful White Willow with its silvery leaves is related to these and grows to a great height. I remember a fine planting of White Willows on the lake shore at Mr. William Robinson's place, Gravetye, England. The trees were finely grouped and the masses of soft silvery foliage were very beautiful seen from the opposite side of the lake. Salix nigra is the native Willow that oftenest grows to a tree of great size.

The forward little Pussy Willow (S. discolor) is, of course, beloved by all and indispensable to hearten us during

That weary time that comes between
The last snow and the earliest green.

Many Willows have conspicuously silvery foliage. One of these—more shrub than tree—is the Rosemary Willow (S. rosmarinifolia), with feathery branches and softly tinted narrow leaves. Unfortunately this is one of the Willows often sold grafted on a hardy stock and so some trouble must be taken to keep down the suckers until the desired plant has become established on its own roots. The Rosemary Willow is most beautiful planted as a broad background for a sweeping mass of Rose Loosestrife (Lythrum Salicaria).

Both Dogwoods and Viburnums number among their ranks shrubs and low trees having brightly coloured bark for winter colour. The best of the Dogwoods for this purpose is the Siberian (Cornus alba), whose blood-red stems gleam strangely against the snow and seem, at the approach of spring, to derive from their reviving life forces almost the quality of flame.

Our native Red Osier (Cornus stolonifera) is almost as highly coloured, and though its blossoms are not as fine as some others of its group, should be extensively planted for winter brightness. Cornus asperifolia has warm brown twigs; C. Amomum, dull purple; and C. circinata and C. alternifolia, fresh green. And all have attractive blossoms, good foliage that colours finely in the fall, and ornamental fruit to contribute to the passing seasons. I have spoken in an earlier chapter of planting Primroses, Forget-me-nots, Daffodils, and other early spring flowers among those shining stems. Marsh Marigolds grow freely in such a position and are gay among the unfolding fronds of young marsh Ferns.

The Viburnums are handsome in flower but their chief glory is the fine colouring of their autumn dress. The Highbush Cranberry* is a good example. The memory of its creamy blossoms is quite effaced when the irregular bush hangs itself all over with flaming scarlet berries that shine brightly through the dull red, bronze, and purple garment of its autumn leafage. V. cassinoides is perhaps the best of the shrubby Viburnums for the waterside. If given the opportunity it assumes a fine form and its changing berries, first green and then rose, then blue-black, are very ornamental. Viburnum lentago (Sweet Viburnum), Sheepberry or Nanny-bush, as it is variously called, is a small tree that develops a beauty of line and proportion, when given sufficient space, quite unsuspected by those who know only its huddled, twisted aspect in the crowded environment of the marsh. There is a delicate, creamy beauty in the flowers of the Sweet Viburnum that distinguishes it above others of its family and in the autumn its dark fruit and ardent colouring again give us pleasure.

Among the Birches we have Betula nigra that thrives even where inundations are common. B. lenta with its spicy-tasting, smooth, dark bark and graceful habit will also grow along the banks of streams or lakes and is a particu-

---

* Viburnum opulus also called Guelder Rose.

larly striking figure in autumn when its foliage turns a clear bright yellow. But none is so charming as the Paper Birch (B. papyrifera), its straight, cream-white trunk reflected upon the surface of the water and its slender branches drooping above a carpet of golden Daffodils; or again a radiant revelation when in autumn its delicate leafage colours to a warm amber.

Nyssa sylvatica, the Sour Gum or Tupelo, is a moisture lover. It is a slow-growing tree but is so handsome when its leathery leaves turn to flaming scarlet that it is worth waiting for. The Tupelo is often to be seen a solitary, dominating figure in pastures or fields for some reason spared when other trees were sacrificed before the march of agriculture. And it is thus it shows to best advantage. It is not a tree for crowded places and by the waterside should stand alone to reach out its horizontal, slightly drooping branches to their full bent.

The Liquidamber, or Sweet Gum, is also a striking tree but less hardy than the Tupelo and quite different in appearance. Its leaves are somewhat like those of the Maple. Harriet Keeler says the "autumnal foliage is not simply a flame, it is a conflagration." Both the Tupelo and the Liquidamber are difficult to transplant, so quite small specimens are best for experiment.

There is not here sufficient space to touch, save lightly, upon the many fine trees that will grow beside and beautify our water margins. There is the Cockspur Thorn (Crataegus Crus-galli), with its curiously directed branches so distinct when leafless; the Swamp Maple (Acer rubrum), that touches with a scarlet finger of warning the winding length of our little river before our hearts have had enough of warmth and sunshine, but ministers to our eagerness in spring by the haste of its rosy flowering; the White Poplar with its slim, straight stalk and restless, silver-lined leaves; and the strange Tamarack, the deciduous conifer, that makes the swamps in northern New Jersey so impregnable to the rambling pedestrian. Nor need we lack true evergreens in low, damp places, for the Norway Spruce and the Douglas Fir thrive whole-heartedly in such situations and I know from observation in my own neighbourhood that the slim Red Cedar rears its strict proportions in many a veritable bog, shouldering the Viburnums and Dogwoods like one born to the marsh.

Of fine shrubs for our water margin there is no end. The exquisite white Swamp Azalea (Azalea viscosa) with its penetrating fragrance creates charming groups with a long flowering in July and August; its lovely sister of the earlier year, the Pinxter Flower (Azalea nudiflora), shakes out its rose-coloured scarf of airy, fringy flowers along the pond to the delight of all loiterers by the way; and the Rhodora, Emerson's "rival of the Rose," that haunts the sluggish streams of the northeast and is a truly beautiful shrub. Thomas Wentworth Higginson wrote of the Rhodora thus happily, "On the margins of some quiet swamp a myriad of bare twigs seem suddenly overspread with purple butterflies, and we know that the Rhodora is in bloom."

Others of the Heath family suitable for our purpose are the Swamp Laurel (Kalmia glauca) a low, slender-stemmed evergreen with lilac-pink flowers in April or early May, and the bell-hung swamp Leucothe (Leucothöe racemosa), which in *Garden & Forest* is described as a "fast-growing shrub which sometimes attains a height of ten feet; its slender branches are covered with dark green leaves which late in the autumn, long after those of every other tree and shrub cultivated in gardens have fallen, assumes a beautiful and brilliant scarlet colour." And still we have the shy Swamp Rose (Rosa carolina); the scented Spice Bush that reaches its branches lovingly out over the water; the fragrant Sweet Pepper Bush (Clethra alnifolia) with spikes of white blossoms late in the summer; the scarlet-berried Indian Currant (Symphoricarpos vulgaris); The Button Bush (Cephalanthus occidentalis) with its white spherical blooms that turn a warm terra-cotta as they mature, and the two water-loving Spiraeas, S. tomentosa and S. salicifolia (the Meadow Sweet).

Plants for the water margin are most effective if they exhibit the rushlike foliage or spiry blossoming that is characteristic of so many water-loving plants. Few are handsomer than our native Cat-tail (Typha latifolia), and the water Irises show the same sort of slender, grasslike foliage with the added beauty of splendid flowers. In our admiration for the great Japanese Iris I think we are apt to overlook the many other good kinds that enjoy the same sort of position. Iris ochroleuca, comfortably established in wet places, grows nearly six feet tall and bears great thick ivory-coloured blossoms with a gold band at the base of the falls. Near this we might have a plantation of Iris aurea, with its buoyant, butter-coloured blossoms, and near again the great Monspur, with deep blue blossoms and the handsomest foliage of all water Irises. Other water-loving kinds are the Siberians, the orientalis group, and I. Delavayi, I. Monnieri, and I. monaurea. The last two are of the fine type of Monspur. Masses of pure white Siberian Irises with their delicate poised blossoms are particularly beautiful following the shore of lake or stream with a background of good green shrubbery. For broad planting none are better than our native I. versicolor and the Yellow English flag (I. pseudacorus).

Next to the Irises in importance for waterside planting are perhaps the Spiraeas and Astilbes that show the magenta colour scale so finely, and provide so many fleecy white varieties to mingle with it, to the betterment of both. Some of the new Astilbes, known as "Astilbe Arendsi hybrids," are particularly handsome, running the scale from soft creamy pink to warm crimson-violet. This is a favourite colour of the marsh and is nowhere else more happily displayed. Seen across a body of water these flowers of the magenta order assume an exquisite softness, merging into the surrounding colours without obvious demarkation. Astilbe Davidi and A. grandis are quite imposing in their height, sometimes attaining six feet if suited, and bearing respectively reddish-purple and white plumes. The Spiraeas are closely related and offer many good species suited to our purpose.

For a tall subject one could scarcely find anything more striking than our native Joe Pye (Eupatorium purpureum) with its encircling ovate leaves and great soft-coloured flower heads. It is so impressive a feature of the autumn landscape, towering upon the borders of the marsh or stream, among Boneset, Milkweed, and tall coarse Ferns, and often most nobly grouped; the wonder is that it is not more frequently made use of in artificial planting. Too often we make the mistake of trying for a bold effect by the use of some unwilling alien, bold enough in its native habitat, but sadly deficient when taken from it, when we have at hand the plant best fitted to bring about the desired effect, that will grow with the joyous luxuriance of the materially and spiritually at peace. Truly

> Eyes of some men travel far
> For the finding of a star.

Our country is rich in valuable material for the garden, but nowhere is it more conspicuously gifted than in its broad marshes and along the water courses and lake shores. We need not bring in a single stranger to achieve a water-side garden of the greatest interest and variety. There are the vibrant Swamp Lilies (L. canadense and L. superbum), the Culverwort, Meadow Rue, Physostegia, Bergamot, Mallows, Turtle-head, Willow Herb, Meadow Parsnip, Loosestrife, Marsh Marigolds, Violets, Gentians, and, among many more, the two Lobelias.

I know a little path—rather oozy—that threads its narrow way across a bit of marsh among pressing black-berry bushes, Swamp Roses, and Viburnums, that no fear of snakes prevents me from traversing in early September to enjoy the glory of blue colour that winds with it. Almost it seems that the extravagant hand of man must have accomplished this lavish planting of the great blue Lobelia. Few flowers boast a finer colour—not even its Red Indian brother that stalks the shady stream-sides, startling us with the fire of his war paint, is more striking.

These are all for broad planting and to be left practically to themselves; but in the treasure store of our country are many other plants which will require more special conditions and which should be bestowed about in nooks and corners to be visited and enjoyed in the season of their flowering as something rare and particularly interesting. There are all the strangely beautiful creations belonging to the Orchidaceae—the quaint Ladies Tresses (Spiranthes); the Rattle-snake Plantain (Goodyera), with its uncomfortably suggestive leafage; the exquisite Arethusa, whose colour Thoreau describes as "crystalline purple"; the pure pink, violet-scented Pogonia and its almost invariable companion, the mauve-pink Calopogon; and the many handsome Orchises grouped under the head of Habenaria and of course the Cypripediums. And besides these we may have the Pitcher Plants and Sundews, Spigela, Sabatia and Grass of Parnassus that will tax our ingenuity to establish in the ordinary marsh.

No dissertation upon waterside planting would be complete without mention of the blue Pickerel Weed that veils the shore in such lovely colour from late July onward. Its stiff flower spikes rise out of the shallow water in closely packed masses and are often accompanied most harmoniously by the white-flowered Arrowhead. The yellow English Flag (Iris pseudacorus) will also grow with its feet in the water as will the Water Arum (Calla palustris), Cat-tail, Golden Club (Oronticum aquaticum), Sweet Flag (Acorus Calmus), the curious Burr Reeds (Sparganium), the Water Plantain (Alisma plantago) whose fresh leafage is beautiful, and others.

I feel very strongly that the use of blue and yellow and pink Water Lilies should be confined to formal pools in "dressed" portions of the grounds. Used upon natural bodies of water, where the surrounding planting is largely of native shrubs and plants, they ever have an alien look to which no pleasure in their peculiar beauty can reconcile us. Whereas the white Lily floats among its shining pads like the exquisite spirit of the wild world, absolutely harmonious with its surroundings, at peace with all about it.

CHAPTER XI

THE POOL IN THE GARDEN

JUNE BOUNTY
JUNE 10TH

*T*HIS riot of colour is characteristic of June's lavish brush. The bright pink Rose on the arbour is Empress of China, the rich-hued Peony below it is Louis Van Houtte. The rest is a tangle of white Peonies Festiva maxima and Duchesse de Nemours, purple-flowered Campanula latifolia macrantha, the gay Pink Beauty Sweet William, and Nepeta Mussini.

In April and May we have along the edge of this border a bright succession of bloom. Patches of bright yellow Daffodils, Tulip Thomas Moore, hardy Candytuft, soft sulphur-coloured Alyssum, Sun Roses, and the new Anchusa myosotidiflora, growing both in the bed and down in the path among Foxgloves, Sweet Williams, and other rovers.

The chronicle of this four-foot border is a gay one throughout the season. Midsummer finds it boasting bright yellow Evening Primroses (Oenotheras Youngi and Afterglow), early white Phlox Miss Lingard, Monkshood, and Spiked Veronica for blue, brilliant Canada Lilies (Lilium canadense), and some yellow Sunflowers that have been removed many times but seem able ever to retain a foothold.

Rich purple Michaelmas Daisies strike the last note here as in so many parts of the garden.

In Plate No. 4 (May 1st) the spring version of this border may be seen painted from the opposite end.

PLATE NO. 10
SEE PLATE NO. 4

THE LAUGHING FACE OF JUNE
JUNE 20TH

*H*ERE are Delphiniums, Anchusa, Goat's Rue, and an old garden Rose, the name of which I do not know, joyously flowering against the north wall. The Rose at the end of the path on the west wall is Newport Fairy and the one in the foreground is Waltham Rambler.

This border appears full to overflowing yet turning to Plate No. 20 (August 6th) it is seen in quite a new dress.

The spring saw many beauties also along this border: patches of Scillas and Snowdrops, a gleaming line of Poet's Narcissus with trails of Golden Alyssum, Arabis, and rich purple Aubrietia. Early May saw the front of the border fluttering with Columbines—pink, cream, mauve, and sky blue with feathery bursts of a little dwarf Spiraea (S. japonica, I think). At the path edge—selfsown—flowered Iceland Poppies, Flax, and a tiny black Johnny-jump-up.

Toward the end of May two great plants of the old-fashioned crimson Peony (Paeonia officinalis) burst into rich-hued bloom beside the arbour post companioned by the gray-white blossoms of Iris florentina and the Anchusa still flowering in the opposite plate.

THE HALF MOON POOL
JUNE 28TH

*T*HE *bed about the overflowing pool is small but large enough to hold many pleasant things with thirsty roots.*

The Irises now in bloom are I. monspur and the gold-banded Iris ochroleuca. Purple and white Horned Violets (Viola cornuta, vars. alba and G. Wenberg) edge the bed where earlier in the spring Forget-me-nots, Polyanthus Primroses, and the scented Gardenia-flowered Narcissus created a gay rim.

In late May and early June the two handsome varieties of Iris orientalis (Snow Queen and Blue King), that flower with unusual freedom in the moist soil, create the picture; and in July a great clump of Rose Loosestrife in the corner against the low wall hoists its magenta plumes behind the rich blue flowers of Iris monspur that still linger.

In August there are bold clumps of frosted Corfu Lilies (Funkia subcordata) in the corners; and for the rest of the season the pool bed is dependent for colour upon the sprightly Horned Violets that are more or less faithful until frost.

CHAPTER XI

THE POOL IN THE GARDEN

When I bring to you coloured toys, my child, I understand why there is such a play of colours on clouds, on water; and why flowers are painted in tints—when I give coloured toys to you, my child.   —TAGORE.

NOTHING so surely adds charm to the expression of the garden as a pool, even of quite small dimensions. Thoreau wrote: "A lake is the landscape's most beautiful and expressive feature. It is the earth's eye." A pool is the eye of the garden in whose candid depths is mirrored its advancing grace. My own little pool is a half moon against the garden wall. Into it, from the mouth of a mild-faced lion, falls a garrulous trickle that threads the heat of summer days with a strand of freshness and relief and breaks in upon our consciousness with a sense of gay companionship. It is a small affair, but in the bed about its overflowing rim is room for many treasures. Here grow water Irises of various kinds: the fine rich blue Iris monspur, I. aurea with its fluted yellow blossoms, I. Snow Queen, and the splendid gold-banded Iris, I. ochroleuca, that sometimes reaches a height of six feet. Against the wall is a clump of Loosestrife for July flowering and about it are some plants of the little Spiraea japonica that bloom before the Irises in June. Here and there is a group of Primula pulverulenta that delights in the damp spot; and everywhere else, pushing their way among the perennials, and carpeting the ground, are alert Horned Violets and self-sowing Forget-me-nots (Myosotis sylvatica) through which rise in early May the lovely blossoms of the Gardenia-flowered Narcissus.

The plants thrive so heartily in the genial dampness of this bed that we must be forever thinning them out, for we would not have them gather so closely about the rim of the pool as to hide the water with its attendant reflections. These reflections are full of charm and suggestion; sometimes the Japanese Cherry enamels a rare design upon the quiet surface of the pool; again will be a gay pattern of Yellow Flowering Currant and Peach Blossoms upon a blue sky ground. To-day my half-moon pool looks like a Japanese fan with an encircling design of blue and white Irises and a roseate glow caught from the Rose pergola over the way. To-night the dark surface will be powdered with star shine.

We do not require a great expanse of water to add this pleasure of reflections to the list of our garden joys. A little round or square pool, or a trio of little rectangular pools; a half moon of a pool, a well head, or even a bird bath will compass it in some degree. And there is no reason why we should not plan a bit for delightful reflections— arrange the Cherry or Hawthorn pattern, place our Irises and Lupines where the pool may mirror their fine designs, and leave the rest to the wind and the clouds.

I should always plant a flowering tree near a pool—one

with graceful, reaching branches—and I should encourage the young stem to lean toward the pool that its beauty be given us again from the clear water and its shadow lend variety to the quiet surface. When the pool is set in an open space of grass it creates, with the little spreading tree, a most delightful picture, and even a quite formal garden might be the more approachable for such a bit of captivating inconsistency.

Quite different, but even more fascinating and suggestive, are the pools of Italian gardens, where only the moon dares brave the sombre guardianship of the sentinel pines to lie upon the surface of the darkened water. These, too, we may have, by marshalling slim Red Cedars about our little basin—quite large ones may be transplanted with care— and will soon create something of the brooding atmosphere of mystery that one associates with the garden pools of Italy.

Here, as by the broader natural waterside, plants of slender rushlike growth and spirelike blossoming give the best effect. Lupines are particularly happy in such a position if the soil is not actually wet, and cast classic reflections. Here, too, we shall enjoy the silvery foliage and blue-green reflections of the Sea Lyme Grass (Elymus arenarius).

For a damp bed about the pool in the garden we have a wide choice of plants. All the Lemon Lilies will thrive here, but it is best to choose some of the finer sorts like Hemerocallis Florham, H. citrinum, or H. luteola major, that are not in quite such haste to populate the world. There the Globe Flowers attain fine proportions and glowing colour; all the Astilbes and herbaceous Spiraeas thrive whole heartedly, as do the beautiful native Physostegias—mauve-pink or white. And Mallows, Funkias, many kinds of Iris including the slim Siberians, the yellow-leaved Sweet Flag (Acorus calamus variegatus), Boconia cordata—if the pool is large—and the Virginian Cowslip (Mertensia virginica) will be found appropriate and well suited. In between the larger subjects may be tucked all kinds of Forget-me-nots, many different sorts of Primula, Horned Violets, and the dainty Anemone rivularis.

The soft magentas and mauve-pinks worn by so many of the Spiraeas and Astilbes are particularly felicitous used by the waterside, the passive tones seeming to merge imperceptibly into the almost colourless tints of the water.

There should always be a seat near by the pool in the garden that we may linger a while to enjoy the beauty of the mirrored flowers. Thoreau says we see reflections only when in an abstract mood. In our rambling trips about the garden the mind is distracted by a thousand sights and sounds, but where there is a seat we are apt to linger, and when we linger in the garden the abstract mood is sure to fall upon us like a magic cloak, endowing us with the power to see much that is hidden from us at busier times—the beauty of wind-stirred reflections, the subtle part played by shadow in the garden's ornamentation, the ways of bees and birds and butterflies, the evening light upon the Cherry-trees. He loses much who has no aptitude for idleness.

CHAPTER XII

WHITE FLOWERS IN THE NIGHT GARDEN

CHAPTER XII

WHITE FLOWERS IN THE NIGHT GARDEN

And still within a summer's night
A something so transporting bright
I clap my hands to see.

—EMILY DICKINSON.

THE garden has its day side and its night side, as different as day and night. The night garden is not the place we know by day; there seems nothing personal or familiar in its simple masses of light and dark. We seem to have had no part in fashioning the vast purple gloom, the pearly visions, the sharp, pale shapes that part the shadows. It is not ours, nor are the tall white forms at our side creatures grown of our fostering love and care. Only the fragrances of the night are familiar—Honeysuckle, White Tobacco, Stock seek us out like the warm pressure of a hand.

We are conscious of a powerful reserve in the graven beauty of the night garden. It gives us little, drawing into itself while yet it presses upon us with a curious impersonal insistence. Its stillness is more exciting than sound, and every small happening seems fraught with significance; the silent flitting of a moth, the delicate rush of a capricious breeze fixes all our attention.

COLOUR IN MY GARDEN

A sally down the garden path has quite the quality of high adventure. We are accompanied by troops of ghostly flowers—nameless at night. At their sign the shadows part before and close in behind us, seeming to cut off retreat. Here a Lily shape is cut against the dark; there a trail of light tells where white Horned Violets "with winged feet" speed into the night; and farther on a shimmering breadth proclaims a group of heavy-headed white Phlox.

The pergola is a purple tunnel. Here shadows press one hard and even the moist cheek-touch of a pink Rose, invisible now, but serves to mark the strangeness, and one is glad to reach the dimly luminous stretch of gravel at the end and hear the familiar prattle of falling water in the half-moon pool. This is all the sound save now and then the sleepy twitter of a nestling bird, or from the song sparrow a sudden silver thread of sound that cuts the darkness like a falling star. And while we stand, held by the imperturbable personality of the night, the moon slips from her garment of clouds and sails round and golden above the garden, transforming it, glorifying it, warming it into the familiar. Shadows flee to the far corners but are sought out by the searching light and must flee again. Lovely forms develop out of gloom and stand forth in "silvered symmetry"; the moon dips into the little pool, and all the garden seems to stir as if breathing full—or is just ourselves released from the stricture of the dark?

Thoreau says it is necessary to see objects by moonlight as well as by sunlight to get a complete notion of them. The moonlit garden is the perfected creation—all our dreams come true. Whatever of beauty we have longed for, striven for in our gardens is graciously vouchsafed. There is no disturbing line, not an imperfect group, not a petal out of place.

> Then veil my too inspecting face
> Lest such a subtle shimmering grace
> Flutter too far for me.

Some day I should like to plant a garden to the night, to be frequented only at dim twilights, by moonlight, or when there is no light save the faint luminousness of white flowers. There should be sombre evergreens for mystery, an ever-playing fountain to break the tenseness, a pool for the moon's quaint artistry, and a seat. And nearly all the flowers should be white and sweet. There should be the wraithlike Shad Bush and Cherry-trees to hang like ghostly balloons among the shadows, waxen Magnolias, sweet blush-blossomed Crabapple trees, and white Hawthorns with crowding blooms lying along the stiff branches like new-fallen snow. Later should come perfumed Mockorange, white Lilac—"ghost of some lone delicate hour"— and great bushes of free-growing white Roses—Stanwell Perpetual, Blanc Double de Coubert, Madame Georges Bruant, Madame Hardy, Frau Karl Druschki, Madame Plantier—dames of unsullied purity. After the Snowdrops and Snowflakes, Arabis, Daffodils, white Tulips, and pale Primroses of the young spring should come Lilies-of-the-Valley, and shy Sweet Woodruff, trails of Candytuft, Alyssum, and frilly white Petunias, Scented Pinks and ranks of chaste Canterbury Bells and Foxgloves; great white Peonies—loose petalled to ensnare the moonbeams—quaint

143

Fraxinella, Dame's Rocket, fragrant Valerian, and Florentine Iris in a gray cowl. Then should come pale Mulleins erect by mounds of gossamer Gypsophila, stately Hollyhocks, sweet Musk Mallows, shining Moon Daisies, white Lilies, sweet white Tobacco, Phlox in broad masses like snow high drifted, and the keen-scented Funkia. Honeysuckle, without doubt, and filmy Clematis and many more— all one's favourites assembled to give form to gloom and by their sweetness to endow the night with subtle consciousness.

The faculty of some flowers to withhold their sweetness from the day and pour it out to the night is often alluded to. Curiously, too, these flowers have small personality by day, but with the twilight seem to rise and expand, laying their white stars, like ivory ornaments, against the dark background of the night. Possessing this peculiarity are Sweet Tobacco and Dame's Rocket (Hesperis matronalis); and the little Night-scented Stock, a drooping, insignificant bit of flowerhood by day that is quite transfigured at the coming of twilight. Then it raises its pale head with assured grace and floods the dusk with a sweetness at once delicate and intense.

Many of the Evening Primroses are more highly scented after nightfall, some of them keeping their petals closed during the day as if to more effectually hold back the perfume. Oenothera biennis, only fit for "God's wide husbandry" is one of these. The closely allied O. Larmarckiana is a more cultivated plant and may be allowed in the garden. Oenothera taraxifolia is a most beautiful Evening Primrose whose blossoms reach their full-

144

est expansion at nightfall. It is a charming lax trailer, drooping its long stems, starred with great white fragrant blooms, most gracefully over steep banks or rocks. O. marginata and O. speciosa are two other lovely species with white flowers gradually changing to pink as they mature. The first sends forth a strong, magnolia-like fragrance at night, and is seldom taller than twelve inches. The other is of somewhat greater height and of shrubby growth. It is a very rampant spreader so should not be put where it will overpower choicer things. The yellow Oenotheras should have a place both in the day and in the night garden. O. fruticosa and its varieties are splendid hardy plants bearing many primrose blossoms over a long period at midsummer. I have a handsome tall Evening Primrose called Afterglow, one of the "mutant" forms of Lamarckiana, that is one of the finest plants in the garden, opening its great yellow blossoms in quick succession throughout the greater part of the summer and shedding a fine fragrance at night.

Nowadays perfume does not bestow upon the flower possessing it the preëminence that it once did. The nose of humanity has become blunted, grown dull to those perfumes that come to it as gifts. We are far less sensitive to the influence of the perfume of flowers than were our forefathers. In early horticultural books one reads constantly that this or that simple flower "rejoyceth the heart of man" or "comforteth his spirits" by its sweet breath. This quality was always mentioned and made much of if it were present, but I remember, a few years ago, when compiling a list of fragrant flowers, going through countless books and catalogues and finding very seldom the word fragrant in the long lists of Peonies, Irises, Tulips, and other plants, though the colours were minutely described. The supply answers the demand. The world is asking for æsthetic colours, multiplied petals, greater height and sturdiness, but not for fragrance. Surely this is irrefutable when such a soulless beauty as the Rose Frau Karl Druschki and the pagan Oriental Poppy enjoy such marvelous vogue. Perhaps perfume magic is beyond the power of the patient hybridists, perhaps it is true that

> To grow flowers is a common thing,
> God alone gives them perfume.

And somehow in the doubling of petals, the enrichment of hues, some divine factor slips from their grasp and something precious is lost that the ingenuity of man may not restore.

It is a pity that we should become less sensitive to the appeal of perfume—should allow any flaunting rag of modern beauty to drive the old-time sweet flowers—"dear for the very fragrance of their names"—back into the dim gardens of the past. Let us plant in some quiet nook a little garden to the night where the old favourites may smile again. Let us tuck in among the white flowers hot-breathed Wallflowers and heady Musk Hyacinths, spicy Clove Pinks, and honey-scented Broom, Mignonette, Rose Geranium, and Lemon Verbena, with patches of Savory Marjoram, Thyme, and Southernwood reaching out into the path that we may brush against them as we pass, invoking a greeting from their aromatic leaves. Let those

146

so fortunate as to possess them divide and multiply and share their roots of double Rocket or fragrant white Violets and let them make slips from their old-fashioned, highly perfumed Roses and distribute them generously among their friends, that the old-fashioned qualities of sweetness and simplicity be not entirely wanting in the gardens of to-day. For it is a true saying that

The glory of the garden lies in more than meets the eye.

CHAPTER XIII
COLOUR FOR THE SHADY BORDER

CHAPTER XIII

COLOUR FOR THE SHADY BORDER

And the North gleams with its own native light.
—BRYANT.

OFTEN it is desirable to have a flower border where trees overshadow it at least in part, or along the north side of a wall where the sun reaches it for part of the day only. Such a border is usually the most troublesome spot in the garden and is frequently seen poorly habited and dull in colour. The mistake generally made is in trying to induce the sun lovers to grow here, or plants that are not reliably hardy, for of course this is the coldest region, subject to the hardest and longest freezings, and receiving less warmth from the sun than other portions of the garden. But there are plenty of good plants for the shady border that, thoughtfully chosen, will provide an attractive variety of colour and type throughout the season.

There we have the opportunity to make use of some of our lovely spring wild flowers.

Along the edge of the border we may plant the shining Bloodroot (Sanguinaria canadensis), Trilliums, yellow Adder's Tongue (Erythronium), quaint Dutchman's Breeches (Dicentra Cucullaria), graceful Solomon's Seal with its

151

creamy pendent bells, double and single Hepaticas, and the Wood Anemones (both our native sorts, and such lovely foreigners as A. apennina, the blue Windflower of the Apennine Mountains), A. nemorosa the British Windflower, with its fine variety Robinsoniana, and the frail-looking but hardy Snowdrop Anemone (A. sylvestris).

If there are stones along the edge of the border, little alpine Campanulas such as C. pusilla, C. Portenschlagiana, and C. caespitosa may be tucked in the crevices, and the pretty Yellow Fumatory will soon create fernlike colonies of itself wherever it can commandeer a bit of space. Campanula carpatica and all the creeping Phloxes are grateful for a position where the sun reaches them for but a part of the day, and the delightful mosslike Sandwort (Arenaria balearica) will creep about and cover the cool sides of the stones with velvet verdure. A particularly fine plant for near the edge of such a border is the Fern-leaved Fumatory (Corydalis cheilanthefolia), a plant with most beautiful dark green leafage that remains in fine condition throughout the season. Its delicate sulphur-coloured flower spikes are born early in the spring.

Many bulbs will thrive in our shady border, but especially grateful for the cool aspect are the lovely Scillas, Snowdrops, the quaint Checker Lilies (Fritillaria meleagris), and the white Daffodils, such as N. albicans, White Lady, Mrs. Thomson, and the fair Musk Daffodil of the Pyrenees (N. moschatus). The Dutch call N. albicans the Musk Daffodil.

One may safely choose a yellow-and-white-and-blue colour scheme for the north border, for these are the hues worn by most of the flowers that will be found to flourish there, unless one is minded to let in the members of the magenta clan, in which case the yellow flowers, all save the palest, are best omitted. A little back from the edge we may have fairy Columbines of all sorts, golden Doronicums, including the tall D. plantagineum excelsum, as well as the dwarfer sorts, the pretty Double Rocket (Hesperis matronalis fl. pl.), Actaeas or Baneberries with their decorative fruit, Epimediums, white and yellow Foxgloves, Geranium ibericum, the yellow Day Lilies (Hemerocallis), and if it is hardy in our locality the curious Welsh Poppy (Meconopsis cambrica). Farther back in the border may come our tall native Snakeroot (Cimicifuga racemosa) and the Japanese variety C. simplex (Syn. Actaea japonica), Veronica virginica, the tall Campanulas—C. latifolia macrantha, C. lactiflora, C. grandis, C. alliarifolia, and C. pyramidalis—Galega officinalis, and all the Aconites.

The Aconites, if the different species are planted, may be had in flower from late June, when the deep blue and rather dwarf A. tauricum blooms, through the Napellus group and the yellow A. pyrenaicum (syn. lycoctonum) for July and August, to A. Wilsoni and the lovely blue A. Fischeri in September, and A. chinense (usually sold in this country as A. autumnale) in October. These are all beautiful plants that give a fine, graceful effect in the garden but whenever they are grown their poisonous qualities should be remembered.

Tiger Lilies as a rule thrive robustly in the north border as do many other Lilies, but as soil is a greater factor in their well-being than aspect, some experimenting must be done to find out which are suited to our particular soil mixture.

Many plants usually counted among the sun worshippers thrive well in the north border if the shade is not too dense. Peonies, Oriental Poppies, Phlox, and Mulleins are among these, their blossoms lasting much longer in perfection when partially shielded from the sun. Mulleins are particularly happy and most effective in such a situation. In Plate 20 may be seen a fine group of Phlox Coquelicot growing in the north border of my garden among Aconitum Napellus, both the dark blue and the bicolour sorts, and our native Culverwort (Veronica virginica).

For late summer and autumn flowering in the shaded border we may have the Corfu Lily (Funkia subcordata) and others of its family, many Michaelmas Daisies, and Eupatorium ageratoides, a fine native plant of about four feet in height with flat heads of white flowers lasting well into October; and the Japanese Anemones, of course.

A few other plants suitable for a northern exposure are:

Astrantia	Iris orientalis	Saxifraga umbrosa
Bleeding Heart	Iris sibirica	Sweet Woodruff
Corydalis nobilis	Lily-of-the-valley	Thalictrum
Dentaria	Lythrum Salicaria	Trollius
Epimedium	Monarda	Viola cornuta
Helleborus niger	Pentstemon Digitalis	Viola gracilis
Heuchera	Rue	Winter Aconite

If the border is wide and shrubs are wanted to fill in at the back the following may be counted upon to thrive:

Amelanchier canadensis	Kalmia latifolia
Benzoin aestivalis	Lonicera fragrantissima

COLOUR IN MY GARDEN

Berberis in variety
Clethra alnifolia
Cornus alba and C. stolonifera
Daphne mezereum
Deutzia gracilis and D. Lemoinei
Forsythia
Hamamelis japonica
Hamamelis virginica

Mahonia Aquifolium
Philadelphus in variety
Privet in variety
Rhododendron
Rhus aromatica
Ribes sanguineum
Symphoricarpos racemosus
Symphoricarpos vulgaris

CHAPTER XIV
MAGENTA THE MALIGNED

CHAPTER XIV

MAGENTA THE MALIGNED

Beauty deprived of its proper foils ceases to be enjoyed as beauty, just as light deprived of all shadow ceases to be enjoyed as light.
—RUSKIN.

THE above quotation supplies the reason that magenta is so universally despised and shunned. Not only is it deprived of its proper foils, but it is nearly always set down beside those colours surest to bring out its worst side. I am very fond of this colour as worn by flowers and have taken some trouble to bring it into harmony with its surroundings. Combative it is, but to be won; fastidious as to its associations, but gentle and beautiful when considered. Surely any one who has seen the sumptuous rim of colour following the banks of the Hudson River and its tributary streams in certain sections where the Rose Loosestrife, a flower of the purest magenta, has naturalized itself, will not deny the possibility of beauty in the use of this colour. Besides the Loosestrife many of the finest hardy plants garb themselves in the maligned hue, and Mr. Schuyler Mathews in his "Field Book of American Wildflowers" gives 73 familiar wild flowers that are enrolled under the magenta banner. But in all my gardening experience I have met only one person who confessed

159

admiration for this colour and I have come across but one garden writer who boldly put down in print his admiration for it. Indeed nearly every writer upon garden topics pauses in his praise of other flower colours to give the despised one a rap in passing. Mr. Bowles writes of "that awful form of floral original sin, magenta"; Miss Jekyll calls it "malignant magenta"; and Mrs. Earl, usually so sympathetic and tender toward all flowers, says that even the word magenta, seen often in the pages of her charming book, "makes the black and white look cheap," and again "if I could turn all magenta flowers pink or purple, I should never think further about garden harmony, all other colours would adjust themselves."

In the thoughtlessness of colour arrangement that prevailed in the gardens of our grandmothers, magenta was recklessly handled—so many sweet and willing flowers wore the now despised hue—but no one felt the horror of such great masses of magenta Phlox and Tiger Lilies, of magenta Foxgloves and scarlet Sweet William that I remember in the charming box-bordered garden of my grandparents in Massachusetts. But now, with this new vision of ours for colour harmony, there is no reason why we should, on account of the past sins of our forefathers and the present sinning of our nurserymen in miscalling it, banish this rich and distinctive colour with all the fine plants that it distinguishes, without some effort to provide for it the proper foils to fully develop its beauty.

I would ask any one possessing Dr. Ridgeway's "Colour Standards and Colour Nomenclature" to open the book at Plate 24 and look at magenta in all its tender gradations of tint and shade.   There is but one magenta, but about it are the gentle sisters of the discredited clan: Liseran purple and rose purple, dull and dusky purple, Indian lake, dahlia car-mine, auricula purple, pale and deep Rosalane pink, all of which we are accustomed to lump as magenta.   And on Plate 12 of that same chart there are yet others that come under the unjust ban: the mallow pinks and purples, amaranths and aster purple.   These are beautiful colours as seen against the soft gray background of the page.   Per-haps if we could strike out the word magenta, so laden with custom-made stigma, and use only these other colour names, all pleasant sounding and suggestive, we should lose much of the antipathy now felt for the flowers that wear it.

When the early writers had magenta to name they usually wrote it as "a little purple mixed with red," and to give it a more poetic but none the less exact description we might reverse Dante's idea of the colour of Apple blossoms —"more than that of roses but less than that of violets."

In my garden I have been able to match but one flower to the magenta of the colour chart.   This is the Rose Loose-strife (Lythrum Salicaria).   It is pure magenta, but in eight catalogues examined it is described as rose pink, or bright pink.   One seedsman ventures so near the taboo name as to call it rosy-purple, another flies from it to the length of describing an improved variety as "glistening cherry red."   Even in the "Cyclopedia of Horticulture" it is described as "rose colour."

It is small wonder that when our minds are set upon, and some garden space prepared for, glistening cherry red, or the ever-cordial and agreeable rose colour, we are exasperated by the arrival of plants that in their flowering show the strange off-tones of the magenta group. It is not among the accepted colours of the garden; we do not plan for it, nor seek it, though it is often thrust upon us; so what chance has the poor colour to come again into its own, for it is believed to have been the "royal purple" of the ancients.

> Custom hangs upon us with a weight
> Heavy as frost and deep almost as life.

It is the custom to despise magenta. It is hustled out of our gardens and out of our consciousness and no one has eyes to see the imperial scarf of magenta Phlox that stoops to bind the dusty roadside, or the riot of tender colour in the neglected cottage dooryard where Petunias have sown and resown themselves and flutter about the gray and rotting porch and squeeze through the gray and rotting palings of the fence in exquisite harmony with the weathered wood.

I am so fond of this colour and its kindred tints and shades that to come across in *The Garden*, December 11, 1915, the following article by Clarence Eliot in its praise, was a great pleasure and I cannot refrain from using it in defence of my beloved magenta blossoms.

In some circles it needs as much moral hardihood to say that one likes magenta as it does to confess that one dislikes cold baths. Some folks seem hardly to like to use the word magenta, as though it were unclean, and resort instead to "rosy-purple." This seems as bad as softening "cold bath" into "soapy-tepid." As a matter of fact, however, real true magenta is a very rare colour among flowers. Callirhoe pulchella is one of the truest examples, and the glossy silky texture of its petals seems to enhance the glowing brilliance of the colour. The most splendid examples

162

of magenta I have ever seen were Bougainvillea cascading over white walls in Madeira, and great trailing slabs of some Mesembryanthemums on the cliffs at the entrance of the harbour of Bonificio. But alas, these two effects cannot be repeated in this country [England] except perhaps on the "Cornish Riviera." . . . I have often thought I should like to try a border of strong magentas with a good many violets and purples and lilacs, a few pinks of the type of Lavatera Olbia, that is with just a suspicion of blue in them, and perhaps a very few white flowers.

Here is Mr. Eliot's list of flowers for a magenta border of which he says, "Comparatively few of them are of the true colour, yet most or all of them are reds and pinks that would accord."

Aubrietias Fire King and Leichtlinii, Epilobium Dodonaei, Calamintha grandiflora, Lythrum alatum, Dianthus Seguieri, Lychnis viscaria splendens, Thymus serpyllum coccineus majus, Betonica grandiflora superba, Cortusa mathiola (shade), Primulas pulverulenta and Veitchii, Lathyrus latifolius (grown on pea sticks), Lavatera Olbia (and near it Nepeta Mussini), Lythrum virgatum Rose Queen, Lythrum Salicaria superbum; Phlox Le Mahdi, Albert Vandal, Reichgraf von Hochberg and Rosenberg for strong colours; and Phlox Eugene Danzanvillers, Phlox pilosa, Phlox subulata compacta, Monarda violacea superba, Verbena venosa (tender but beautiful), Lunaria biennis, Callirhoe, pulchella and Mesembryanthemum tricolor.

To this good list I must add a few of my own favourites: the exquisite, sprawling Callirhoe involucrata, Lychnis Coronaria the Mullein Pink, Kansas Gay Feather, purple Foxglove, Azalea amoena, Rhododendron catawbiense, the splendid Ironweed, Lychnis alpina, Spiraea Davidii, Centaurea dealbata Desmodium penduliflorum, and some fine Michaelmas Daisies of the novae-Angliae ruber type.

COLOUR IN MY GARDEN

I am well aware that this list will simply stand as a warning to most gardeners, but while my aim is not so high as Mr. Eliot's in hoping to inspire a magenta border, yet I do hope to start even a small revulsion of feeling in favour of this tender, hushed colour, to give it in these pages as I have in my garden some of the associations that silence its combativeness that it may raise its erstwhile imperial head, not as of old in the terrible if joyous racket of Tiger Lilies and Sunflowers, but in assured and reposeful harmony.

The first time I saw magenta flowers used with thoughtful consideration was in the wondrous gardens of Drummond Castle in Scotland. There a double border running on either side of a grass walk for nearly a quarter of a mile, between dark, severely clipped Hollies and Yews, was planted in blocks of about twelve feet in two alternating colours—blue and magenta! I do not now recall all the plants used in the border, but among them were Loosestrife and Monkshood, Spiraea Rutlandi and Veronica, magenta and bluish-violet Phloxes. Standing at one end and looking along the narrowing perspective one's eye was carried from great richness of effect to an indescribable softness that finally seemed to melt away like a trail of smoke.

The best colours to associate with magenta are deeper and paler tones of itself, the dim blue of such as Monkshood, pale buff, sky blue like that of Salvia azurea, white, the mallow pinks—that is, those pinks that have a bluish cast, lavender, and gray foliage. Indeed, I think it safe to say that all colours are in harmony with it save strong yellow, red, scarlet, orange, cherry, and the salmon pinks.

COLOUR IN MY GARDEN

Magenta does not come into conspicuous life in the garden before June, when enter Foxgloves and Sweet Williams. Before this, however, we have little patches of it here and there where creeping Phloxes and Aubrietias, Lychnis alpina and Viscaria splendens wind the border verges with a soft-hued scarf in front of sweeps of nodding, pale-coloured Star Daffodils and hoary-leaved Nepeta gleaming the lovelier for the shadow of a full-flowered Cherry-tree. Many Rhododendrons and Azaleas affect the colour. In a friend's garden Azalea amoena is broadly massed against dark evergreens, producing a most striking effect.

All the gray-foliaged plants are particularly happy with the dear magenta culprits, and gray stone is a perfect background for them. The tall magenta Foxgloves we plant with Southernwood or Wormwood and perhaps a few soft blue Peach-leaved Bellflowers or lavender Canterbury Bells. Mullein Pink (Lychnis Coronaria) is splendid with the gray leafage and lilac flower spikes of Nepeta Mussini, or shining through a haze of Gypsophila with a background of creamy Mulleins. This plant which, as near as I can match its velvet depths, answers on the colour chart to aster-purple, is described in various catalogues as "blood red," "purple or scarlet," "beautiful pink," "bright rose," "rosy crimson," and "red"; no two alike and all keeping well out of the danger zone of truth. It is an old-fashioned plant seldom seen in new-fashioned gardens, but its glowing colour and gray velvet leafage should give it entrance everywhere. I am glad to say that it seldom fails to win admiration from visitors to my garden. The white form is fine but far less beautiful.

COLOUR IN MY GARDEN

The Rose Loosestrife blooms for about six weeks at mid-summer and is one of the best hardy plants of its season. There are several "improved" forms that, while not changed in colour perceptibly, are perhaps of a slightly purer tone. The illustration, Plate 17, shows it growing behind Verbascum Miss Willmott and white Mullein Pink with a touch of bold yellow from Centaurea macrocephala. It is lovely in groups with Aconitum Napellus and Gypsophila. The creamy forms of Anthemis tinctoria are quite safe to plant with it as is the soft lavender of Erigeron speciosa. No plant is finer for water-side planting. I would suggest massing it at the water's edge where we may have the added beauty of wind-stirred reflections, and against it bold groups of the deep blue water Iris monspur.

A little later in the summer come the Gayfeathers (Liatris), whose impetuous, hurtling aspect has suggested to the children the name of "sky rockets." These grown in groups behind Lyme Grass or Rue and mingled with clumps of white Moon Daisies are very effective. They are prairie plants requiring a dry soil and a sunny aspect. Later we have the delightful Trefoil or Bush Clover (Desmodium penduliflorum) with slender, wandlike branches closely hung with tiny winged blossoms in two shades of magenta. It grows in my garden against a stone wall in company with the opaque lavender flowers of Clematis Davidiana and plenty of pale yellow Snapdragons. Later still there is Vernonia arkansana, to be worn in the garden like a festal plume, with Phlox Peachblow and Lyme Grass to set off its peculiar glowing colour. And last of all we have the Michaelmas Daisies, with many a good member

A FAVOURITE COMPOSITION
JULY 1ST

PLATES No. 3 (April 28th) and No. 7 (May 21st) have shown the earlier displays offered by this bit of ground and now we have this happy arrangement of Yellow Meadow-rue (Thalictrum glaucum), Delphinium, and Lyme Grass against the fading pink Rose Mrs. R. W. Flight that festoons the arbour.

Between the clumps of Meadow-rue are planted a few roots of the pinkish Michaelmas Daisy Novelty, which, in October, adds its heads of heath-like blossoms to the setting of soft gray foliage.

This pleasant picture lasts well into November and is the more precious as the brighter colours of the garden give way before the frost.

PLATE NO. 13
SEE PLATES NOS. 3 AND 7

MY GARDEN CELEBRATES
JULY 4TH

THIS patriotic arrangement of Delphiniums, English Field Poppies, and early white Phlox Miss Lingard came about by chance. It is a region generally given over to much gray foliage and soft-hued flowers.

The border edges are bound with velvet-leaved Woundwort (Stachys lanata), Nepeta Mussini, gray tufts of Pinks, and cascades of the "Moonlit" creeping Phlox, behind which the great lavender cups of Tulip Nora Ware open in May with a few pale yellow ones (Miss Willmott). A large standard Wistaria flowers with them.

A little later clumps of pink Oriental Poppies flower in lovely harmony with the Lyme Grass and tall stems of gray-pink Valerian. Their subsequent defection is covered by a haze of Gypsophila paniculata as seen in the present picture.

Later still lavender Fleabane (Erigeron speciosus) and tall pale Mullein Miss Willmott, white and buff and pale pink Hollyhocks make the picture; and in the autumn this whole region is hidden beneath clouds of lavender, purple, and pale mauve Michaelmas Daisies. (Plate No. 24. October 10th.)

PLATE NO. 14
SEE PLATE NO. 24

that may be said to belong among these unappreciated treasures.

I do not deny that there are poor and wishy-washy tones of magenta and that these are not desirable; but where the colour is frank and pure and used with a right intermingling of green and other soft friendly hues, there is none more beautiful and distinctive. It requires only such consideration as we give as a matter of course to blue or scarlet, but which is certainly not vouchsafed magenta in the gardens of to-day.

CHAPTER XV
THE PHLOXES

CHAPTER XV

THE PHLOXES

Every thing beautiful impresses us as sufficient to itself.
—THOREAU.

THE Phlox family is one upon which we should look with special interest, for it is American in 47 of the 48 species allowed it in the "Standard Cyclopedia of Horticulture." A few other plants have this distinction, the American Cowslip (Dodecatheon) for one, but none other has attained such worldwide fame as to make it an object of national pride.

Of the many species few are grown. Indeed, save for the tall midsummer Phloxes, hybrids of Phlox decussata and suffruticosa, only two perennials are seen with any frequency in this their native land—P. divaricata and the little creeping P. subulata. This is a pity, for while we strive for success with unwilling aliens that frequently reward us in a sorry manner, these natives, accustomed to our climatic excesses, would give us far more luxuriant and satisfactory results. As is too often the case, it remains for our cousins across the water to sing the praises of an American flower. Mr. Reginald Farrer writes of the dwarf Phlox species as "a race of indispensables beyond all indispensables for the

171

rock garden." It is Mr. Farrer, too, who notes the "moonlit blue" of Phlox subulata G. F. Wilson, and the "French-gray" of the charming P. Stellaria, "a beautiful lax trailer, like a rather large subulata, making mossy cascades down the rock work." Phlox divaricata wears this moonlit blue also, one of the tenderest and most beautiful of flower colours, but among the rest of the dwarf Phloxes that colour is rife which early writers refer to tactfully as "a little purple mixed with red." Worn by these round, simple flowers, however, it is very pure and bright and not by any means to be despised.

These dwarf Phloxes are not Alpines but they do very well on the rockery or planted in rich, sandy soil along the front of stone-edged borders where the roots may find a cool run and the trailing stems spread themselves in comfort. A dry-built wall, too, offers a suitable home for them if the exposure is a cool one. Small bits inserted in the crevices in spring soon make strong plants to festoon the wall face. The best of the species are amoena, carolina, Douglasii, stolonifera, nivalis (perhaps a form of subulata), Stellaria, subulata, and divaricata. They bloom in April and May. Phlox amoena exhibits the characteristic trailing habit and gives its lovely magenta blossoms with freedom. P. stolonifera (syn. reptens) is even more lax in growth but very pretty. P. Stellaria is vigorous and has a white sort besides the French gray one, and P. Douglasii is low, tufted, and pubescent, with pale coloured flowers. It is a Western species.

The well-known P. subulata, called Moss Pink or Flowering Moss, has many fine garden varieties, the most beautiful of which are, I think, G. F. Wilson of the moonlit blue colour and the gleaming white Nelsoni that is much less spreading in habit than the former.

Phlox divaricata, sometimes known as the Wild Sweet William, is one of the most charming of spring flowers. It loves a bit of shade and nothing is prettier to plant in the shadow of early-flowering shrubs. My yellow blossoming Currant Bushes (Ribes aureum) have a carpet of this cool lavender flower that is lovely and lasts a long time in perfection. P. divaricata is co-parent with P. paniculata of a race that I think will in time hold an important place in the floral world. It is known as Phlox Arendsii. The plants are vigorous in growth and about eighteen inches in height. They flower toward the end of May, bridging the space between the creeping Phloxes and the suffruticosa group, of which Miss Lingard is so prominent a member. The colours of this new race are not all that can be desired as yet, but some are of the lovely tint of divaricata. Louise is one of these and is further beautified by some little flecks of deeper colour about the centre. Grete is good also, with buds opening a delicate mallow pink but paling as they expand.

Of the so-called Early-flowering Phloxes, Miss Lingard is the best known and is certainly one of the very best of hardy plants. In Nettie Stewart we have a lovely sort, very pale mallow pink, and in the newer Enchantress this colour is deepened. Indian Chief is one that many will not care for on account of its pure mallow purple colour, but it is a plant of fine habit and in slightly shaded situations, among gray foliage and delicate white flowers, it is very effective.

These midseason Phloxes are extremely useful, for they come at that period which is the most difficult to gardeners— late June and early July. Very gay and striking is a mass of Miss Lingard interplanted with Pentstemon barbatus, whose graceful stalks hung with scarlet bells curve gracefully above the Phlox. Lovely, too, is this white Phlox planted behind lavender Erigeron speciosus—a splendid new form of this plant is Quakeress—with some Lyme Grass and tufts of the little blue Fescue Grass (Festuca glauca) at the edge of the border. The mallow-pink Phloxes are charming with the gray-leaved Mullein Pinks—both the white and the rich aster-purple sorts with little clouds of Gypsophila between.

Early August is the festal season of the decussata Phloxes. They are perhaps the very best of hardy plants, seeming to embody all the qualities desirable in a plant—hardiness, upright carriage, fine foliage, beautiful and various colours, fragrance, and immunity from disease. And yet, fine as they are, I think the average garden, my own included, is too much given up to them at the season of their blooming. Especially are we apt to have too many of the pink and scarlet sorts which, in such generous masses as we are used to plant them, do certainly produce a cloying effect—like too many sweets. Freer use of the violet and lavender sorts, which are many and fine, would go a long way toward remedying this fault. The reason that these are not more freely made use of is, I believe, because of the very misleading descriptions given of them in the catalogues. Phloxes are under suspicion, for the magenta principle is never more than a generation or two back, and we have grown wary of the nurseryman's easy application of mauve and violet, rose and crimson, especially to these flowers. Last summer I went through an important nursery and made careful note of all the Phloxes that came within the magenta danger zone. Many of them are very pure and beautiful in colour, but they are certainly not suitable in situations planned for pink or lavender. Here is the list:

Australie	Richard Straus
Bacchante	Indian Chief (early)
Champs Elysée	Forward (early)
Eclaireur	Widar
La Vague	Rossingnol
Rosenberg	L'Aiglon
Ringleader (early)	Antonin Mercie
Champignol	L'Esperance
Redacteur Flammer	Miramer
Jules Cambon	Albert Leteau
Amarante	Edmund Rostand
Henri Martin	Le Prophete

As I have said, the lavender and white sorts will relieve the Phlox situation appreciably; not planted among the pinks but in generous groups to themselves, one kind at a time, mingled with the slender yellow Monkshood (Aconitum Lycoctonum pyrenaicum), sheaves of flaming Montbretias, tall yellow and cream coloured Mulleins, patches of Ageratum, dull gold Zinnias, lemon and white Hollyhocks, groups of Lilium Henryi, Moon Daisies, and late-flowering Lemon Lilies. Of course a variety like Wanadis, that adds the beauty of a Tyrian eye to its Hortense violet petals, would need to be kept away from yellow. Rose Loosestrife would be fine with it or any of the soft white flowers of the season. The following is a list of the prettiest lavender and purple Phlox that I have seen:

CENDRILLON: White shaded delicate gray. Buds and tubes soft blue. Late flowering. 2½ ft.

LADY GRISEL: White shaded gray. Buds dim blue. Early. 3½ ft.

CRÈPUSCLE: Silvery mauve with Tyrian eye. 2½ ft.

DERVICHE: Lilac-blue with white centre. Late. 3 ft.

EUGENE DANZANVILLIERS: Mauve and white. 3 ft.

IRIS: Bluish-violet self. 3½ ft

PHARON: Mauve with white eye. 2 ft.

LE MAHDI: Dark bluish-violet self. 2½ ft.

PAPILLON: Grayish-white, with violet tubes. 3 ft.

WANADIS: Hortense violet with Tyrian eye. 2½ ft.

Maeterlinck writes of the loud laughter of the jolly, easy-going Phlox, and while this is hardly complimentary there is yet much truth in the simile and in the wheel-like regularity of its blossoms, the perfection of its flower heads, the symmetry of its growth, there is certainly monotony. To my thinking the Phlox needs a deal of neutralizing. Thus counterbalanced, however, by plants of diffuse habit or spirelike growth, with many blue flowers and much silver foliage and pretty white garnitures, no plant confers so gracious a boon upon the garden. Nothing is finer for association with the Phloxes than the blue and silver Sea Hollies and Globe Thistles (Eryngiums Oliverianum, planum and amethystinum and Echinops Ritro and bannaticus). These, grown in groups of six or eight among the Phloxes, create a fine effect. Gypsophila, too, is lovely with them and the August-flowering Aconites, Veronica virginica,

Salvia virgata nemorosa (with light pink), and Salvia Blue Beard. Also Salvia uliginosa and S. azurea grandiflora, the Campanulas lactiflora and pyramidalis, Clematis Davidiana, Statice latifolia, Platycodons, White Verbascums, Rue, Elymus arenarius, Santolina incana, Nepeta, and many others.

The four prettiest pink Phloxes that I know are Elizabeth Campbell, said to be outclassed by Lindfield Beauty but this is difficult to believe; Madame Paul Dutrie, of pale mallow-pink hue so lovely with the metallic blue of Sea Hollies and Globe Thistles; America, a variety of fairly recent introduction, with pure pink blossoms of enormous size and a Tyrian eye; and Peachblow, a lovely soft-coloured thing with a very descriptive name, that seems little known. While all these sorts are pink, they are very unhappy in each other's neighbourhood. Elizabeth Campbell is salmon pink, Madame Paul Dutrie is more blue pink, Peachblow leans to mauve, and the Tyrian eye of America interferes with amicable relations. Rijnstroom is a striking full rose-pink variety of splendid habit and may take the place of the older Pantheon which it much resembles. The sky-blue Salvia uliginosa is lovely with it.

The scarlet Phloxes are many and fine. Perhaps a selection of four might be Coquelicot, not very tall; General von Heutsz, salmon scarlet with a cool gray eye; Baron von Dedem, a dazzling thing with very large flowers, 3 ft., and Dr. Konigshofer, very brilliant with a darker eye. Cool blues are the best association for these high-coloured Phloxes, though if one wants to sound a very vibrant chord the Tiger Lilies, orange-scarlet, Hemerocallis Kwanso and Montbretias, will furnish the means. Scarlet and white is

177

always gay and pretty and the garden picture maker will do well to put some clumps of Campanula lactiflora alba, white, and the gray-blue E. Molineaux among his scarlet Phloxes. General von Heutsz is particularly fine with Platycodons of dim blue colour or with soft lavender Goat's Rue. The dark blue Monkshood (Aconitum Napellus) is fine in a group with white Goat's Rue (Galega officinalis) and Phlox Baron von Dedem.

Africa is a fairly new Phlox of a deep Tyrian rose colour, with an amaranth purple eye. It is very rich in effect and only less handsome than the deeper toned Compt von Hochberg, pure amaranth purple in colour. These two sorts are very amenable to arrangement. Pure pink flowers, Zinnias, Clarkia, Mallows, or Snapdragons are fine in their neighbourhood and also flowers of mauve and lavender colouring. Compt Von Hochberg is one of the longest flowering Phloxes I know. I have a group of it that starts flowering through a mist of double-flowered Gypsophila and is still in great beauty when the wandlike branches of Aster Top Sawyer colour softly about it and over the spent Gypsophila.

Good white Phloxes are many. The one I find the most valuable is the late-flowering Jeanne d'Arc (syn. Pearl). It is the very best white flower in bloom with the Michaelmas Daisies. It is an old-fashioned sort and many nurserymen have dropped it from their lists to make room for some of the newer sorts with enormous trusses of great wheel-like blossoms, but if I might have but one white Phlox it would be Jeanne d'Arc. I find many uses for it; but one group against the garden wall is particularly soft and tender amidst the gay trumpeting of autumn flowers. It is made up of the mallow-purple wands of Aster Mrs. J. F. Raynor, white Phlox, and fine masses of gray Lyme Grass, and over the stones at the edge of the border sprawls in luxuriant, warm-toned beauty the bright magenta Poppy Mallow (Callirhoe involucrata).

The newer and earlier flowering white Phloxes are Frau Antoine Buchner, F. G. von Lassburg, and Mrs. Jenkins. Henri Murger and Josephine Gerbeaux have pink centres, and Helen Vacaresco and Tapis Blanc are very dwarf white varieties, the latter but eight inches in height, that take their place at the front of the border. I love these gleaming white Phloxes with masses of Lyme Grass and Rue, with tall silver Globe Thistles (Echinops sphaerocephalus, and Eryngium giganteum), with many bloom-hung branches of Desmodium penduliflorum or some other flower of its lovely rich colouring.

I do not like white Phlox mixed through the groups of pink and scarlet sorts; it breaks them up into sharp units disturbing to the eye. With the lavenders they are of course all right, but plants of quite other form are better calculated to heighten the beauty of all.

It is well known that Phlox to be had in perfection requires a deep, rich loam, leaning neither to clay nor to sand, and plenty of water in dry weather. Thus humoured, the wedge-shaped flower heads expand to a great size, while the individual blossoms are as large as silver dollars. If the first panicle is cut off directly it is spent, the plant will bloom modestly well into the autumn. Phlox plants require to be divided frequently. Four or five flowering stalks are sufficient to a plant if large flower heads are expected. Seedlings should on no account be allowed to spring up about the parent plant; these are nearly always of inferior quality and will speedily run out the better variety besides spoiling our colour groups by their poor habiliments.

CHAPTER XVI
AUGUST COMPOSITIONS

CHAPTER XVI

AUGUST COMPOSITIONS

The one that could repeat the summer's day
Were greater than itself, though he
Minutest of mankind might be.
—EMILY DICKINSON.

AUGUST is a month of coarse foliage and robust colour. There is less poetry and suggestion in its expression than at any other period and we must be at some pains to prevent an appearance of vulgar obtrusiveness. Comely order is the first precaution. The mature garden must be well groomed and strictly kept. The pretty disorder, so easily tolerated in the spring, is no longer attractive. The paths must be raked and swept to a nice tidiness, the beds and borders relieved of all faded blooms and spent flower stalks, and all remaining plants made to toe the mark by being firmly and carefully staked. Vines must be rigidly trained, shrubs cut back where their branches encroach too boldly upon the paths, and the whole place made free of weeds. Even those determined interlopers have some charm in their svelte springtime, but in maturity none at all.

The next precaution is to choose one's August-flowering plants with discernment. It is a composite-ridden month, and many of these plants are too lacking in refinement and too pervasive in character for any save Nature's bold and broad planting. Others, however, are invaluable for filling out the lines of the late summer and autumn garden, but they should be adroitly mingled with flowers of more intricate design and polished habit. It is the Daisy type of composite that makes so many late summer gardens monotonous in appearance, and while many of these are important, a good word should be said for those of the family that are less typical. All the Thistles, including the handsome Globe Thistles, are members of the order, the splendid Ironweed, the useful Achilleas, Artemisias, Liatris, and Golden Rods. These are quite as useful in relieving the Daisy type, among which belong Dahlias, Cosmos, Chrysanthemums, Centaureas, Sunflowers, Heleniums, Michaelmas Daisies, Zinnias, and a host of others, as are plants of any other order.

No plants are more easily grown than the composites of the Daisy type, and we are too quick to make use of them and too prone to let them spread unchecked until the hearty countenance of the August garden has quite lost the charm of varied expression and we have moreover mats and tangles of almost invincible roots and fecund rootlets below the surface of the soil to cause us endless trouble for years to come.

It is well too, in the August garden to consider the subject of coolness in its colour scheme, for while we would not shut out the bright-coloured blossoms a cool picture here and there is a welcome relief to the eye. Such a picture is now at its height in my garden, and to no other do

COLOUR IN MY GARDEN

I turn with so strong a sense of satisfaction. Gray foliage is its dominant feature. There are broad masses of Lyme Grass and nicely rounded Rue bushes with great clumps of white Phlox. At the back the taller gray of Thalictrum glaucum, now out of bloom, tall Silver Thistles (Echinops sphaerocephalus), and many slender spikes of Veronica virginica. At the front and reaching to the edging of gray-leaved Pinks and lavender and white Ageratum is a mass of shining Moon Daisies.

A plant which produces a feeling of freshness at this warm season is the old Plantain or Corfu Lily (Funkia sub-cordata). Its broadly spreading pale green leaves are delightfully cool in appearance as are its fragrant, frosted Lilies. Planted in front of lavender-coloured Phlox it makes a pleasant picture that lasts a long time in perfection.

The great Sea Lavender (Statice latifolia), by reason of its lightness and delicacy, is also of great value in this season of coarse growth and hearty colour. It does for August what Gypsophila does for the preceding month. If left year after year without division the clumps grow strong and broad, sending up many stems bearing great heads of mist-like bloom that, as a result of the tiny white buds mingled with the tiny lavender expanded blossoms, have a curiously frosted appearance. We interplant the clumps of Sea Lavender with speciosum Lilies, thus accomplishing the double purpose of shading the Lily bulbs and lower stems and providing the beautiful blossoms with a charming setting. In front of them are patches of Nepeta Mussini that contribute their second blossoming to the group, and behind the Lilies and Sea Lavender is a mass of Phlox

COLOUR IN MY GARDEN

Eugene Danzanvilliers, pale lilac in colour. The heavy heads of the Sea Lavender require to be staked, but the stakes should be so arranged that they will not show and spoil the airy, poised effect of the flower sprays.

More use should be made in the August garden of our native Veronica virginica. I do not often see it, but have grown it myself for a long time and consider it of the first value as a hardy plant. At this season, when so much is rankly luxuriant and diffuse in habit, the slender but firmly erect stalks of the Culverwort, terminating in clusters of gray-white tapering flower spikes, have a special, refined beauty. It grows in rich, heavy soil six feet tall, but in dry soil will not reach a greater height than four feet. There is a handsome group made up of scarlet Phlox Etna, dark blue Aconite, and this white Veronica, and again it is most effective where it is set between clumps of the splendid double Orange Day Lily (Hemerocallis Kwanso), with which it blooms.

Salvia azurea belongs to the gentler side of August. Its delicate sky-blue wands are in charming accord with such a Phlox as Peachblow and I have it also set among some clumps of the splendid long-flowering Mullein Pink (Lychnis Coronaria), whose rich magenta colouring is wonderfully enhanced by the delicate blue. Even of greater merit than Salvia azurea is a giant form of recent introduction in this country, listed as S. uliginosa.* It grows five feet tall, is stronger and more substantial in all its parts, and has not the disconcerting habit of S. azurea, of being overthrown by

---

*This plant is not reliably hardy in the vicinity of New York unless well protected. The roots may be carried over in a frame.

every high wind. Salvia azurea and its improved variety, grandiflora, should be planted where Rue bushes, Phlox, or some other sturdy plant may be used as a prop. Stout clumps of Salvia uliginosa are fine set out with the lovely magenta Loosestrife, and such a delicately coloured Phlox as Madame Paul Dutrie would be a good third in the group.

This is but the half of August's robust symphony. The rest is set to a much deeper tone and rolls forward sonorously to meet the great autumn requiem. One of its grandest notes is sounded by the Tiger Lily.

The Tiger Lily is, next to the Phlox, the most important plant in the early August garden, but I am sometimes sadly put to it to prevent noisy warfare between these rivals. Of course the curious "grenadine" colour of the Tiger Lilies cannot be trusted to stand amiably in the vicinity of any of the innumerable pink Phloxes, though with some of the sharp scarlet sorts and a few of the coolest of the lavenders it does well enough. My garden, through the arrangement of architectural features, the placing of flowering trees or tall-growing perennials, is contrived into many small sections. It is not possible at any time to see all over it from any viewpoint and so I may have my Tiger Lilies, great masses of them, and my pink Phlox to the point of satiation, without fear of open discord. Again we have recourse to the cool blues—the Aconites, Sea Hollies, Veronica spicata, Globe Thistles, Campanula pyramidalis, and the pale E. Molineux to companion this bold plant. It lends itself well to interplanting and nothing is better for this purpose than the dark blue Monkshood (Aconitum Napellus) and its pretty blue-and-white variety, bicolor. The great candelabra-like stalks of Lilies are very splendid mingled with the more lightly made panicles of hooded flowers, and the more the two spread and crowd each other the more splendid is the display. A bold group shows the Tiger Lily planted with tall spires of pale Mullein and masses of partly spent Veronica spicata, with a few stalks of Hemerocallis Kwanso that almost repeats the colour of the Lily. One still bolder has our Lily interplanted with Veronica virginica with a foreground of Phlox Coquelicot and a pale, late-flowering Lemon Lily that I think is Hemerocallis citrina. At its feet blue and white Carpathian Harebells flower tumultuously, and over its head, swinging from a cedar arch, are the strange scarlet urn-shaped blossoms of Clematis coccinea. The scarlet Trumpet Creeper might well climb the wall at the back of this group among the English Ivy which is already there.

The Tiger Lily is one of the few Lilies that grows like any other hardy plant under ordinary garden conditions. It "seeds" itself prolifically as well as carrying on operations underground and one may very shortly give away Tiger Lily bulbs as one gives roots of Phlox and Michaelmas Daisies. I know several places in Orange County that are completely overrun with it—the great stalks of nodding Lilies rising close to the dusty roadside. Hemerocallis flava, the orange Day Lily, is also often called the Tiger Lily, and it is frequently found growing along the roadside.

Lilium Henryi is a beautiful August-flowering Lily of recent introduction that promises to be of the gracious managable-ness of L. tigrinum. I have but a few bulbs of it so far, as they are still rather expensive, but it is already showing the spreading ways of the former and apparently asks no special treatment. Its flowers, that are of the form of the speciosum Lilies, wear a splendid golden apricot colour, and the stalks grow very tall and strong. I think it might appear well with the porcelain blue blossoms of Clematis Davidiana, the new varieties of which, Profusion, Crepuscle, and Gerbe Fleuri, are real improvements over the old.

Another indispensable flower of strong colour is the Torch Lily (Kniphofia). Although usually regarded as one of September's gayest decorations, there are varieties that give their best to August, and the great spears thrust through a mass of cool blue or lavender or white are arresting indeed. Some of these early bloomers are Express, a beautiful coral red; Leichtlini, Pfitzeri, Torchlight, and Tysoni, a splendid sort with bluish foliage and soft scarlet and yellow torches. All the Kniphofias require care over the winter in the vicinity of New York; south of Philadelphia they are hardy enough. Mr. Farr says the best way to protect them is "to heel them in by digging a shallow trench and laying them close together in a slanting position in a dry location, covering them with about six inches of earth. . . . They may also be kept in dry earth in a cool cellar." If left in the garden the plants should not be cut down in the fall, nor divided, but given a heavy covering of straw. They should always be set out in spring.

Eight or ten of these Torch Lilies is not too large a number for a group in a large garden and with them may be set Veronica longifolia and V. virginica, blue and white Chinese Bellflowers, Campanula lactiflora and C. pyramidalis,

COLOUR IN MY GARDEN

Corn Flowers, Love-in-a-mist, the great Sea Lavender, Salvia Blue Beard, lavender coloured annual Larkspur, salmon and flame-coloured Zinnias and Snapdragons, flaming Montbretias in groups of a dozen or fifteen, lavender China Asters, and little spreads of soft-coloured Ageratum.

With the Sunflowers and Coneflowers (Rudbeckia) we get rather harsh colour though it is not nearly so objectionable as it would have been in the earlier year. Most of the members of these two families are too coarse and pervasive for the dressed flower garden and are more at home among the jolly Joe Pyes and Golden Rods of the August meadows. The annual Cut-and-come-agains I do not sow any more even for cutting, though some of the pale coloured sorts are rather pretty.

The double forms of Helianthus multiflorus—Golden Ball, Soleil d'Or, and plenus—are among the best of hardy plants, having shining, persistent foliage and upright carriage. The rigidus type to which belong Miss Mellish, Rev. C. Wolly Dod, and Daniel Dewar, should, I think, be excluded from the flower garden. Many years ago I set out a few roots in a long border against the garden wall and now it is only by means of the most strenuous measures that any other plant can get so much as a root-hold in this border. Every year we dig it out at least a foot and remove every smallest particle of root that we can find and yet, when August comes round, there is always the brazen din of those Sunflowers sounding above the deeper notes of imperial Ironweed and old purple Phlox that grow in the same border. The association is very pretty and one would

190

be glad enough to have a few bunches of the gay yellow things about the garden, for their growth is graceful and they may be drawn down over bare spaces in the borders. But while all their ways are so gay and careless above ground, beneath the surface their intentions are sinister: they are forming an almost impregnable mat of roots in the loose garden soil that spells destruction to any plant that we are so unwise as to place near them. There is a sort known as H. Maximilianii that I think may be a variety of giganteus, whose great proportions would not be tolerated within the garden enclosure save that it is often to be found blooming in November.

With the yellow Sunflowers I love to grow fluffy Boltonia and the warm-coloured Ironweed (Vernonia arkansana). For this last plant I am always pleased at the opportunity to say a good word, for though it is a wild plant, quite un-improved, and little used to cultivation, all its ways are seemly. Its roots are stay-at-homes, its growth splendidly upright, its colour imperial and gracious. There is no finer plant of the late summer and early autumn for the back of the border. There with sprays of yellow Sunflowers, in spite of our efforts, groups of bluish Rue bushes and masses of late white Phlox, it creates one of my favourite pictures. The Ironweed is one of the few American plants that I do not find appreciated by English gardeners. Now and then I come upon it in lists of plants for special purposes, but there is never the warm praise of its beauty and usefulness that it undoubtedly deserves.

For bold groups in the shrubbery there are several yellow composites too large in scale for the borders. Of these, the cure-all of our Grandmothers' days, Inula Helenium or Elecampane is handsome, with its gray-green leaves and tall stems of great yellow flowers. The Giant Groundsel of China, Senecio clivorum, is a striking subject for damp situations or in partial shade where the sun will not scorch its enormous leathery leaves. Bupthalmium cordatum, with large heart-shaped leaves and handsome orange-coloured flowers four or five inches across, might also have a place where broad planting is practised.

CHAPTER XVII
A WORD FOR COLOURED FOLIAGE

CHAPTER XVII

A WORD FOR COLOURED FOLIAGE

You ought to love colour and to think nothing quite beautiful or perfect without it.　　　　　　　　　　　　　　　　　　　　—Ruskin.

IN AMERICA, where the sun-hastened flowers have a short individual life tenure, it takes an immense variety of plants to maintain a succession of bloom in our gardens, and we do not sufficiently appreciate the importance of fine foliage of a permanent character that will enable us to keep the borders fresh and full when the flowers are not in evidence. That this fine foliage should also be handsomely coloured is in some cases an added advantage and one that we should be quick to make use of when we feel that persistent colour is desirable.

Of course coloured leaved plants and shrubs have been so unfortunately used in the past as lawn specimens and in bedding out that they are at present out of favour. Many of them, too, are quite too ginger-bready for any beauty at all, but there are others freshly variegated, soft gray, or rich purplish-maroon that are both fine and distinct and which, when carefully chosen and used with restraint, will add much to the borders and shrubberies.

After its spring flowering the shrubbery, for the most

part, settles into an inert greenness too uniform in tone for beauty. This period of monotony may be greatly relieved by a thoughtful grouping of some of the best of the coloured leaved shrubs. These should never be dotted about promiscuously, however, but massed, one kind at a time, and the harmonious setting of each group carefully considered. The so-called "purple-leaved" trees and shrubs are very handsome. Two of the best are the purple-leaved Plum (Prunus Pissardi) and the "blood-leaved" Peach (Prunus persica foliis rubris). The Peach is a bit lighter in colour than the other and all through the summer continues to send forth young shoots clothed in almost transparent leafage that has the colour of a ruby, giving the little tree a most attractive variety of tone and texture. Both these trees experience an ecstatic blossoming in April—just a moment when they stand arrayed, as for some mystic festival, before the warm leafage claims the twigs and branches. We plant Crocuses beneath them to make a picture with the blossoms, and later when the rich foliage has developed we love to see gay pink and cherry coloured Tulips streaming away from beneath the shadowing branches.

In my own garden a Dorothy Perkins Rose climbs the wall beside my group of Purple Plum-trees and throws its great trusses of pink blossoms across the purple branches with fine effect.

The purple Barberry (Berberis vulgaris foliis purpureis) is a handsome shrub. I like to see it well massed as a foreground for a group of Paul's Scarlet Thorn, with clumps of Tulip, Pride of Haarlem or Clara Butt, set against its richly sombre foliage. In the garden borders it is very effective used behind Irises of the pinky-mauve tones, Fraxinella, hybrid Pyrethrums, and for an autumn picture, grouped with the beautiful Desmodium penduliflorum.

The Purple Beech is perhaps the finest of its kind but it becomes too large a tree for use in the shrubbery or in the flower borders. There is also a purple-leaved Filbert (Corylus avellana purpurea) that is both distinct and beautiful and the purple Sumach (Rhus Cotinus purpurea), of which good use might be made. Some of the vivacious little Japanese Maples could be better employed massed among other shrubs or used as spots of high colour in the flower borders than as at present—like ships on fire and calling for help in a waste of green grass ocean. The best of these—I hesitate to write its terrible name—is Acer polymorphum atropurpureum nigrum. This is the true blood-leaved variety and keeps its colour throughout the season. Such a variety as versicolor, with red, green, and white leaves, is a bit fantastic for good taste.

The yellow and white variegated plants and shrubs are a bit more difficult to manage and should be used only after careful consideration of their surroundings. Of the herbaceous things especially, many are poorly coloured and of weedy character, and there is a decided choice among the shrubs.

The Golden Privet is, I think, one of the best of the yellow-leaved shrubs. In the herbaceous border it is very attractive used in a section of the border where dim blue flowers, Campanulas, Veronicas, and Aconites prevail; or employed to accentuate the sunshiny effect of groups of yellow and white flowers. The golden Elder, too, is a very good shrub and there is a pretty Mock-orange (Philadelphus coronarius foliis aureis) whose small creamy blossoms are in delightful accord with its "golden" leafage. As the season advances this variety loses some of its colour. Besides these we have "golden" Box, Euonymus, Retinispora, Arborvitae, Japanese Maples, Dogwoods, Weigelas, Hibiscus, Kerria, Ribes, and Filberts from which any who are interested may choose.

I am very fond of the Japanese Honeysuckle (Lonicera japonica), the leaves of which are finely variegated. It climbs a trellis with a fluffy white Rose called Bennett's Seedling and all through the season plays an important part in the colour scheme of its neighbourhood, where white and buff Hollyhocks, white Musk Mallows, Creamy Mulleins, and yellow Evening Primroses make their home.

For the golden-leaved herbaceous plants I cannot confess to so much admiration, though I think their usefulness in some situations is undoubted. Certainly the rampant Goutweed (Aegipodium Podograria), that old-fashioned folk call Soapsuds, is a delightful underplanting for shrubs in by-places where there is no danger of this prodigious "doer" overrunning and annihilating choicer subjects. The variegated Funkia, too, that one sees so often edging the paths or encircling the lozenge-shaped beds in country gardens, is particularly fresh and cheerful.

Not so well known is Arrhenanthemum bulbosum folia variegata—a wee thing to stagger under such an astounding name. It is a small grass, only about six inches in height, freshly striped yellow and green, and really makes a delightful edging. Then there is, of course, the tall striped grass—

HOLLYHOCKS AND DELPHINIUM
JULY 7TH

*T*HE Rose on the arbour is Trier, the Rose over the gate is Wm. C. Egan. The buff and pink Hollyhocks are the result of chance crosses between the yellow Fig-leaved Hollyhock (*Althaea ficifolia*) and the ordinary pink and crimson sorts. Phlox Elizabeth Campbell and Aster Climax are set behind the Hollyhocks and a few white Musk Mallows just in front.

White and pink Peonies are along the edge of this bed for earlier bloom with the pretty pink and white Cottage Tulip Picotee planted in groups between and showing charmingly among the crimson Peony shoots at the time of their flowering in early May.

The Delphiniums and Yellow Foxgloves (*Digitalis ambigua*) of the picture are in another bed across a narrow path. The Foxgloves are interplanted with Sea Lavender (*Statice latifolia*), whose great heads of lavender mist-like bloom expand in August and hide the decapitated stalks.

About the Delphiniums grow Campanula lactiflora alba magnifica, and the beautiful russet Helenium autumnale rubrum for late summer and autumn bloom.

PLATE NO. 15

AN ARRANGEMENT IN PINK
JULY 10TH

*T*HIS bed is the same that is seen in the Frontispiece. It is important because of its conspicuous position and must be kept well dressed from spring to autumn. It has an edging of bright yellow early Tulip Chrysolora growing in front of patches of pale Daffodil Mrs. Langtry. On the low retaining wall behind the bed are large pots of lavender-blue Hyacinths.

A band of Pink Beauty Sweet William follows the bulbs, and with it bloom, in late May and June, masses of pink and white Canterbury Bells behind a broad grouping of Iris pallida dalmatica with its great lavender flowers. Two bushes of blue-spiked Baptisia australis also bloom at this season and there is often a sprinkling of self-sown Yellow Foxglove (Digitalis ambigua).

In July the Hollyhocks, Goat's-rue (Galega officinalis), and Phlox Selma, seen in the picture, hold sway for several weeks, when the long branches of purple and mauve-pink Michaelmas Daisies that are set between the Phlox and Canterbury Bells begin faintly to colour and finally fill the bed with a soft haze.

Behind the Hollyhocks pink and white Boltonias are planted, their long branches to be drawn forward to hide the final untidiness of the former.

PLATE NO. 16
SEE PLATE NO. 1. FRONTISPIECE

A FAVOURITE MIDSUMMER GROUP
JULY 15TH

HERE we see the rose Loosestrife, the white Mullein (*Verbascum Miss Willmott*), Mullein Pinks (*Lychnis Coronaria*), and the yellow Knapweed (*Centaurea macrocephala*).

Along the edge of the border in spring flower Daffodils and the rich purple Aubrietia Dr. Mules; and Silene acaulis with its many tiny white flowers interplanting tall orange-coloured Tulips.

A little later blue and white hybrid Columbines have the corner to themselves.

The Mullein Pinks and true Mulleins have a long period of blossoming, and the Loosestrife at the back retains its form and foliage late in the fall, so no third flowering has been arranged for this group; but there might well be an interplanting of late-flowering Aconites or Torch Lilies (Kniphofia).

PLATE NO. 17

HIGH NOON
JULY 28TH

*T*HIS *bit of border is characteristic of the rich colouring of the midsummer garden. The flowers shown are Tiger Lilies, Mulleins (Verbascum phlomoides), the double orange Day Lily (Hemerocallis Kwanso), blue Spiked Veronica, Chinese Bellflowers, and Globe Thistles (Echinops Ritro).*

By turning to Plate No. 23 (September 10th) it may be seen how in a few weeks the picture may be completely reconstructed. The long branches of tall-growing plants at the back have been drawn down to cover their passé predecessors, and the border again blooms as freshly as before.

Nor in the earlier seasons was this spot devoid of bloom, for along the stone edging rioted the lovely white Sandwort (Arenaria montana), yellow and creamy Sun Roses (Helianthemum), a trail of Daffodils, and some groups of lavender Tulip Dream.

These in turn are followed by the blossoming of a large clump of Iris Madame Chereau accompanied by a few heads of lacelike Valerian and some yellow Columbines (Aquilegia chrysantha). Farther along in this border the beautiful Lilium Brownii has grown and increased for many years.

PLATE NO. 18
SEE PLATE NO. 23

COLOUR IN MY GARDEN

Ribbon Grass or Gardeners' Garters—known to all frequenters of old gardens, or loiterers along country by-ways, that seems to belong naturally among Sweet Williams and Foxgloves and faint lavender Canterbury Bells and is not by any means to be despised as a garden decoration.

The well-known Golden Feather (Pyrethrum parthenifolium aureum), upon which the faith of all bedders-out used once to be pinned to insure a permanent yellow glare, is yet a pretty edging for blue and yellow and white flowers. To keep it shapely and full its aspiring tendencies may be nipped back, and it should be started in the house in February or March.

There are many other plants of varying merit with "golden" or "silver" variegated foliage; the quaint, country-looking Euphorbia, known as Snow-on-the-mountain, the golden-leaved Coltsfoot (Tussilago), good for a ground cover beneath shrubs, or to spread over banks of heavy clay where little else will grow; the pretty Periwinkle, perhaps the most used to-day of these plants; the very old-fashioned Valeriana Phu aurea; the really charming golden-leaved Thyme, and many others.

But of all the coloured leaved plants and shrubs none is so really beautiful and so entirely indispensable as those that wear the silvery or bluish tones. These fill a place in the garden that no other plants can fill; among the gay garden flowers, the trails and mounds and breadths of soft neutral foliage soothe our colour-excited nerves and give us great æsthetic pleasure. We do not usually take gray into consideration as a garden colour, yet there are so many really fine plants that wear it, or variations upon its quiet theme, that we are enabled to enjoy it as freely in the garden as we do elsewhere.

Particularly in gardens where there is much stone work, this gentle, mediating tone is of marked value, seeming to draw the widely differing materials that go to make up the garden into a more sympathetic relationship. And in autumn, when the clamour of gay colours is silenced, the gray-leaved plants gleam with a special significance and beauty, keeping our garden fresh and well adorned for yet many weeks.

To be wholly effective, these sober-hued plants should be used with a fairly lavish hand, not dotted about among gayer colours where their quiet sway would scarcely be felt. They are most effective among light-coloured flowers, mauves and pinks, pale buff, and particularly with white flowers.

I do not know of many gray-leaved shrubs. A number of the Willows have fine silvery foliage and grow satisfactorily in other situations than by the waterside. Salix rosmarinifolia is one of the best, and we have Salix alba argentea that grows to quite a good-sized tree, the Royal Willow, and several others. The Silver-leaved Oleasters (Eleagnus argentea and angustifolium) are Willow-like shrubs with delicate gray foliage and ornamental fruit. The Sea Buckthorn (Hippophöe rhamnoides) has grayish foliage and there are two new Japanese Bush-honeysuckles (Lonicera Korolkowii and L. thibetica) said to be very fine, with fragrant pink blossoms and silver-green foliage. Besides these there are "silver" Elms, Ashes, Lindens, Hollies, and a number of evergreens that show a silvered or hoary surface. The Blue Spruce, relieved of its existence as a lawn specimen, might be most effectively massed as a background for pink Phlox, or grouped with purple-leaved Maples.

Of gray plants for the border none is finer than the Sea Lyme Grass (Elymus arenarius, listed in some catalogues as E. glaucus) that is well shown in Plates 13 and 14. All through the summer and autumn and until snow is on the ground its strong, grasslike foliage retains the beautiful colour, taking its place harmoniously with whatever scheme of colour is the fashion of the moment in its neighbourhood, and outlasting them all. Stachys lanata is another of great beauty and usefulness. This is a low-growing plant with long silver velvet leaves that bind the border verge in company with patches of pink Thrift and lavender Nepeta Mussini with an effect most delightful. The Nepeta itself has charming gray-green foliage that accords pleasantly with its mauve flower spikes.

Rue (Ruta graveolens) is a plant of rare beauty and elegance. It is the old time-honoured medicinal herb, but is quite fit to serve a less material use in the garden world. Its delicately cut foliage shines with metallic lights that increase in lustre as the season advances. The bush grows almost three feet tall and should be well cut over occasionally to keep it in form. Few finer accompaniments could be found for pink Phlox, Michaelmas Daisies, or any flowers belonging to the magenta group. Other fine gray-leaved plants are:

Lychnis Coronaria (Mullein Pink), both the aster-purple and the white sorts, 3 ft.; June through August. Easily raised from seed.

Artemisia abrotanum (Southernwood), shrubby, 3 ft.; foliage hoary and fragrant.

Artemisia Stellariana (Old Woman), 18 in.; foliage delicate and silvery, increases rapidly and is one of the best.

Artemisia vulgaris (Mugwort), tall rather coarse herb with whitish leaves finely cut. Handsome for groups in shrubbery. Grown from seed. Also Artemisia frigida and pedemontana.

Cerastium tomentosum (Snow-in-Summer), trailing; silver foliage and white flowers in May.

Antennaria tomentosa, creeping; white flowers.

Malva officinalis (Common Mallow), seed; 4 ft.; gray velvet leaves and small mauve-pink blossoms—lovely.

Salvia officinalis (Garden Sage), hoary leafage and spikes of blue flowers.

Santolina incana (Lavender Cotton), bushy, 18 in.; very fine.

Festuca glauca (Blue Fescue Grass), low tufted grass, very pretty as an edging among lavender and purple Violas and pink Thrift.

Pyrethrum leucophyllum, dwarf; only a few inches tall; silvery, finely cut foliage. Seed.

Thalictrum glaucum (Glaucous Meadow Rue), 6 ft.; yellow flowers; beautiful foliage.

Veronica incana (Gray-leaved Speedwell), 6 in.; blue flowers. Seed.

Anthemis montana, and A. Cupaniana 1 ft. white flowers and finely cut foliage. Seed.

Funkia Sieboldiana and Fortunei, 18 in. broad, spreading; blue-green leaves.

COLOUR IN MY GARDEN

Other plants of gray or glaucous leafage are: Sedum Sieboldi, Sedum glaucum and Sedum spectabilis, Mulleins, Globe Thistles, Sea Hollies, Pinks in large and enchanting variety, Arabis, yellow Alyssum, Thymus lanuginosus, Iris pallida dalmatica, Linaria dalmatica, Centaurea dealbata, Baptisia australis, Helychrysum angustifolium.

Some annuals have good gray foliage. Chief among these are the plants known as Dusty Miller, Centaurea candidissima and Cineraria maritima. These were once extensively used in ribbon gardening and bedding, but are as fine and useful in the more graceful and gracious gardening of our own day. They should be started indoors or in a frame in February or March and set out when settled weather is assured.

I am ever on the lookout for new gray-leaved plants. There is always the possibility in visiting a nursery or in reading a garden book that I shall see or have news of a new one. Miss Jekyll, who, I think, first directed our attention to the beauty and usefulness of this class of plants, speaks of two that I have not yet had the opportunity to try— the Jerusalem Sage (Phlomis fruticosa) and Euphorbia characias.

A free use of these quiet-toned plants seems to soothe all the conflicting elements of the garden into a happy relationship and creates in the mind of the beholder an impression of tranquil unity and accord.

CHAPTER XVIII
BEDDING OUT

CHAPTER XVIII

BEDDING OUT

Nothing is more the child of art than a garden.
—Sir Walter Scott.

IT REQUIRES some fortitude in this day to express approval of the bedding-out system. It has departed, or should have, with the days of antimacassars and hand-painted tambourines, and no one wants this period of terrible and useless ornament to return; yet it seems to me that there are times and places where we may still "bed out" with propriety and even grace.

Where there are flower beds on a terrace that extends along the façade of the dwelling there would be reason to resort to this sort of planting. Such a conspicuous situation should not be at the mercy of the ups and downs, the defections and general uncertainness that prevails in the region devoted to perennials and annuals, where their half-wild ways are simply an additional charm. On the contrary, in such a position we should enjoy a display of persistent colour and exact arrangement, only to be attained by the use of law-abiding bedders, long trained to march in rows and to suppress any ideas of their own about spreading and general emancipation. A spot so treated can never be regarded as the *garden*. It is what John Sedding calls "the betweenity," neither house nor garden, but relating to both; a seemly setting for the house and a little breathing space of preparedness before we descend the steps or round the corner into the gay special atmosphere of the garden.

Again, when an owner has not the time or perhaps the taste for gardening, the constant bedders will rescue his plot from the stolid dominance of the Hydrangea and the meagre forlornity of the pining Roses one sees in such impersonally conducted places, and keep it bright and personable from frost to frost.

Of course while there are so many happily grubbing gardeners in the world, bedding will never again gain any real foothold upon the land, and yet there are situations where its fresh and persistent colour and precise outlines would be a relief to the eye; not arranged in the intricacies of the parterres de broderie of old, but with what grace and prettiness we may command.

The very phrase, "Spring Bedding," is delightfully suggestive to me. The world is so fresh and tidy in the spring; one sees the strict young greensward with its cleanly interrupting beds of moist brown mould and one's imagination sets to work washing in the colours upon its expectant surface. Of course we paint in Tulips—not as of old—Duc van Tholl, scarlet; Chrysolora, yellow; and some white sort in stars and circles—but having recourse to all the exquisite tints and shades to be suggested by the most extravagant mind, used in graceful if formal association with plants of quite other forms. The only bedding out I ever did was in two beds in my flower garden that were destined for perennials still in seedhood. They were planted respectively with white Arabis and pink Cottage Maid Tulips and Forget-me-nots and early yellow Tulips—such spreads of fresh and sprightly colours! They did not last half long enough for me to look my fill.

The so-called "early" Tulips seem to lend themselves with particular propriety to bedding. Their shorter stems and crisp, upstanding habit better fit the conventional treatment than do the long, willowy stemmed blooms of the May or Cottage Tulips. The Darwins are of more upright carriage but they linger overlong and make us late with our summer bedding. There are numbers of pretty plants to be used as a ground cover for the Tulips—Arabis, Golden Alyssum, Aubrietia, Violas, Polyanthus Primroses, Forget-me-nots, Pansies, and English Daisies. Wallflowers make lovely spring beds in themselves—brown and russet and gold, but grow rather too tall and bushy to accompany the Tulips.

All these cover plants should be raised from seed sown in spring in a by-place where they may remain until they are wanted. Then in the autumn when the summer bedders have succumbed these may be cleared away and the nice little tufts of spring promise set in even rows or circles in the beds with Tulips, or if one likes, Hyacinths set between. Perhaps Daffodils are a bit giddy for such conventional treatment, yet they would be lovely shining above purple Pansies or frollicking among Forget-me-nots. A few combinations for spring beds that might be tried are:

Aubrietia Dr. Mules and Tulip Chrysolora.
Aubrietia Fire King and Tulip White Hawk.
Aubrietia Lavender and pink Hyacinth Jacques.

COLOUR IN MY GARDEN

Forget-me-nots and white Tulip Queen of Whites.
Forget-me-nots and rose Tulip Flamingo.
Forget-me-nots and yellow Tulip Golden King.
Arabis and blue Hyacinth Czar Peter.
Arabis and Tulip Joost von Vondle.
Primula polyanthus, and Tulip Thomas Moore.
Primula polyanthus and Forget-me-nots.
English Daisies and Pansies.
English Daisies and pink Tulips.

While I am certainly for bedding out within certain limits and with certain plants, I am all against it done in those plants that once made up the "turgid mosaics" against which Maeterlinck writes so feelingly. Here is the taboo list: Alternanthera, Caladiums, Caster-oil Plants, Dracaena indivisa, Coleus, Coxcomb, Cannas, Cupheas, Abutilon Savitzii and Achyranthes, Acalypha, Begonia Rex, Crotons and Echeveria. Lantanas were favourite bedding plants of yore. I remember that my father always stood out for two lozenge-shaped beds of Lantanas on the terrace in front of our old stone house, and how he gloried in their vivacious colours and ignored their terrible odour. This peculiarly sickening odour is as fresh in my memory as when I vainly strove to share my mother's gently amused tolerance of my father's favourites. I have not seen Lantanas since we closed the gate upon the dear Maryland garden, but some-one must still be setting them out in lozenge-shaped beds, for they are to be found in all the plantsmen's lists of bedding plants to-day.

Without resorting to the taboo list there is much good material at hand for use in summer bedding. I am very fond of Geraniums, myself. There is much beauty in their frank, pure colours, untroubled foliage, and the warm scent is always agreeable. I think a bed of such a satiny salmon-coloured Geranium as Mrs. Lawrence, with an edge of dwarf Ageratum, would be charming. Lavender and white Horned Violets would make pleasant bindings for beds of scarlet, pink, or white Geraniums; and dwarf Snapdragons, Mignonette, Verbenas, Phlox Drummondii, in suitable colours, might also be used.

No bedding plant is so sweet and reposeful in appearance as Heliotrope. A bed of Heliotrope, or Cherry Pie, as it was once called, edged with white Horned Violets or frilly white Petunias is a delight to the eye and "comforts the spirits" by its rich fragrance all through the summer and early autumn. I have seen such a bed interplanted with pale pink Gladiolus like America, or with the handsome summer Hyacinth (Galtonia), but I like best the simpler arrangement.

The waxen Tuberous Begonias—that "tribe of turbulent fighting-cocks"—need not be altogether scorned as bedders. They are a bit artificial in appearance, yet the colours are very splendid and beds of them make gay breaks in a stone terrace or shine handsomely upon the greensward. They prefer a light, rich loam with some sand. They should be lifted at the first hint of frost and allowed to dry before being packed away in sand in a frost-proof cellar. The dwarf-growing forms of Begonia semperflorens are better for bedding.

For beds in shady places nothing is more graceful than Fuchsias, with their pendent, warm-coloured flowers—soft crimson and purple, old rose and scarlet. They might be thickly underplanted with the rich purple Horned Violet G. Wenberg. Mr. E. T. Cook says: "Cuttings of the young plants strike root readily in spring and the plants so obtained may be grown in various ways. If the tops are pinched out two or three times when the plants are young they form neat bushes; next, allowed to grow at will with the leading shoots tied to a stake, they assume naturally more or less of a pyramidal habit, while standards, which are admired by many, are formed by tying the plants upright, and removing all the side shoots until the required height is attained, when the upper portion of the plant which is to form the head may be allowed to branch out."

The least expensive, and often very pretty, bedding may be done with annuals, though of course there is an element of uncertainty and a bit of waywardness not present when use is made of the regular bedders. To insure an early blossoming annuals should be raised in a hotbed or frame, or in a box in a sunny window. Seed thus started in February or March, pricked out into other boxes or tiny pots when the plants are possessed of two or three leaves, provides thrifty little plants for the beds by the time danger of frost is past. Seed for this purpose should not be bought "mixed," and only varieties that flower the whole season should be chosen. Some useful kinds are: Verbenas, pink and white and scarlet; French Marigolds, Calendulas, Zinnias; Petunias Rosy Morn, Double White, and the handsome violet-blue Velchenblau; Snapdragons, Intermediate varieties and the Tom Thumbs, Stocks (Cut-and-come-again varieties), Alyssum Little Gem or White Fleece, Browallia speciosa major, Calceolaria

Golden Bedder, Salvia patens and S. Bluebeard, Dimorphoteca aurantiaca, Ageratum tall and dwarf, both mauve and white; Lobelia Crystal Palace for its intense blue flowers and bronzy foliage, Emperor William for a lighter shade, Snowball for white; Matricaria Bridal Robe, Nicotiana, Pentstemon Southgate Gem and Sensation; and the three Dusty Millers—Cineraria maritima, Centaurea candidissima, and C. gymnocarpa.

If tall plants like Nicotiana are used, they should be carefully staked, for a beaten-down bed is irrevocably ruined. All faded blossoms should be removed that the beds may maintain a neat appearance and the plants continue to bloom freely.

Here are a few beds that would be attractive: Salmon Zinnias edged with light Ageratum; deep-coloured Ageratum with Alyssum White Fleece; Calendula Lemon Queen and white Phlox Drummondii; Nicotiana and Blue Lobelia; Salvia patens and Petunia Rosy Morn; Salvia Bluebeard and California Poppies; Snapdragon Rose Doré and Dusty Miller; Snapdragon Orange King and Ageratum.

Perhaps the most beautiful of summer and autumn beds are made with China Roses and Nepeta Mussini, or thickly carpeted with lavender, purple, or white Viola cornuta. For this purpose one variety of China Rose only should be used in a bed. Cramoisi Superieur is a glowing crimson Rose that blossoms freely from May until frost and is charming with a ground cover of vivacious little lavender and white Viola Papilio. The Rose and Amber Comtesse du Cayla is brilliant above a shadow of dark purple Viola G. Wenberg. Some of the best of the China and Bengal Roses are:

213

COLOUR IN MY GARDEN

Madame Eugene Resal, pink and orange; Mlle. de la Vellette, very brilliant orange and vermilion; Queen Mab, soft blush and yellow; Laurette Messimy, rose and amber; Arethusa, apricot and yellow; Ducher, white, and Mrs. Bosanquet, blush. Beds of the "Old Blush" China Rose and Nepeta Mussini are charming all through the season. Violas may be raised from seed and started indoors in March and will commence to bloom in July, continuing until frost, and starting in again in late May with the Roses.

Of course all such beds must be looked after very carefully; plants kept from straggling, edges trimmed with precision, weeds removed, and the whole kept watered and cultivated. In such conventional planting we may admit of no dwindling or pining, no sprawling or untidiness of any sort, for it is upon the crisp artificiality of its perfection that the beauty and usefulness of bedding out is contingent.

CHAPTER XIX
MICHAELMAS DAISIES

CHAPTER XIX
MICHAELMAS DAISIES

A symphony in purple, the colour of the organ peal are they.
—MARTHA FLINT.

SOMEWHERE I have read that there are ten thousand members of the ubiquitous clan Compositae, but sad to tell most of them are the most graceless weeds. Among the rowdy crew we find Horseweed, Ragweed, Beggar-ticks, Burdock, Dandelion, Hawkweed, Mayweed, Wild Lettuce, and a host of others that deserve to be frowned upon, but like the little girl in the nursery rhyme, when they are good the composites are very, very good, and never do they attain to such an eminence of goodness as in the Michaelmas Daisy. There are few more useful and charming flowers for use in the hardy garden. Many flowers, however, suffer the fate of prophets and have no honour in their own country. Our Michaelmas Daisy is one of these.

More than three hundred years ago young Tradescant, son of the great gardener of the seventeenth century, took back with him from America to the Royal Gardens in England a number of our wild flowers, among them the pretty wild Aster or Michaelmas Daisy that bears his name (Aster Tra-

descanti).   Since then many other wild Asters of the United
States have crossed the water and occupy proud places in the
finest gardens; while here, though their charm challenges us
from .every roadside and woodland tangle, our autumn
gardens are still largely held in the harsh grip of Cannas and
Salvias whose strident clamour is silenced by the first
onslaught of the frost king.   The Michaelmas Daisy, on
the contrary, blooms in its different species and varieties,
from August until November finds it still softly gleaming
unharmed by fierce frosts and little dismayed by the signs
of hasty departure all about.   It seems most extraordinary
that these flowers have been so slow to win the appreciation that they most certainly merit.   Few are so easy
to grow and to increase, few have so sturdy a constitution
and none, known to me, fill the garden with such a tide of
gracious and harmonious colour.   How often are we blind
to the things "beneath our shoon," looking abroad for
novelties and rarities that more often than not give a
meagre showing for all our pains, while all about us are
native flowers fit to grace the finest gardens.

Our nurserymen are now offering us long lists of Michaelmas Daisies.   Most of these are native wild species or have
been developed from them.   For those of the acris, amellus
and alpinus sections, however, we must credit Europe, and
Aster Thomsoni, a distinct species, comes from the Him-
alayas.   In many cases the wild species has been superseded
by a garden variety of greater merit.   The weediness inherent in all the composites is being gradually eliminated,
but the peculiar grace that is the birthright of the Michaelmas
Daisy remains to fit them for almost any position.   In wild

218

gardening they adorn the landscape as fittingly as a cloud the sky, and in the most formal arrangements they are no less at home. In colour they seem, save for a few Tyrian pink and magenta sorts, almost incapable of inharmony. The faint grayish tones, the hundred tints and shades of lavender, mallow pink, mauve, and heliotrope, and even the deep-toned violet and purple sorts lend themselves happily to almost any association.

The great body of hardy Asters or Michaelmas Daisies belongs to September, but August has a few and October and November also. The amellus group flowers in August and early September; and thereafter until frost occasional flowering stems are developed. The flowers are large, sometimes two inches across, and wear soft, porcelain-like tones of lavender and heliotrope. The flower stems rise from a tuft of attractive leafage to a height of from ten inches to two feet. Three of the best varieties are Beauté Parfaite, Beauty of Ronsdorf, and Rudolph von Goethe. These are plants for the front of the border, for while the flowering stems reach a fair height they have not the sturdy bushy habit of other Michaelmas Daisies and the tuft of leaves would be smothered among the taller growing plants of the early summer. It is necessary to divide nearly all the kinds of hardy Asters every other year, but Aster amellus is of more deliberate growth and may often be left undisturbed for three or four years without signs of deterioration.

Toward the end of August Aster acris asserts its fluffy bloom. It is distinct in appearance and very lovely when well grown. It grows about two feet high, its slender branches closely set with linear leaves and at the top a carelessly fashioned head of long-rayed flowers. The variety nana grows but a foot tall and is a delightful subject for the front ranks of the borders; Thomsoni is another fairly early bloomer. It is a twiggy little plant about two feet in height that contributes its sober gray-lilac bloom a bit apologetically to this season of lavish gaiety.

September, of course, is the heydey of the Michaelmas Daisies. My garden is aswarm with them. All summer long they have bided their time, pushing their way up through the other perennials, keeping fresh and green their sections of the borders, screening the blank places left by biennials, until now, when here and there the Woodbine throws out a scarlet signal, they sweep over the garden in such a blend of tender colour and transcendent grace that even the June garden in its crisp young maturity and bountiful beauty is not fairer. All the crudeness of the late summer is neutralized by the tide of tender colour, all bare spaces are filled by the slender bloom-clouded branches. This last festival of the garden is of a most rare and satisfying character.

The lists of Michaelmas Daisies now offered us have reached such a length that it is difficult to choose six or a dozen sorts with which to deck out the autumn garden, but there is a decided choice among them. Of the mallow-pink sorts two stand preëminent—St. Egwin and Mrs. Perry Improved. Both form sturdy bushes three to four feet in height completely covered with large flowers a full inch across. Mrs. Perry and Perry's Pink are of the same type and are nearly as fine. The former has the delicate mallow-pink colour of St. Egwin and the latter is a tone or two paler. Leaving out Mrs. Perry, the other three give a charming scale of colour. Mrs. Perry Improved is at least two tones deeper than St. Egwin. With these one may plant much soft gray foliage, Lyme Grass and Stachys, Rue and Lavender Cotton, and venture now and then a sheaf of sky-blue Salvia azurea or S. uliginosa, white Japanese Windflowers, and some groups of Aconitum Wilsoni. Still deeper in the pink scale is Aster novae-angliae rubra which is improved in Mrs. J. F. Raynor. These flowers, that approach magenta in colour, are lovely planted among the fleecy Boltonias, the tall stiff stems reaching well up among the crowding white blossoms.

Of the clear lavender sorts perhaps nothing finer has yet been produced than Feltham Blue of the New York Aster or novi-belgii type, though the newer Climax has many admirers. Top Sawyer, Robert Parker, and the later flowering Chapmani are tall-growing old sorts full of grace and soft-coloured beauty, and some of the laevis group have a spraylike growth that is very attractive. Gertrude is rather dwarf and most floriferous, and Perry's Blue with erect, dark stems showing through a haze of lavender bloom is not to be dispensed with. We might add T. S. Ware, the Hon. Edith Gibbs, King Edward the Seventh, and the two double sorts—Beauty of Colwall and Glory of Colwall, and not be overstocked.

Of the strong purple sorts there is, of course, our native novae-angliae, but far better are Melpomene and Rycroft Purple, both of the same group; and F. W. Burbidge belonging to the New York Starworts.

221

Good white Michaelmas Daisies are scarce. Peter's White, Finchly White (October), and White Queen are only fair. The little Heath Aster (A. ericoides), blooming late in the month, is perhaps the best, and some of the vimineus varieties are very like it. For white at this season it is best to turn to Boltonia, the ever-valuable Pyrethrum uliginosum, Chrysanthemum nipponicum, white Japanese Anemones, and Phlox Jeanne D'Arc. I am frequently asked for a list of the twelve best September flowering Michaelmas Daisies. I think the following would be my choice:

St. Egwin, 3 ft. Mallow pink.
Mrs. Perry Improved. Deep mallow pink.
Perry's Pink. 3½ ft. Pale mallow pink.
Feltham Blue. 4 ft. Clear lavender.
Climax. 5 ft. Clear lavender—late in the month.
Mrs. J. F. Raynor. 5 ft. Magenta. Late in the month.
Top Sawyer. 4–5 ft. Lavender.
Gertrude. 3 ft. Lavender.
F. W. Burbidge. 4 ft. Purple.
Cordifolius magnificus. 4 ft. Lavender.
Wm. Marshall. 4 ft. Clear violet.
Chapmani. 4–5 ft. Lavender. Late in month.

Blooming in October and November are Novelty, grandiflorus, cordifolius Ideal, amellus elegans, and tataricus. Of these A. tataricus, an Asiatic species, is the latest to bloom but has not great beauty to recommend it. Aster grandiflorus is a splendid native growing through Virginia and southward. It has strong, erect stems and bears large purple flowers. Novelty is a good tall sort of heathlike aspect and pale pinkish flowers crowded on the wiry stems.

COLOUR IN MY GARDEN

From very small gardens the strong-growing Asters like those of the novae-angliae and novi-beligii sections are best excluded and choice made among the more slender growing amellus, acris, ericoides, and cordifolius varieties.

No plants at our disposal are more suitable and effective for naturalizing than the Hardy Asters. They are entirely able to take care of themselves in waste places, along stream-sides, or upon dry, rough banks, soon spreading into great breadths of lovely colour and mingling with the Golden Rod, Sunflowers, and flaming autumn leaves in entire felicity. They should be planted in broad, irregular groups, the tall, strong-growing novae-angliae and novi-belgii, tataricus and grandiflorus varieties toward the back with the more slender and dwarf sorts in a careless fringe along the edge of the plantation. Many will grow in shady places. Of these are cordifolius, corymbosus, laevis, undulatus, divaricatus, and acuminatus. Others crave the boggy comfort of swamps and stream-sides. There we find radula, Tradescanti, longifolius, and puniceus pulcherrimus. This last is a very fine plant growing five feet tall and bearing great pyramidal heads of faintly coloured blossoms with curiously incurved petals and yellow centres.

For two of the wild Asters (unimproved) I have a special fondness. One is A. cordifolius, the Heart-leaved Aster, also called Bee Weed and Bee Tongue; the other is A. linariifolius. Aster cordifolius is a graceful thing of dense, spraylike flowering in late September. Its colour is in-determinate, now gray, now white, now faintly flushed, according to the light and probably influenced by the soil in which it grows. My children say it is the colour of the

hoar frost and have christened it Frost Bloom; and indeed
where it covers a dry bank beneath great maple trees near
our home one might well imagine that the white invader
had arrived in strength and pitched his silvered tents. Its
height is variable, from one to three feet, but its stems are
so willowy and slender that we seldom see it upright. I
have used it here with nice results as an underplanting to
shrubs, and at no time is the shrubbery so attractive as
when it shows the silver hem of Frost Bloom beneath its
reddening garment. Aster cordifolius has its being also in
an improved state. Lists of named varieties are given in
some catalogues, but I have not seen them. Ideal is said
to bloom in October; Photograph is a pale blue-lavender sort;
Profusion, Diana, and Sweet Lavender all sound delightful.
Of course these improved varieties are best for the flower
borders, but for wild shaded banks, the shrubbery, and in
half-waste places, the Frost Bloom with its wayward charm
is surely the loveliest.

My other favourite, A. linariifolius, is a bristly, tufted
little plant, not more than a foot in height. Its rough,
erect stems are closely set with narrow, stiff leaves, and bear
a single lavender flower of a peculiar porcelain-like quality.
I cannot learn that this little Aster is handled by the trade.
We find it in an abandoned upland pasture where slim Red
Cedars, sure followers upon the heels of neglect, and spreading Dogwoods have claimed the land. There growing
thriftily in the dry grass between sumptuous spreads of
Fringed Gentian we find now and then a tuft of Aster
linariifolius. I have never found it in any quantity. I have
brought it into the flower garden, planting it along the edge

of a dry, sunny border with some Corydalis for company and am hoping that it will not too much miss the scarlet Wood Lilies, the heavenly Gentians, the tiny Ladies' Tresses, and all the rest of the rare company that hold that upland pasture, and will give us the pleasure of its quaintly stiff blossoming next September.

CHAPTER XX
THIS SIDE THE SNOWS

CHAPTER XX

THIS SIDE THE SNOWS

The maple wears a gayer scarf,
The field a scarlet gown,
Lest I should be old fashioned
I'll put a trinket on.

—EMILY DICKENSON.

HOWEVER we may feel about strong colour during the spring and summer, there are few who do not welcome it in the autumn garden. It is as if we wished to fill our souls with warmth and gaiety against the time when winter with its cold white silence shall lie upon the land. Purple, scarlet, and gold are the colours of the autumn garden and however bizarre and extravagant their assemblage, the eye is made quiet, not only by means of its harmony with the season, but through its accordance with the moods of our own mind.

Yellow and red is of all colour combinations to me the most unpleasant. All summer I avoid it, snatching the chance Coreopsis seedling from the neighbourhood of the scarlet Lychnis, taking strenuous measures where California Poppies and English Field Poppies attempt affiliation, but now I am moved only to ardent admiration by the groups of blazing Torch Lilies and Helenium, Scarlet Snapdragons,

229

COLOUR IN MY GARDEN

Marigolds and Nasturtiums. Gaillardias I particularly dislike, save the pure yellow Lady Rolleston, on account of their red and yellow colour scheme, yet I always admire them warmly when seen in my friends' autumn gardens. Scarlet and purple would jar the colour sensibilities of many during the summer months, yet how delighted are we now at the massing of purple Michaelmas Daisies against the flaming Virginia Creeper both in the garden and along the roadside. All over my own garden after the tenth of September flows a tide of Michaelmas Daisies, filling the garden with soft colour through which burst with telling effect the conflagrations of scarlet and gold, the whole so splendid and satisfying as to make me quite forget the tender beauty of spring or the brave days of the Iris and the June Roses.

My favourite flowers in the autumn garden, after the hardy Asters, are Heleniums. Helenium autumnale is one of the best yellow flowers of the entire year. It wears a warm full tone, yet soft and entirely lacking in the garish quality that spoils the Sunflowers; the variety pumilum shows the same fine tone of yellow, but is of lesser stature, growing only about two feet tall while the other reaches six in good soil. Helenium autumnale rubrum, with its round russet-coloured blossoms, is perhaps the most decorative flower of the season. It is splendid grouped with the lavender hardy Aster Climax and such a shining Torch Lily as Kniphofia Golconda. H. autumnale striatum, with its yellow petals flushed and streaked with scarlet, is less fine than the other two, but is worth planting where there is room for a number.

A COOL PICTURE
AUGUST 1ST

PLEASANTLY cool in appearance in the heat of midsummer is this corner where white Phlox, Silver Thistles, Moonpenny Daisies, and Lyme Grass are assembled. The group of Rose Loosestrife just behind gives the needed touch of colour.

In May and June the picture here is just as lovely, for it is composed of tall white Canterbury Bells, pale yellow Lupines, and a charming mauve-pink Iris Her Majesty.

In September the Hardy Aster Perry's Pink, planted between the Thistles, refurbishes the group and lasts well into October.

PLATE NO. 19

COLOUR IN A NORTH BORDER
AUGUST 6TH

*I*T IS *perhaps difficult to see, when looking at the June picture of this bit of border, Plate No. 11 (June 20th), where all the plants shown in the opposite picture could have been hiding during the all-covering exuberance of that flowery month. There they were, however, awaiting their chance, and here they are making us forget in the richness of their display the more frivolous loveliness of young summer.*

Of course the white Goat's Rue is a "hand-me-down" from the earlier season and is good for a full fortnight yet. The Delphiniums and Anchusas of the earlier picture were interplanted with Aconites (Aconitum Napellus and its variety bicolor) whose sprays of blue and white flowers are conspicuous in the picture. The tall white-flowered plant is the Culverwort (Veronica virginica), and the scarlet Phlox is Coquelicot.

As autumn claims the garden for her own long branches of a hardy Aster, hitherto unnoticed, suddenly burst into a heathlike flowering. The name of the Aster is Novelty. Its colour is a curious soft pink which is in nice accord with the cold blue Aconites (Aconitum autumnale) that are arranged to companion it.

PLATE NO. 20
SEE PLATE NO. 11

SUMMER MOONLIGHT
AUGUST 10TH

HERE in the transfiguring light of the *Lady Moon* we see the tender pink *Phlox Peachblow*, the long grasslike leaves of *Lyme Grass*, and across the path the strong foliage of *Iris*.

Earlier upon this spot bloomed insistent scarlet *Poppies* and lace-like *Valerian*. *Plate No. 8* (*May 28th*).

PLATE NO. 21
SEE PLATE NO. 8

GARDEN OUTLAWS
AUGUST 29TH

*B*OTH the Old Purple Phlox and the Sun-flowers have been many times removed from this border, but a season of relaxed vigilance sees them again in possession as shown in the present illustration.

Growing with them is the pale and lovely Phlox Madam Paul Dutrie, Rue, and, in the foreground, the shrubby Clematis Davidiana. A little later the filmy inflorescence of white Boltonias and the purple plumes of Ironweed will be added to the group, carrying it along until mid-autumn.

In the spring, after the Daffodils have passed, this border edge is buried beneath a fluttering cloud of azure Flax and gay Spanish Poppies (Papaver rupifragum) through which gleam here and there pure-white Columbines.

In June Iris Albert Victor and white Fox-gloves create the picture, and in July the flowers seen in this portion of the border are the tall yellow Evening Primrose Afterglow and blue Spiked Veronica.

COLOUR IN MY GARDEN

I am extravagantly fond of Torch Lilies (Kniphofias), not grown as one sees them all too often, drawn up in fierce array upon a spread of meek greensward, but used in gracious combination with the hardy plants and annuals of their season. The flaming scarlets, warm coral reds, and golden apricots of the torches are in fine harmony or bold contrast with all the autumn flowers, save those that wear the pinkish magenta tones, and even from these in accidental juxtaposition we do not shrink as we should have in the earlier year. The great flower heads are particularly striking piercing a haze of lavender Michaelmas Daisies; late Aconites are most effective planted with them, and they may be delightfully used with white Japanese Anemones and the pretty lavender-flowered Eupatorium coelestinum, or with the late white Phlox Jeanne d'Arc with a foreground of dwarf Nasturtiums and Ageratum.

One of the best and most reliable of these Kniphofias is K. Pfitzeri (syn. corallina). It is of a fine coral colour and sends up its great torches on stems three feet tall from August until November. The old Red Hot Poker (K. Uvaria; syn. aloides) is perhaps the hardiest and the best for general use. It blooms late and its red and yellow flowers rise on stems five feet tall. But the wonderful colours of some of the newer sorts are not to be resisted. K. caulescens, for instance, has handsome glaucous foliage and reddish-salmon flowers of a most beautiful tone. Golconda, too, is a beauty and Leichtlinii, both with warm golden-apricot torches. The flower spikes of Chloris are tarnished gold and particularly rich in combination with deep purple Michaelmas Daisies like Melpomene. Bright-

hued annuals that celebrate the autumn festival handsomely are Snapdragons like Orange King, Fireflame,
Sunset, and Orange Prince; Nemesias, Marigolds, Calendulas, Zinnias in the scarlet, buff, and burnt orange shades;
and the fine African Daisy, Dimorphotheca aurantiaca.

The new early-flowering hardy Chrysanthemums are also
in bloom in the early fall and too much may not be said in
favour of their inclusion among our autumn flowers. They,
of course, can never take the place in our hearts of the old-
fashioned hardy little plants of the November garden—
the little brown buttons, the ashen pink tufts, and the
ragged yellow fellows—but they give us the beauty of
Chrysanthemums many weeks before we should have the
old-fashioned ones and add much to the scope of our autumn
planning. In fine harmony with the scheme of the season
are Sevenoaks, pure bright yellow; Nina Blick, golden
bronze; Harvest Home, of much the same colouring as the
last; October Gold and Billancourt, rich terra cotta. The
early pale-coloured sorts like Fée Japonaise, Normandie,
and Dorothy are a valuable addition to the garden's supply
of light colours and some of the pink and crimson sorts will
be found fine in association with the pretty Blue Spiraea
(Caryopteris Mastacanthus, or more properly C. incana) or
the lavender Eupatorium. Single-flowered Chrysanthemums
are also coming into favour and show many fine colours.

English people make much use of Golden Rod, not only
in their natural planting but in the hardy borders, and our
nurserymen are offering a number of kinds. To me they
ever have an alien look in the prescribed atmosphere of the
dressed garden. They seem true creatures of the wild, born

to gypsy roving, to preach the cult of beauty from the highway to all who care to listen; but in the garden they appear like shy country folk at a city rout, their native beauty and grace unfelt because of their manifest unfitness for the occasion. Not all wild flowers seem to me appropriate for garden decoration. I cannot bear to see the Cardinal Flower in captivity and feel that all its wild soul must be reaching out and yearning for the seclusion of the shaded stream-sides, and the freedom of the wild world. No one, I believe, has yet been able to tame the free spirit of the Fringed Gentian and it is better so that we may yet have something to draw our footsteps from out the narrow windings of the garden paths to windy uplands and broad sun-tanned marsh-meadows, away from the prescribed and personal to the contemplation of infinity.

Blue is represented in the autumn garden by Aconitum autumnale and A. Wilsoni, the fine Chimney Bellflower (Campanula pyramidalis), Salvia azurea and S. uliginosa still lingering and the charming little Leadwort (Plumbago Larpentae) of so warm and rich a blue. This lovely jewel of the waning year is not reliably hardy in all soils. It likes not the flesh pots of the garden, but thrives best in well-drained gravelly loam. In spring it makes so tardy an appearance above ground that we are apt to abandon hope of ever seeing it again and often injure or quite annihilate the little plants in the spring digging and cultivating. All these blue flowers are fine and rich in association with those soft colour tones held up to scorn as rosy magenta, the pinkish Hardy Asters, Ironweed, and the beautiful Desmodium penduliflorum.

The autumn perennials last long in beauty. They do not

give way to panic before the onslaughts of early frosts as do many of the more succulent annuals, resolving at once into pulpy masses of blackened matter dreadful to look upon, but bear themselves bravely and light the garden well into brown November. The latest flowering perennials that I know are Helianthus Maximilianii, Chrysanthemum nipponicum, Anemone japonica, Hardy Chrysanthemums, Aconitum autumnale; Asters Novelty, grandiflorus, and amellus elegans; and Eupatorium ageratoides.

The last-named plant is a native that may with great propriety and benefit be brought into the garden. It grows four feet tall and has broad, flat flower heads of a soft gray-white colour and it thrives in the shade. This with the handsome Chrysanthemum nipponicum, Phlox Jeanne d'Arc, and Japanese Anemones provide about all the good white flowers for our autumn scheming, but as a matter of fact we need white flowers at this time less than at any other. They interrupt the rich and dignified ensemble which most completely satisfies the eye at this season.

Few shrubs and trees bloom in the autumn, but many contribute decorative fruit or glowing foliage to the last festival of the garden's life. The little Abelia chinensis continues to offer its waxen flowers well into the autumn and keeps its leafage halfway through the winter. The Rose of Sharon, too, is handsome and conspicuous in the autumn garden. I like particularly the slaty-lavender sorts and some that are a rich old rose. A few other shrubs that blossom late are Buddleia Davidii Veitchiana, Tamarix pentandra or aestivalis, T. gallica indica, and Hamamelis virginica, our native Witch Hazel.

234

COLOUR IN MY GARDEN

One of the gayest autumn pictures in my own garden is where a group of Waahoo and Snowberries occupies an angle of the wall. The Waahoo grows tall like a little tree, and in the autumn after the leaves have fallen is hung all over with the most fetching rose-coloured seed receptacles that finally burst and hang out scarlet ear drops that cling nearly all winter. The Snowberry (Symphoricarpos racemosus) is a very old-fashioned shrub now generally overlooked in the rush for exotic novelties, but this should not be, for its autumn beauty is undoubted and in the spring the tiny blossoms provide a rare feast for the honey bees. The Waahoo grows wild in my neighbourhood, making the roadsides and neglected dooryards delightfully bright in autumn. The birds do not seem fond of the scarlet ear drops but eat the Snowberries with relish. The two together are charmingly gay.

Among the shrubs and trees that have scarlet berries are the following: the Washington Thorn (Crataegus cordata), C. nitida, the Cockspur Thorn (C. Crus-galli), the English May (C. oxyacantha), the Mountain Ash (Sorbus Aucuparia), the Dogwood (Cornus florida), the native Holly (Ilex opaca), Black Alder (Ilex verticillata), I. Sieboldi, Japanese Bush-honeysuckle (Lonicera Morrowii and L. tatarica), Berberis vulgaris, B. Thunbergii, the Highbush Cranberry (Viburnum americanum), Sambucus racemosa, and Cotoneaster horizontalis.

And as the weeks steal one upon the other "mesmeric fingers softly touch" the glowing beauty of the garden. Now the scarlet flush is gently smoothed away, the yellow light put softly out, and the garden stands tender and wistful in second mourning colours—purple and lavender and gray, but showing here and there a mutinous spark of brilliant colour.

A walk about the garden in November is productive of a sort of mournful ecstasy. There have been many hard frosts, and all but the most faithful plants are gone, and these seem far more precious than all the beauties of the summer. It is Indian Summer and within my sheltering garden walls many a plant is tricked by the "blue and gold mistake" and ventures a timid resurrection. Beside me where I sit upon the sun-warmed garden steps, wrapped in the golden warmth—"almost myself deceived," a little Corydalis in the wall has burst forth in a springlike flowering above a gay colony of purple and white Horned Violets assembled in the path. Nepeta flowers again delicately from a low wall top and a single apricot-coloured Poppy sways above it. China Roses bloom undismayed, and a great white Rugosa Rose, like the ghost of June, presses its wan cheek against the sunny wall.

Perhaps all summer I have not paused to notice Sweet Marjoram, but now how grateful I am for its warm purplish-pink spread and spicy fragrance. Aconitum autumnale still flowers—a chill-appearing presence, rising above the cold rounds of Chrysanthemum nipponicum. One border verge is quite freshly blue and white where Salvia Blue-beard and Sweet Alyssum riot unharmed. Snapdragons and California Poppies gleam here and there in sheltered corners, and in a stone jar Petunias, bizarre and careless,

COLOUR IN MY GARDEN

flaunt their rose and purple skirts in the face of the grim
presence.

> These few pale autumn flowers,
> How beautiful they are!
> Than all that went before
> Than all the Summer store
> How lovelier far!

CHAPTER XXI
FAMILIAR PLANT NAMES—A DIGRESSION

CHAPTER XXI

FAMILIAR PLANT NAMES—A DIGRESSION

The name that dwells on every tongue
No minstrell needs.
—Don Jorge Manrique.

NOWADAYS we are become so learned in the matter of Latin plant names that there is some danger that the familiar English names, their pet names, will disappear from our garden vocabulary and finally, perhaps, be altogether forgotten. More and more often do we hear the words Dianthus, Digitalis, Lychnis tripping easily from the tongues of young gardeners, and less and less the friendly, time-endeared appellations—Pink, Foxglove, Campion; and our garden conversations lose much of piquancy and agreeable intimacy in consequence. It is, of course, essential that we know the Latin names of our plants, for by no other means may we accurately designate them, but the passing of the old vernacular names would be a real loss. They are the connecting links between us and the flower lovers of all the ages—men, women, and children, a long line of them—stretching across the years through countless gardens, high and humble, through woods and meadows and marshes to the little gatherings of potent herbs and edible roots nestled against the protecting walls of ancient monasteries wherein were kept the first records of flowers and their names. Out of the simplicity and sweetness of each age these names were born and linger yet with the freshness and charm of the flowers themselves.

In "English Plant Names" the Rev. John Earl says: "The fascination of plant names is founded on two instincts —love of nature and curiosity about language." It lies deeper than this, it seems to me; these old names are a bond between the gardeners of to-day and generations of congenial spirits who loved and laboured in their gardens as do we; they are the artless records of centuries of pleasant work, of country-spent leisure, and they reach us across the years like messages from old friends. More than this, many of these quaint titles—Gillyflower, None-so-pretty, London Tufts, Sops-in-wine, Honesty, to take a few at random— have the power to spread a magic carpet for the mind and send it voyaging into the gardens of the past. They not only place us on a more friendly footing in our own gardens, but open the gate of many a one long claimed by oblivion, and even acquaint us somewhat with the gardener, his fancy, and his station in life.

One may not search old horticultural works without gleaning the knowledge that it was the housewife who in most cases had the garden under her jurisdiction; and it seems highly probable that her mind and the minds of her children, fitted to the narrow circumference of home and garden, blossomed into many of the pretty whimsical titles with which we are familiar to-day. One seems to detect a woman's fancy in many of them, a woman's note of detail. There is ample testimony in the old flower books in support of this supposition. The ancient writers again and again give "our women" or our "English Gentlewomen" credit for the fanciful christenings of flowers. "Some English Gentlewomen," says Parkinson, "call the white Grape-flower Pearles of Spain," and of the gay scarlet Poppy "Our English women call it by a name, Ione Siluer Pinne: sub-auditor, Faire without and fowle within." Here, too, is the case of the "Frenticke or Foolish Cowslip," "come lately into our gardens whose floures are curled and wrinkled after a most strange manner, which our women have called Jacknapes-on-horse-back." "Our women" it was, too, one feels sure, whose tender scrutiny caught the resemblance between another Cowslip and a sort of old-fashioned foot-gear and called it the Cowslip, Galligaskins; and fitted the double Cowslips, whose rounds of petals set one within the other, so nicely with the name of Hose-in-hose.

The burnished little Hawkweed (Hieracium aurantiacum), a traveller to our roadsides and meadows from over seas, was once a garden flower in good standing with a string of friendly names to its credit. One of these names is Grim-the-colliar—seemingly obscure enough as to origin—and yet here we have old John Gerade informing us across three hundred years in this wise: "The stalkes and cups of the floures are all set thick with a blackish downe or hairiness as it were the dust of coles; whence the women who keep it in gardens for noueltie sake, have called it Grim the Colliar."

Mr. Frederick Hulm offers further elucidation of the origin of this curious name by telling us that during the reign of Queen Elizabeth a comedy called "Grim the Colliar of

Croydon" enjoyed wide popularity and from this seeming coincidence he assumes that "the grimy hero of the populace stood god-father to our plant." If we may accept this supposition we have, not only Gerade's account of its derivation, but we learn that the woman who bestowed the name belonged, not to a remote rural neighbourhood, but was more or less urban in her associations and while spending at least part of the year in the country, was no stranger to the gay doings of London Town.

How fascinating to trace out the beginnings of these old plant names! The origin of some is, of course, obvious enough, as for instance, Shepherd's Warning and Poor-man's-weather-glass, for the Scarlet Pimpernell, that closes its tiny blossoms at the approach of a storm; Butter and Eggs for such flowers as display the fresh colours of those good country products; Guinea-hen-flower and Checker Lily for the Little Fritillary whose bell is well checkered over with deeper colour; Hod-the-rake (hold-the-rake) and Rest Harrow (Arrest harrow) for meadow plants having such thickly growing roots that they impede the operation of rakes and harrows.

Many plants have received names indicatory of their habits; thus Four-o'clocks, Morning Glory, Evening Glory, John-go-to-bed-at-noon, Ten o'clock Lady, Flower-of-an-hour, Good-night-at-noon; and so also Turnesol (turning toward the sun), Catch-fly, Fly-trap, and so on.

Creeping plants with insistent colonizing proclivities usually receive some such name as Meg-many-feet, Gill-over-the-ground, Robin-run-in-the-hedge, Roaming Charlie, Creeping Jenny, Jack-jump-about, or Mother-of-thousands.

Hundreds were named from some real or fancied resemblance to some object; thus Monkshood, Bluebell, Turtlehead, Ladies-tresses, Snow-in-summer, Adder's-tongue, Snowdrop, Quaker Bonnets, Dutchman's-breeches, Maltese Cross, Larkspur, Bird's-foot, Pussy-toes, and so on indefinitely. The words Bull or Horse used as a prefix to certain others, as Bull-rush and Horse-mint, simply indicate a coarser variety of rush or mint. Many twining plants were christened by sentimentalists Love-bind and Bind-with-love.

Several centuries ago John Parkinson wrote "I would not two things should be called by one name, for the mistaking and misusing of them." If there was this danger in Parkinson's day, it has increased a hundredfold in ours. Few of these old plant names are at all fixed in their application, many doing duty for numerous quite different and unrelated plants and others making part of a string of names of anywhere from two or three to fifty or sixty designating the same plant. Nearly all neat, rather small, round flowers have been called at some time or in some locality Bachelors Buttons; many flowers with soft whitish leaves Dusty Miller, and those having fringed petals were frequently called Ragged Robin or Ragged Sailor. There are countless Prince's Feathers, Bird's-eyes, Sweet Nancys, Cowslips, London Prides, Nonesuch, Cuckoo Flowers, Honeysuckles, Long-purples, Sweet Marys, Ladders-to-heaven, Forget-me-nots, Buttercups, Roses of Heaven, Butter and Eggs, Willow-herbs, Sweet Williams, and Ox-eyes—to name a few; and the number of Meadow Pinks, Indian Pinks, Squaw-roots, and May-flowers that flourish in our own floral kingdom would astonish the curious searcher into such matters.

The word Gillyflower, one of the softest and prettiest of all flower names, plunges us into a most pleasurable confusion. It seems to have been a sort of pet name given to many greatly admired flowers having no attributes in common save a delightful fragrance. The Clove Carnation was, I believe, preëminently the Gillyflower, though the Wallflower and the Stock, and numerous others, shared with it the distinction of the pretty name. The Carnation's claim lies in the assumption that from the Latin Caryophyllum, a clove, grew the Italian garofalo, the French giroflée, and finally by way of the capricious spelling common to those days, the English Gillofer or Gillyflower.

July-flower was another corruption of Gillyflower. Drayton wrote of the "curious, choice Clove July-flower," probably meaning the Carnation; and Wallflowers also came to be known as July-flowers.

Old Gervaise Markham in "The Country Housewife's Garden" (1626) speaks of "July-flowers (I call them so because they flower in July), they have the name of cloves of their scent." These must have been Carnations, but he also notes "July-flowers of the wall, or Bee-flowers, or winter July-flowers, because growing in the walls even in Winter, and good for Bees."

The name Carnation comes from coronation because of the constant use of this flower in garlands and wreaths. In France the Pink is Oeillet—Petite Oeillet, or Oeillet de Poete, but the fragrant flowers sold to-day in the Paris markets as Giroflé are Wallflowers, "Gold blossoms frecked with iron brown." A friend tells me that in her grandmother's garden in New York State Wallflowers were always called Gillyflowers.

Stocks were also called Gillyflowers and sometimes also White Wallflowers; and our Sweet Rocket (Hesperis matronalis) was known as Queen's Gillyflower. A sort of Campion was the Marsh Gillyflower, and the great Thrift was known as Sea Gillyflower; and there were doubtless many others that shared the name.

I think the flower with the greatest number of names must be the Marsh Marigold. Mrs. Earl says it is the proud possessor of fifty-six. The Pansy, a loved flower of all ages, has attached to itself almost as many. The flower that comes down the years without winning one or more pet names has somehow failed to draw close to the lives of the human beings beside whom it has grown. There are not many old-fashioned flowers of which this may be said, but it is a curious fact that a flower so appealing and distinctive as the Crocus should be one. Crocuses have been grown in gardens since the early part of the seventeenth century but none as far as I can ascertain has acquired a common name save Crocus sativus, which was called Saffron or Saff-flower. Its relative the Colchicum, on the other hand, boasts quite a number, the quaintness and intimate character of which seem to imply a special affection for the jaunty little autumn flower.

The Zinnia, a flower of the nineteenth century introduction, has drawn to itself a most old-fashioned sounding name, that of Youth-and-old-age, but the Dahlia and the Cosmos, which also are of yesterday have, so far, in spite of the admiration lavished upon them, only their given names.

It is probable that future introductions to the plant world will receive only the most commonplace of common names, unless children come to our aid. We are grown much more self-conscious than of old, more hesitant in expressing our fancy, and we feel to a greater degree than did our gardening forefathers and foremothers the necessity for accuracy.

Of course the present day is almost entirely deprived of one most productive source of vernacular plant names— that of superstition. The superstitious peasantry of all ages contributed enormously to the number of plant names. The great number that have been in the past credited with magical power may be understood from the many that bear such names as Enchanter's-herb or Sorcerer's Violet. The Vervain was known by the former name and Drayton wrote

> Trefoil, Vervain, Johnswort, Dill,
> Hinder witches of their will.

The unassuming little Periwinkle won the name of Sorcerer's Violet from the assumption that it was one of the chosen flowers of the "wise folk" in their magic-working operations. Plants associated with witches, pixies, Puck, fairies, elves, and even with his satanic majesty are too many to mention.

A great many plants also are dedicated to the Virgin Mary and a few to our Saviour. The saints have a long list, as St. Johnswort, St. Barbara's Cress, St. Peter's Wreath, St. Patrick's Cabbage. These, I believe it is generally assumed, have been so named because they bloomed near the days which are dedicated to the same saints.

"Once whatever was scientific in the art of medicine was centred in the study of herbs and the materials of the healing art were wholly vegetable." Thus it is not surprising that many plants acquired their names through a real or fancied power to alleviate certain human ills. The little Pansy was deemed a potent heart remedy or cordial and so received its name of Heartsease, and so also we have Lungwort, Throatwort, Consumption Root, Ague-weed, Palseywort, Pleurisy-root, Eye-bright and Woundwort. Some were believed to be so universal in their curative powers that they received the name of All-heal or Cure-all.

To the curious old cult called the Doctrine of Signatures, which at one time certainly won the credulity of suffering humanity, is traceable many plant names. "This was a system for discovering the medical uses of a plant from something in its external appearance that resembled the disease it would cure" or the portion of the body to be cured. In "The Art of Simpling" we read "Though Sin and Satan have plunged mankind into an Ocean of Infirmaties, yet the mercy of God, which is over all His works, maketh Grasse to grow upon the Mountains and Herbes, for the use of men, and hath not only stamped upon them a distinct form, but also give them particular signatures, whereby a man may read, even in legible characters the use of them." Imaginations must have run riot in the compilation of a pharmacopœia based upon this wild theory, and even after a lapse of several centuries one must feel pity for the poor creatures treated with Quaking Grass for chills, with Nettle tea for nettle rash, with Gromwell (on account of its hard seeds) for gall-stones, with Scabiosa (by reason of its scaly pappus) for all affections of the skin, even unto leprosy. A heart-shaped leaf was good for the heart, a kidney-shaped leaf for the kidneys; a yellow flower cured jaundice, and a red one assuaged blood.

> Thus lived our sires ere doctors learned to kill
> And multiply with theirs the monthly bill.

And our heritage from these strange and seemingly terrible practices is a thousand flower names that serve to throw some light to-day upon the customs of those ancient times.

One might continue indefinitely to work out the origins of the old plant names; of many we are able to find the key for ourselves, and the old horticultural works teem with more or less plausible explanations. There are the many plants of a poisonous nature which bear testimony to the grim fact in such names as Death-come-quickly, Death-cup, Deadly Night-shade, Poison-berry; there are those associated with the ceremony of the bridal, as Bridal-wreath, Bride-sweet, Bridewort, Wedding Posy; those named from some quality of fragrance as the Heliotrope, which is said to bear the name of Cherry Pie because of the resemblance of its perfume to that of the homely dainty; the many named in honour of the gods, as Jupiter's Beard, Flower of Jove, Juno's Rose, Venus' Looking Glass; those derived from natural history as Bird Cherry, Duck-weed, Cat-mint, Chickweed, Bee-nettle, and those which are corrupted or translated from a foreign word. Examples of these are Mallow from the Latin Malve, Fumatory from the French

Fume-terre (Earth-smoke), Herb Bennet from Herba Bene-
dicta (Blessed Herb).

Mr. Leonard Barron tells me of an interesting case that
came within his experience of the manner in which a Latin
name was most curiously changed. A nurseryman in a
communicative mood told some children who were playing
in a meadow near by the nursery that the name of the
flower with which they were decorating themselves was
Rudbeckia. The children received this unwieldy word,
tossed it to and fro in their play until the harsh edges were
softened and finally had it as Rosy Betty—a strange name
indeed for the swarthy Black-eyed Susan—but one by which
it is now generally known in that one locality. By some
such incidents as this must we account for the many plant
names to which we can find no clew; to such intriguing
appellations as Jump-up-and-kiss-me, Impudent Lawyers,
Meet-me-love, Blooming-down, Little-washer-women, Cast-
me-down, Lad's Love, Kiss-me-behind-the-garden-gate,
Cats and Keys, Seven-years-love, Sweet Mary Ann, Vetter-
voo, Stickadose, Suckie-sue, and innumerable others.

The familiar plant nomenclature of our own country
is a sort of composite of that of many others; as widely
various in origin as our population. Among the most
poignant memories brought by the early settlers to our
shores were doubtless those of the flowers that flourished in
the gardens and along the familiar roadsides at home; so
that it is small wonder that we find record not only of
these flowers themselves early brought to the gardens and
naturalized in the wild of the new land, but many cases
where some homely flower name, the mere speaking of

which must have eased the homesick hearts, had been fitted to an American flower bearing some resemblance to one that grew in the old country.

The names of such plants as are indigenous to this country may, with a fair amount of certainty, be labelled "made in America," and I dare say in a few cases we have bestowed titles upon the comers from over seas. Without doubt we have added Boston Pink to the many aliases by which pretty Bouncing Bet (Saponaria officinalis) is known in various localities, and it is safe to say, I think, that another of her names is of fairly recent American Origin. This is Lady-by-the-gate, for it is only of recent years that Bet has chosen to toss aside her birthright as a garden child in exchange for the doubtful sociability of the open road. Now she is the Lady-by-the-gate—outside the gate and one may not travel through any rural neighbourhood where are the remains of old gardens and not appreciate the applicability of this name. Around my own white gate-posts and along the paling fence that encloses my dooryard this erst-while favourite crowds closely, dreaming wistfully, I believe, of the sheltered days when she grew in seemly rows with her sister Pinks and Campions and sweet-breathed Stocks and was hailed by all World's Wonder.

Another flower quaintly associated with gates, though perhaps we may not conclusively claim for this name American origin, is the Cypress Spurge, sometimes known as Welcome-to-our-home. In my neighbourhood, where many old gardens have been left deserted or neglected by the ebbing tide of human interest or affection, this curious little plant crowds about the rotting gate-posts and straggles up the weed-claimed garden paths, providing still a green welcome where the human one is lacking to the searcher in old gardens and their precincts.

Naturally many American plant names are associated with the Indians. Thus we have a great number of such as Squawroot, Indian-boys-and-girls, Indian Posy, Papooseroot, Moccasin-flower, Indian Currant, Indian Pipe, Indian Tobacco, and Indian Pink. Few real Indian names linger, however, to "sound a note of the wilderness, a voice from the 'house of ash and fir.'" This is a pity, for besides being so truly of the soil, the Indian names are peculiarly agreeable in sound and suggestion. Pipissewa, whose liquid syllables someone has likened to the piping of a bird, and Miscodeed (Spring Beauty) are two that should be saved for posterity. Tamarack, Tupelo, Waahoo, Scuppernong, Catawba, Chinkapin, Catalpa, Yucca, Dockmackie, and Hickory are happily in fairly general use, but in Martha Flint's "Garden of Simples" she gives these others which might with great gain be added to our list of familiar plant names:

Cassena, or Youpon—Ilex cassine.
Cohosh—Cimicifuga racemosa.
Cushaw, Kershaw—Cucurbita.
Dahoon—Ilex dahoon.
Hackmatack—Larix americana, Spiraea tomentosa.
Kinnikinnik—Cornus sericea.
Macock—Cucurbuta.
Maize—Zea Mays.
Musquash—Cicuta maculata.

COLOUR IN MY GARDEN

Quamash—Camassia Fraseri.
Pocan—Phytolaca decandra.
Puccoon—Sanguinaria canadensis.
Tacamahac—Populus balsamifera.
Unkum—Senecio aureus.
Waukapin, Youkapin—Nelumbo lutea.
Whohoo—Ulmus alata.
Wicopy—Dirca palustris.

Perhaps in my enthusiasm for the old-fashioned and familiar plant names I have not laid sufficient stress upon the importance of mastering the Latin names. I have not intended that this eulogy should in any way discount the necessity for exact knowledge along this line, and surely enough testimony has been offered to show what confusion would result were only the vernacular names made use of. My desire is simply that the friendly old names shall not be forgotten, that they shall be sometimes used in the bosom of our own gardens and in those of understanding friends that they and all they have stood for in past ages be not lost to the gardeners that shall come after us. Many of the Latin names, far from being simply difficult and uninteresting, repay a careful study and are quite charming in their meanings and derivations, and while some are truly terrible in their harshness and length, names "which no one can speak and no one can spell," others are quite pleasant-sounding enough to take their places by the side of the softest of the old "by-names."

The following glossary does not claim to be at all exhaustive. I have listed only the names that have come my way during intercourse with other gardeners, in conversations with country folk in many localities, through visitors to my garden, and in the ordinary course of reading garden literature. Through lack of space I have been able to include only garden flowers and such of the wild flowers as are sometimes grown in gardens, and a few trees. Unregenerate weeds I have been constrained to shut out of this book of my garden as I must from the garden itself. This has caused me more than one struggle; for those plants which either through their supposed medicinal virtues or from their naughty persistence in defying the efforts of man to accomplish law and order upon the land, are the ones with the very quaintest and most interesting of flower names.

PERIODS OF FLOWERING

PERIODS OF FLOWERING

I T HAS been my custom for a good many years to set down in my day book each week the flowers in bloom in the garden. The following chart is the result of these notes and shows from April first to October first the plants upon which we may count for a display during each week of this period. An allowance of a week should be made for each hundred miles north or south of the latitude of New York. That is, in Boston the group for May first should be read May eighth, and in Richmond these early May flowers will bloom soon after the middle of April. There are no marked differences due merely to longitude. Flowers growing in a light soil are apt to come into bloom more precipitately and to be of shorter duration than those dwelling in stiff clay, and of course the exposure of the garden has somewhat to do with the blossoming time of its flowers. But with allowance made for these accidents of soil and exposure, the chart has served me well in my simple colour scheming, and I trust will be of use to others. Those listed do not at all exhaust the possibilities of garden flowers; they are simply the ones that have been under my eye for more than one season in my own garden.

The colour divisions have been made as simple as is compatible with clarity. The first group is made up of the pure reds and scarlets such as one sees in Oriental Poppies— the reds with no blue in their composition. The generally

called red of the old red Paeony (P. officinalis) is relegated
to the last group, the crimson and magenta, because, it
seems to me, to be more closely allied to these than to the
spectrum reds. Among these first reds, however, I have
put the rich dark red Sweet William because it seemed not
to belong properly in any other group. This has been the
case also with the deep terracotta Helenium autumnale
rubrum, and in the yellow and orange group with the
tawny Tiger Lilies and the fuscous Orange Day Lilies
(Hemerocallis fulva and H. Kwanso). With these excep-
tions I trust the chart will prove accurate enough to render
the making of lovely colour groups perfectly simple even
for the beginner, when used in conjunction with the illustrations and the text of the book.

The third group, lavender and purple, includes lavender,
mauve (a pinkish lavender), pure purple like the colour of
Clematis Jackmani, and reddish purple like that of Iris
Crimson King, which is yet not red enough to be placed in
the crimson and magenta group.

The blues are, as nearly as my eye can judge, pure blues
with but little admixture of purple in their composition.
The pinks are true pink, not leaning toward magenta, unless
some may cavil at the inclusion of Malva moschata.

The last group, magenta and crimson, represents those
colours which are neither red nor purple but are closely
related to both. They are called variously and indiscrimi-
nately, as a rule, magenta, crimson, crimson-lake, rosy
purple, and amaranth. The flowers in this group will be
found to harmonize with each other, and with an admixture
of gray foliage and white flowers create lovely pictures.

COLOUR IN MY GARDEN

In compiling this chart I have simply dropped from the list each week the plants that have ceased to flower and added those that have begun to bloom. Annuals may be counted upon for a display from July until frost.

It may be noted here that the nomenclature and style adopted follows generally the 1917 official code of "Standardized Plant Names" as being the most generally acceptable in a book that is designed for practical garden use—but in a very few cases it has seemed better to follow more popular garden terminology.

CHART FOR COLOUR AND PERIOD OF BLOOM

RED AND SCARLET	WHITE AND CREAM	LAVENDER AND PURPLE	YELLOW AND ORANGE	DARK BLUE AND LIGHT BLUE	PINK AND ROSE	MAGENTA AND CRIMSON
			APRIL 1ST			
	Galanthus nivalis	Crocus Imperati	Jasminum nudiflorum	Scilla sibirica	Daphne Mezereum	
	Galanthus Elwesii	Crocus biflorus	Crocus susianus			
	Crocus, Dutch vars.	Crocus, Dutch vars.	Crocus, Dutch vars.			
	Sanguinaria canadensis	Iris reticulata	Eranthus hyemalis			
	Leucojum vernum	Bulbocodium vernum	Benzoin aestivale			
			Erythronium americanum			
			APRIL 8TH			
	Galanthus nivalis	Crocus Imperati	Jasminum nudiflorum	Scilla sibirica	Daphne Mezereum	Aubrietia
	Galanthus Elwesii	Crocus, Dutch vars.	Crocus susianus	Scilla amoena		
	Crocus, Dutch vars.	Iris reticulata	Crocus, Dutch vars.	Muscari botryoides		
	Sanguinaria canadensis	Bulbocodium vernum	Benzoin aestivale	Chionodoxa sardensis		
	Leucojum vernum	Viola tricolor	Erythronium americanum	Chionodoxa Luciliae		
	Dicentra Cucullaria	Aubrietia, many vars.	Adonis vernalis			
	Amelanchier canadensis					
	Lonicera fragrantissima					
			APRIL 16TH			
Cydonia japonica	Crocus, Dutch vars.	Crocus, Dutch vars.	Crocus, Dutch vars.	Scilla sibirica	Daphne Mezereum	Aubrietia
	Sanguinaria canadensis	Iris reticulata	Erythronium americanum	Scilla amoena		Phlox subulata

261

COLOUR IN MY GARDEN

RED AND SCARLET	WHITE AND CREAM	LAVENDER AND PURPLE	YELLOW AND ORANGE	DARK BLUE AND LIGHT BLUE	PINK AND ROSE	MAGENTA AND CRIMSON
			APRIL 16TH—*Continued*			
	Dicentra Cucullaria	Viola tricolor	Adonis vernalis	Muscari botryoides		
	Lonicera fragrantissima	Aubrietia, many vars.	Narcissus minor	Chionodoxa sardensis		
	Amelanchier canadensis	Anemone Pulsatilla	Narcissus Princeps	Chionodoxa Luciliae		
	Arabis alpina	Anemone Hepatica	Narcissus Golden Spur			
	Spiraea Thunbergii	Phlox subulata var. G. F. Wilson	Narcissus obvallaris			
	Magnolia stellata		Tulipa sylvestris			
	Anemone Hepatica		Corydalis cheilanthifolia			
	Anemone Pulsatilla		Forsythia, several vars.			
	Phlox subulata, Nelsoni					
	Muscari botryoides alba					
			APRIL 24TH			
Cydonia japonica	Arabis alpina	Viola tricolor, many vars.	Narcissus, many vars.	Muscari botryoides	Prunus japonica	Aubrietia
Aquilegia canadensis	Spiraea Thunbergii	Anemone Pulsatilla	Tulipa sylvestris	Chionodoxa sardensis	Prunus triloba	Phlox subulata
Primula polyanthus	Magnolia stellata	Phlox subulata G. F. Wilson	Corydalis cheilanthifolia	Myosotis sylvatica	Tulips, early	Primula polyanthus
Tulipa Early Dutch	Anemone Hepatica	Anemone Hepatica	Forsythia			
Cheiranthus Cheiri	Anemone Pulsatilla	Aubrietia, many vars.	Fritillaria imperialis			
	Phlox subulata, Nelsoni	Puschkinia libanotica	Tulips, Early Dutch			
	Narcissus albicans		Primula veris			
	Fritillaria meleagris alba		Primula vulgaris			
	Spiraea prunifolia		Cheiranthus Cheiri			
	Spiraea Van Houttei		Ribes odoratum (aureum)			
	Tulips, early Dutch					
	Myosotis sylvatica alba					
	Cherries, orchard					
	Plums, orchard					
	Prunus cerasifera Pissardi					
	Magnolia conspicua					

EARLY AUTUMN IN THE GARDEN
SEPTEMBER 10TH

*B*Y TURNING to Plate No. 18 (July 28th),
which portrays the same space of border
against the eastern wall of the garden, it may be
seen how the long branches of Helenium, Boltonia, and Michaelmas Daisies have been drawn
over and through the Lilies, Veronicas, and other
plants composing the midsummer display so as
to leave no blanks either of foliage or flowers.

These tall plants are set in fair-sized clumps
at the very back of the border so that they con-
stitute a fresh green background for the earlier
flowering plants and finally cover their departure
with their own fair flowering.

SUMMER'S OBSEQUIES
OCTOBER 10TH

THE earlier history of this part of the garden is told opposite Plate No. 14 (July 4th).

Now frost has silenced the annuals, and the day of most of the perennials is past. But these faithful ones, the Michaelmas Daisies and the gray-leaved things, will linger on, a trifle faded as to their soft-hued garment but showing patches of warm colour here and there, until the first of November and even longer if the weather is mild.

PLATE NO. 24
SEE PLATE NO. 14

COLOUR IN MY GARDEN

RED AND SCARLET	WHITE AND CREAM	LAVENDER AND PURPLE	YELLOW AND ORANGE	DARK BLUE AND LIGHT BLUE	PINK AND ROSE	MAGENTA AND CRIMSON

MAY 1ST

RED AND SCARLET	WHITE AND CREAM	LAVENDER AND PURPLE	YELLOW AND ORANGE	DARK BLUE AND LIGHT BLUE	PINK AND ROSE	MAGENTA AND CRIMSON
Cydonia japonica	Narcissus albicans	Viola tricolor	Narcissus, many vars.	Muscari botryoides	Prunus japonica	Phlox subulata
Aquilegia canadensis	Tulips, early	Aubrietia, many vars.	Tulips, early Dutch	Myosotis sylvatica	Prunus triloba	Aubrietia
Primula polyanthus	Fritillaria alba	Phlox subulata G. F. Wilson	Corydalis cheilanthifolia	Myosotis, in var.	Persica vulgaris	Primula polyanthus
Tulips, early Dutch	Spiraea prunifolia	Aquilegia vulgaris	Forsythia	Polemonium coeruleum	Tulips, early Dutch	Cersis canadensis
Cheiranthus Cheiri, many vars.	Arabis alpina	Phlox divaricata	Fritillaria Imperialis	Polemonium reptans	Dicentra spectabilis	Lunaria biennis
	Phlox subulata Nelsoni	Camassia esculenta	Primula veris	Anchusa myosotidiflora	Armeria cephalotes	
	Spiraea Van Houttei Thunbergii	Iris pumila	Primula vulgaris	Scilla festalis	Armeria maritima	
	Spiraea prunifolia	Iris olbiensis	Cheiranthus Cheiri, many vars.		Daphne Cneorum	
	Myosotis dissitiflora alba		Ribes odoratum (aureum)		Cherries, Japanese	
	Prunus cerasifera Pissardi		Alyssum saxatile			
	Phlox divaricata alba		Alyssum montanum			
	Camassia alba		Aquilegia hybrids			
	Iris pumila alba		Doronicums, in var.			
	Iberis sempervirens		Iris Chamaeiris			
	Armeria maritima alba		Erysimum rupestre			
	Lunaria biennis alba		Trollius, in var.			
	Polemoniums		Kerria japonica			
	Stellaria Holostea					
	Corydalis nobilis					
	Cherries, Japanese					
	Cornus florida					

MAY 8TH

RED AND SCARLET	WHITE AND CREAM	LAVENDER AND PURPLE	YELLOW AND ORANGE	DARK BLUE AND LIGHT BLUE	PINK AND ROSE	MAGENTA AND CRIMSON
Cydonia japonica	Narcissus poeticus	Viola tricolor	Primulas, in var.	Myosotis, in var.	Dicentra spectabilis	Aubrietia
Aquilegia canadensis	Fritillaria alba	Aubrietia, many vars.	Cheiranthus Cheiri, in var.	Polemonium coeruleum, in var.	Armeria, in var.	Phlox subulata
Primula polyanthus	Spiraeas, in var.	Phlox subulata G. F. Wilson	Ribes odoratum (aureum)	Polemonium reptans	Daphne Cneorum	Cersis canadensis
Cheiranthus Cheiri, many vars.	Arabis alpina	Aquilegia vulgaris	Alyssum saxatile	Anchusa myosotidiflora	Cherries, Japanese	Lunaria biennis
	Phlox subulata Nelsoni	Phlox divaricata			Aquilegia Hybrids	Iris lurida

RED AND SCARLET	WHITE AND CREAM	LAVENDER AND PURPLE	YELLOW AND ORANGE	DARK BLUE AND LIGHT BLUE	PINK AND ROSE	MAGENTA AND CRIMSON

MAY 8TH—*Continued*

RED AND SCARLET	WHITE AND CREAM	LAVENDER AND PURPLE	YELLOW AND ORANGE	DARK BLUE AND LIGHT BLUE	PINK AND ROSE	MAGENTA AND CRIMSON
Tulips, Cottage and Darwins	Myosotis, in var.	Camassia esculenta	Alyssum montanum	Scilla festalis	Tulips, Darwin and Cottage vars.	Lychnis alpina
Geum Heldreichii	Phlox divaricata	Iris pumila, Chamieiris, olbiensis, cristata	Aquilegia hybrids	Scilla hispanica	Pyrus spectabilis	
	Camassia	Tulips, Darwin vars.	Iris Chamieiris lutescens	Aquilegia coerulea	Pyrus floribunda	
	Iberis sempervirens	Viola cornuta	Erysimum rupestre	Lithospermum prostratum	Papaver nudicaule	
	Armeria	Hyacinthus orientalis, many vars.	Trollius, in var.	Linum perenne	Hyacinthus orientalis, many vars.	
	Lunaria biennis		Kerria japonica	Linum narbonnense	Rhododendron nudiflorum	
	Polemoniums		Viola lutea	Houstonia coerulea	Aethionemas	
	Stellaria Holostea		Geum montanum	Mertensia virginica		
	Corydalis nobilis		Papaver nudicaule			
	Cherries, Japanese		Papaver rupifragum			
	Cornus florida		Tulips, Cottage vars.			
	Aquilegia vulgaris nivea grandiflora		Corydalis lutea			
	Iris pumila		Papaver alpinum			
	Tulips, Cottage vars.					
	Papaver nudicaule alba					
	Cerastium tomentosum					
	Linum perenne album					
	Viola cornuta alba					
	Hyacinthus orientalis, many vars.					

MAY 16TH

RED AND SCARLET	WHITE AND CREAM	LAVENDER AND PURPLE	YELLOW AND ORANGE	DARK BLUE AND LIGHT BLUE	PINK AND ROSE	MAGENTA AND CRIMSON
Aquilegia canadensis	Narcissus poeticus	Viola tricolor	Primulas, in var.	Myosotis, in var.	Dicentra spectabilis	Aubrietia
Papaver nudicaule	Spiraeas, in var.	Aubrietia, in var.	Cheiranthus Cheiri	Polemonium, in var.	Dicentra eximia	Cercis canadensis
Primula polyanthus	Arabis alpina	Phlox divaricata	Ribes odoratum (aureum)	Anchusa myosotidiflora	Apples, orchard	Lunaria biennis
Cheiranthus Cheiri	Phlox subulata Nelsoni	Camassia esculenta	Alyssum saxatile	Scilla hispanica	Papaver nudicaule	Iris lurida
Tulips, Cottage and Darwins	Myosotis, in var.	Iris pumila and I. olbiensis	Alyssum montanum	Aquilegia coerulea	Dianthus neglectus	Lychnis alpina
Geum Heldreichii	Phlox divaricata	Tulips, Darwin vars.	Alyssum rostratum	Aquilegia Stuarti	Dianthus, Mule vars.	Lychnis viscaria
Dianthus Napoleon III	Camassia	Iris cristata	Aquilegia chrysantha	Lithospermum prostratum	Dicentra spectabilis	Paeonia officinalis rubra
	Iberis sempervirens				Dicentra eximia	Paeonia Moutan

RED AND SCARLET	WHITE AND CREAM	LAVENDER AND PURPLE	YELLOW AND ORANGE	DARK BLUE AND LIGHT BLUE	PINK AND ROSE	MAGENTA AND CRIMSON

MAY 16TH—*Continued*

RED AND SCARLET	WHITE AND CREAM	LAVENDER AND PURPLE	YELLOW AND ORANGE	DARK BLUE AND LIGHT BLUE	PINK AND ROSE	MAGENTA AND CRIMSON
	Lunaria biennis alba	Hyacinthus orientalis, many vars.	Erysimum rupestre	Linum perenne	Armerias, in var.	Azalea amoena
	Polemoniums	Viola cornuta, many vars.	Trollius, in var.	Linum narbonnense	Daphne Cneorum	Salvia pratensis rosea
	Stellaria Holostea	Iris benacensis	Kerria japonica	Houstonia coerulea	Aquilegia hybrids	
	Aquilegia, vulgaris nivea grandiflora	Iris germanica, many vars.	Viola lutea	Veronica prostrata	Tulips, Darwin and Cottage vars.	
	Iris pumila alba	Iris Cengialti	Iris lutescens	Veronica repens	Pyrus spectabilis	
	Tulips, Cottage vars.	Aster alpinus	Iris, intermediate vars.	Veronica gentianoides	Pyrus floribunda	
	Papaver nudicaule alba	Lilacs, many vars.	Geum montanum	Salvia pratensis	Weigela	
	Cerastium tomentosum	Nepeta Mussini	Papaver nudicaule	Globularia trichosantha	Saponaria ocymoides	
	Linum perenne album		Papaver alpinum	Tradescantia virginica		
	Viola cornuta alba		Papaver rupifragum	Mertensia virginica		
	Hyacinthus orientalis, many vars.		Tulips, Cottage vars.			
	Convallaria majalis		Corydalis lutea			
	Apples, orchard		Laburnum vulgare			
	Crataegus oxyacantha		Achillea tomentosa			
	Asperula odorata		Euphorbia epithymoides (polychroma)			
	Iris albicans		Doronicums, in var.			
	Iris, intermediate vars.					
	Weigela candida					
	Lilacs, many vars.					
	Lychnis alpina alba					
	Lychnis Viscaria alba					

MAY 24TH

RED AND SCARLET	WHITE AND CREAM	LAVENDER AND PURPLE	YELLOW AND ORANGE	DARK BLUE AND LIGHT BLUE	PINK AND ROSE	MAGENTA AND CRIMSON
Papaver nudicaule	Narcissus poeticus	Viola tricolor	Aquilegia chrysantha	Myosotis, in var.	Dicentra eximia	Aubrietia
Primula polyanthus	Arabis alpina	Aubrietia	Trollius, in var.	Scilla hispanica	Papaver nudicaule	Lunaria biennis
Cheiranthus Cheiri	Myosotis, in var.	Tulips, Darwin vars.	Viola lutea	Lithospermum prostratum	Dianthus neglectus; Mule vars.; arenarius; sylvestris; petraeus; plumarius; caesius; Prichardii	Lychnis alpina
Tulips, Cottage and Darwins	Phlox divaricata alba	Hyacinthus orientalis	Iris lutescens; intermediate; pseudacorus; "German" and Spanish vars.	Linum perenne; narbonnense		Lychnis Viscaria
Geum Heldreichii	Iberis sempervirens	Viola cornuta		Veronica prostrata		Paeonia officinalis rubra
		Iris benacensis; Cengialti;				Paeonia Moutan

MAY 24TH—*Continued*

RED AND SCARLET	WHITE AND CREAM	LAVENDER AND PURPLE	YELLOW AND ORANGE	DARK BLUE AND LIGHT BLUE	PINK AND ROSE	MAGENTA AND CRIMSON
Dianthus Napoleon III	Polemoniums	Iris tectorum; Biliotti; germanica vars. pallida; sibirica	Geum montanum	Veronica repens; gentianoides	Armerias	Azalea amoena
Heuchera Pluie de Feu	Stellaria Holostea		Papaver nudicaule; alpinum; rupifragum; orientale	Salvia pratensis	Daphne Cneorum	Salvia pratensis rosea
Papaver orientale	Aquilegias	Aster alpinus	Tulips, Cottage vars.	Globularia	Aquilegia hybrids	Silene asterias
Geum coccineum	Tulips, Cottage vars.	Lilacs	Corydalis lutea	Tradescantia virginica	Tulips, Cottage and Darwins	Centaurea dealbata
	Papaver nudicaule	Nepeta Mussini	Achillea tomentosa	Lupines	Pyrus floribunda	Chrysanthemum coccineum
	Cerastium tomentosum	Campanula glomerata	Euphorbia polychroma	Centaurea montana	Pyrus ioensis	Dictamnus albus ruber
	Linum perenne album	Lupines, many vars.	Laburnum vulgare	Baptisia australis	Saponaria ocymoides	Lychnis dioica
	Viola cornuta alba	Hesperis matronalis violacea	Alyssum saxatile	Anchusa	Lupines	
	Hyacinthus orientalis, many vars.	Iris versicolor; graminea; Blue King; Xiphium; sambucina	Alyssum rostratum		Heucheras, many vars.	
	Convallaria majalis		Hemerocallis flava; graminea		Paeonia, single vars.	
	Crataegus oxyacantha				Papaver orientale, many vars.	
	Asperula odorata				Chrysanthemum coccineum	
	Iris albicans; intermediate; florentina; Innocence				Crucianella stylosa	
	Weigela candida					
	Lilacs, many vars.					
	Lychnis alpina alba					
	Lychnis viscaria alba					
	Lupines					
	Tradescantia virginica alba					
	Heuchera Virginale					
	Salvia pratensis alba					
	Silene maritima					
	Iris siberica alba; tectorum alba					
	Arenaria montana; balearica					
	Centaurea montana alba					

RED AND SCARLET	WHITE AND CREAM	LAVENDER AND PURPLE	YELLOW AND ORANGE	DARK BLUE AND LIGHT BLUE	PINK AND ROSE	MAGENTA AND CRIMSON

MAY 24TH—Continued

RED AND SCARLET	WHITE AND CREAM	LAVENDER AND PURPLE	YELLOW AND ORANGE	DARK BLUE AND LIGHT BLUE	PINK AND ROSE	MAGENTA AND CRIMSON
	Hesperis matronalis alba					
	Philadelphus coronaria					
	Paeonia officinalis alba					
	Paeonia albiflora The Bride					
	Campanula glomerata alba					
	Ornithogalum arabicum					
	Deutzias, in var.					
	Dianthus arenarius					
	Papaver orientale Perry's White					
	Chrysanthemum coccineum					
	Cerasus avium flore pleno					
	Viburnum Opulus					

JUNE 1ST

RED AND SCARLET	WHITE AND CREAM	LAVENDER AND PURPLE	YELLOW AND ORANGE	DARK BLUE AND LIGHT BLUE	PINK AND ROSE	MAGENTA AND CRIMSON
Papaver nudicaule	Iberis sempervirens	Viola tricolor	Aquilegia chrysantha	Lithospermum prostratum	Dicentra eximia	Aubrietia
Geum Heldreichi; coccineum	Stellaria Holostea	Aubrietia	Trollius, in var.	Linum perenne	Papaver nudicaule	Lunaria biennis
Dianthus Napoleon III	Aquilegias	Viola cornuta	Viola lutea	Linum narbonnense	Dianthus neglectus; Mule vars.; sylvestris; petraeus; plumarius; caesius; Prichardii; deltoides; graniticus	Lychnis Viscaria
Heuchera Pluie de Feu	Papaver nudicaule	Iris benacensis; Biliotti; sambucina; Cengialti; tectorum; pallida; German vars.; Spanish; English; Blue King; versicolor; graminea	Iris Pseudacorus; German vars.; Spanish	Veronica prostrata; repens; gentianoides	Armerias	Salvia pratensis rosea
Papaver orientale	Cerastium tomentosum	Aster alpinus	Papaver nudicaule; rupifragum; alpinum; orientale;	Salvia pratensis	Daphne Cneorum	Silene Asterias
China Rose Leuchtfeuer	Linum perenne album	Nepeta Mussini	Corydalis lutea	Tradescantia virginica	Pyrus ioensis	Centaurea dealbata
Dianthus atrorubens	Viola cornuta alba	Lilacs	Achillea tomentosa	Lupines	Saponaria ocymoides	Chrysanthemum coccineum
	Asperula odorata	Lupines	Achillea sericea	Centaurea montana	Lupines	Dictamnus albus ruber
	Iris albicans; florentina; German vars.; tectorum alba; sibirica alba; SnowQueen;	Campanula glomerata	Euphorbia polychroma	Baptisia australis	Heucheras	Lychnis dioica
		Hesperis matronalis violacea	Laburnum vulgare		Paeonia, many vars.	Digitalis purpurea
			Alyssum saxatile		Papaver orientale, Pink vars.	Achillea Millefolium

RED AND SCARLET	WHITE AND CREAM	LAVENDER AND PURPLE	YELLOW AND ORANGE	DARK BLUE AND LIGHT BLUE	PINK AND ROSE	MAGENTA AND CRIMSON
			JUNE 1ST—*Continued*			
	Iris Spanish; English	Thalictrum aquilegifolium	Alyssum rostratum		Chrysanthemum coccineum	
	Weigela candida	Dodecatheon Meadia	Hemerocallis flava; graminea; Dumortieri; Middendorfii; Gold Dust; Florham; Apricot		Crucianella stylosa	
	Lilacs				Helianthemum vulgare, pink and rose vars.	
	Lychnis Viscaria alba					
	Lupines		Helianthemum vulgare			
	Tradescantia virginica alba		Cytisus scoparius			
	Heuchera virginale					
	Salvia pratensis alba		Orobus auranticus aurea			
	Silene maritima		Linum flavum			
	Arenaria montana; balearica		Baptisia tinctoria			
	Centaurea montana alba					
	Hesperis matronalis alba					
	Philadelphus coronaria					
	Campanula glomerata alba					
	Deutzias, in var.					
	Dianthus arenarius; deltoides alba; Mrs. Sinkins					
	Paeonia, many vars.					
	Dianthus Her Majesty; plumarius					
	Papaver orientale Perry's White					
	Chrysanthemum coccineum					
	Viburnum Opulus					
	Thalictrum polyganum					
	Gypsophila repens					
	Valeriana officinalis					
	Digitalis purpurea alba					
	Dictamnus albus					

RED AND SCARLET	WHITE AND CREAM	LAVENDER AND PURPLE	YELLOW AND ORANGE	DARK BLUE AND LIGHT BLUE	PINK AND ROSE	MAGENTA AND CRIMSON
			JUNE 1ST—*Continued*			
	Helianthemum vulgare album					
	Achillea ptarmica fl. pl.					
	Asperula hexaphylla					
	Dodecatheon Meadia alba					
	Tiarella cordifolia					
			JUNE 8TH			
Papaver nudicaule	Linum perenne album	Viola tricolor	Aquilegia chrysantha	Linum perenne	Dicentra eximia	Aubrietia
Papaver orientale	Viola cornuta alba	Viola cornuta	Viola lutea	Linum narbonnense	Papaver nudicaule	Lychnis Viscaria
Geum Heldreichii; coccineum	Iris German vars.; tectorum album; sibirica; Snow Queen	Iris German vars.; sibirica Blue King; Spanish; English; versicolor	Iris pseudacorus; German vars.; Spanish	Veronica prostrata	Papaver orientale, pink vars.	Salvia pratensis rosea
Dianthus Napoleon III	Lychnis Viscaria alba	Aster alpinus	Papaver nudicaule	Veronica repens	Dianthus neglectus; Mule vars. caesius; Prichardii; deltoides; sylvestris; plumarius; graniticus	Silene Asterias
Dianthus atrorubens	Lupines	Nepeta Mussini	Papaver rupifragum; orientale	Veronica incana	Armerias	Centaurea dealbata
Heuchera Pluie de Feu	Tradescantia virginica alba	Lupines	Corydalis lutea	Salvia pratensis	Saponaria ocymoides	Chrysanthemum coccineum!
Sweet William Scarlet Beauty; Dark Red	Heuchera virginale	Hesperis matronalis violacea	Achillea sericea	Tradescantia virginica	Lupines	Dictamnus albus ruber
Gaillardia grandiflora	Salvia pratensis alba	Thalictrum aquilegifolium	Alyssum rostratum	Lupines	Heucheras	Lychnis dioica
Lychnis chalcedonica; fulgens; Haageana	Silene alpestris	Campanula glomerata	Hemerocallis flava; Dumortieri; Middendorfii; Gold Dust; Florham; Apricot	Centaurea montana	Paeonia, many vars.	Digitalis purpurea
Lilium tenuifolium	Arenaria montana	Geranium ibericum	Helianthemum vulgare	Baptisia australis	Chrysanthemum coccineum	Achillea Millefolium
	Centaurea montana alba	Pentstemon diffusus; grandiflorus	Cytisus scoparius	Anchusa italica	Crucianella stylosa	Sweet Williams
	Hesperis matronalis alba	Phlox Arendsi	Orobus auranticus aureus	Campanula persicifolia	Helianthemum vulgare, pink and rose vars.	Lychnis Coronaria
	Campanula glomerata alba		Linum flavum	Delphinium grandiflorum; cashmerianum	Sweet William Newport Pink; Pink Beauty	
	Campanula persicifolia alba		Baptisia tinctoria		Tunica saxifraga	
	Dianthus arenarius; Mrs. Sinkins; Her Majesty; deltoides alba; plumarius; fimbriatus		Laburnum vulgare			
			Asphodeline lutea			
			Gaillardias			
			Digitalis ambigua; orientalis			
			Linaria dalmatica			

RED AND SCARLET	WHITE AND CREAM	LAVENDER AND PURPLE	YELLOW AND ORANGE	DARK BLUE AND LIGHT BLUE	PINK AND ROSE	MAGENTA AND CRIMSON
		JUNE 8TH—*Continued*				
	Papaver orientale Perry's White					
	Chrysanthemum coccineum					
	Thalictrum polygamum					
	Gypsophila repens					
	Valeriana officinalis					
	Digitalis purpurea alba					
	Dictamnus albus					
	Helianthemum vulgare alba					
	Achillea ptarmica fl. pl.					
	Asperula hexaphylla					
	Lychnis chalcedonica alba					
	Pentstemon laevigatus; Digitalis					
	Sweet William, White					
	Aruncus sylvester					
	Geranium sanguineum album					
	Paeonia, many vars.					
	Lychnis Coronaria alba					

JUNE 16TH

RED AND SCARLET	WHITE AND CREAM	LAVENDER AND PURPLE	YELLOW AND ORANGE	DARK BLUE AND LIGHT BLUE	PINK AND ROSE	MAGENTA AND CRIMSON
Papaver nudicaule; orientale	Linum perenne album	Aster alpinus	Aquilegia chrysantha	Linum perenne	Dicentra eximia	Aubrietia
Geum Heldreichii; coccineum	Viola cornuta alba	Nepeta Mussini	Viola lutea	Linum narbonnense	Dianthus Mule vars.; deltoides; plumarius; graniticus; caesius	Salvia pratensis rosea
Dianthus Napoleon III	Iris German vars.; Snow Queen; ochroleuca; Spanish	Lupines	Iris Pseudacorus; German vars.; Spanish; Monnieri; aurea	Veronica prostrata; incana	Armerias	Centaurea dealbata
Heuchera Pluie de Feu	Lychnis Viscaria alba	Hesperis matronalis violacea	Papaver nudicaule; orientale; rupifragum	Salvia pratensis	Saponaria ocymoides	Pyrethrum coccineum
Sweet William Scarlet Beauty; Dark Red		Thalictrum aquilegifolium	Corydalis lutea	Tradescantia virginica	Lupines	Digitalis purpurea
Gaillardia		Campanula glomerata; latifolia; macrantha		Lupines	Heucheras	Lychnis dioica
				Centaurea montana	Chrysanthemum coccineum	Dictamnus albus ruber

270

RED AND SCARLET	WHITE AND CREAM	LAVENDER AND PURPLE	YELLOW AND ORANGE	DARK BLUE AND LIGHT BLUE	PINK AND ROSE	MAGENTA AND CRIMSON

JUNE 16TH—*Continued*

RED AND SCARLET	WHITE AND CREAM	LAVENDER AND PURPLE	YELLOW AND ORANGE	DARK BLUE AND LIGHT BLUE	PINK AND ROSE	MAGENTA AND CRIMSON
Lychnis chalcedonica; Haageana; fulgens	Lupines	Geranium ibericum	Achillea sericea	Baptisia australis	Crucianella stylosa	Achillea Millefolium
Lilium tenuifolium; elegans; fulgens; grandiflorum	Tradescantia virginica alba	Pentstemon grandiflorus; diffusus; ovatus	Alyssum rostratum	Anchusa italica var.	Helianthemum vulgare, pink and rose vars.	Sweet William
	Salvia pratensis alba	Viola cornuta	Hemerocallis flava; Dumortieri; Middendorfii;	Campanula persicifolia; carpatica; rotundifolia	Sweet William Newport Pink; Pink Beauty	Lychnis coronaria
	Heuchera Virginale	Iris German vars; Spanish; Blue King; Japanese	Gold Dust; Florham; Apricot; Queen of May; Sovereign	Delphinium grandiflorum; belladonna; cashmirianum	Tunica saxifraga	Centranthus ruber
	Silene alpestris					Epilobium angustifolium
	Arenaria montana	Campanula Medium, purple and lavender vars.	Helianthemum vulgare	Iris monspur	Campanula Medium	Geranium sanguineum
	Centaurea montana alba	Phlox Arendsii	Cytisus scoparius			Phlox Arendsii
	Hesperis matronalis alba		Orobus auranticus aureus			
	Campanula persicifolia alba; carpatica alba; latifolia flore albo; medium alba		Linum flavum			
			Baptisia tinctoria			
	Dianthus arenarius; plumarius; Her Majesty; Mrs. Sinkins; deltoides; fimbriatus		Asphodelus luteus			
			Gaillardia			
			Digitalis ambigua; orientale			
	Chrysanthemum coccineum		Linaria dalmatica			
	Thalictrum polygamum		Coreopsis grandiflora			
	Gypsophila repens		Sedum kamtschaticum			
	Valeriana officinalis		Lilium elegans vars. aureum, citrinium, and Prince of Orange			
	Digitalis purpurea alba					
	Helianthemum vulgare		Scabiosa ochroleuca			
	Achillea ptarmica fl. pl.		Thermopsis caroliniana			
	Asperula hexaphylla		Cephalaria alpina			
	Lychnis chalcedonica alba					
	Pentstemon digitalis					
	Sweet William, White					
	Aruncus sylvester					

RED AND SCARLET	WHITE AND CREAM	LAVENDER AND PURPLE	YELLOW AND ORANGE	DARK BLUE AND LIGHT BLUE	PINK AND ROSE	MAGENTA AND CRIMSON

JUNE 16TH—Continued

RED AND SCARLET	WHITE AND CREAM	LAVENDER AND PURPLE	YELLOW AND ORANGE	DARK BLUE AND LIGHT BLUE	PINK AND ROSE	MAGENTA AND CRIMSON
	Filipendula hexapetala fl. pl.					
	Astilbe japonica					
	Geranium sanguineum album					
	Lychnis coronaria alba					
	Scabiosa caucasica alba					
	Clematis recta					
	Saxifraga umbrosa					
	Delphinium cashmiri-anum album					
	Centranthus ruber albus					

JUNE 24TH

RED AND SCARLET	WHITE AND CREAM	LAVENDER AND PURPLE	YELLOW AND ORANGE	DARK BLUE AND LIGHT BLUE	PINK AND ROSE	MAGENTA AND CRIMSON
Papaver nudicaule	Linum perenne album	Nepeta Mussini	Aquilegia chrysantha	Linum perenne	Dicentra eximia	Salvia pratensis
Geum coccineum	Viola cornuta alba	Lupines	Viola lutea	Linum narbonnense	Dianthus, Mule vars.	Centaurea dealbata
Dianthus Napoleon III	Iris ochroleuca, Spanish, Japanese	Hesperis matronalis violacea	Iris Monnieri aurea	Veronica incana	Dianthus deltoides	Chrysanthemum coccineum
Heuchera Pluie de Feu	Lychnis Viscaria alba	Campanula glomerata	Papaver nudicaule	Veronica spicata	Armerias	Digitalis purpurea
Sweet William Scarlet Beauty; Dark Red	Lupines	Campanula latifolia macrantha	Papaver rupifragum	Salvia pratensis	Saponaria ocymoides	Lychnis dioica
Gaillardia	Tradescantia virginica alba	Geranium ibericum	Corydalis lutea	Tradescantia virginica	Saponaria officinalis fl. pl.	Sidalcea malvaeflora
Lychnis chalcedonica	Heuchera Virginale	Pentstemon diffusus	Achillea sericea	Lupines	Heucheras	Lychnis coronaria
Lychnis fulgens	Salvia pratensis alba	Pentstemon ovatus	Alyssum rostratum	Centaurea montana	Chrysanthemum coccineum	Centranthus ruber
Lychnis Haageana	Silene alpestris	Veronica amethystina	Hemerocallis Dumortieri, Middendorfii,	Anchusa italica in var.	Sweet William, Newport Pink, Pink Beauty	Epilobium angustifolium
Lilium tenuifolium	Centaurea montana alba	Viola cornuta	Gold Dust, Florham, Apricot, Queen of May, Sovereign	Campanula persicifolia	Helianthemum, pink and rose vars.	Geranium sanguineum
Lilium elegans, vars. fulgens and grandiflorum	Campanula persicifolia alba	Iris, Japanese	Helianthemum vulgare	Campanula carpatica	Tunica saxifraga	Phlox Arendsii
Potentillas, many vars.	Campanula carpatica alba	Campanula Medium	Cytisus scoparius	Campanula rotundifolia	Roses, Climbing	Lythrum Salicaria
Clematis coccinea	Campanula latifolia flore albo	Phlox Arendsii	Linum flavum	Campanula pusilla	Campanula Medium	Phlox suffruticosa, many vars.
Pentstemon barbatus	Campanula Medium album	Erigeron speciosus	Baptisia tinctoria	Delphinium grandiflorum	Potentilla nepalensis	Erodium Manescavi
		Stachys lanata	Asphodelus luteus	Delphinium belladonna	Phlox Enchantress, NettieStuart	Lychnis Flos-cuculi
		Scabiosa japonica	Gaillardia	Delphinium cashmiri-anum		Veronica spicata rosea
		Lavendula		Delphinium, hybrid vars.		
		Salvia Sclarea		Iris monspur		

RED AND SCARLET	WHITE AND CREAM	LAVENDER AND PURPLE	YELLOW AND ORANGE	DARK BLUE AND LIGHT BLUE	PINK AND ROSE	MAGENTA AND CRIMSON

JUNE 24TH—*Continued*

RED AND SCARLET	WHITE AND CREAM	LAVENDER AND PURPLE	YELLOW AND ORANGE	DARK BLUE AND LIGHT BLUE	PINK AND ROSE	MAGENTA AND CRIMSON
	Campanula rotundifolia alba		Digitalis ambigua	Aconitum tauricum	Coronilla varia	Spiraea Peach Blossom
	Campanula pusilla alba		Digitalis orientale		Robinia hispida	Spiraea palmata
	Dianthus plumarius, deltoides, fimbriatus, Mrs. Sinkins		Linaria dalmatica		Calystegia pubescens	
	Chrysanthemum coccineum		Coreopsis grandiflora		Sidalcea Lysteri	
	Gypsophila repens		Sedum kamtschaticum			
	Valeriana officinalis		Lilium elegans, vars. aureum, citrinum, Prince of Orange			
	Digitalis purpurea alba		Scabiosa ochroleuca			
	Asperula hexaphylla		Thermopsis caroliniana			
	Lychnis chalcedonica alba		Cephalaria alpina			
	Pentstemon laevigatus		Potentillas, many vars.			
	Digitalis		Oenothera fruticosa			
	Sweet William, White		Verbascum phloimoides			
	Aruncus sylvester		Aconitum pyrenaicum			
	Filipendula hexapetala fl. pl.		Lilium croceum, Hansoni			
	Astilbe japonica		Helenium Hoopesii			
	Geranium sanguineum album		Sedum acre			
	Lychnis coronaria alba		Anthemis tinctoria			
	Scabiosa caucasica alba		Thalictrum glaucum			
	Clematis recta					
	Saxifraga umbrosa					
	Delphinium grandiflorum album					
	Delphinium cashmirianum alba					
	Centranthus ruber alba					
	Anthemis tinctoria alba					

273

RED AND SCARLET	WHITE AND CREAM	LAVENDER AND PURPLE	YELLOW AND ORANGE	DARK BLUE AND LIGHT BLUE	PINK AND ROSE	MAGENTA AND CRIMSON

JUNE 24TH—*Continued*

RED AND SCARLET	WHITE AND CREAM	LAVENDER AND PURPLE	YELLOW AND ORANGE	DARK BLUE AND LIGHT BLUE	PINK AND ROSE	MAGENTA AND CRIMSON
	Phlox Miss Lingard					
	Veronica spicata alba					
	Iris, Japanese					
	Phlox Arendsii					
	Lilium candidum					
	Sidalcea candida					

JULY 1ST

RED AND SCARLET	WHITE AND CREAM	LAVENDER AND PURPLE	YELLOW AND ORANGE	DARK BLUE AND LIGHT BLUE	PINK AND ROSE	MAGENTA AND CRIMSON
Papaver nudicaule	Linum perenne album	Nepeta Mussini	Aquilegia chrysantha	Linum perenne	Dicentra eximia	Salvia pratensis rosea
Geum coccineum	Viola cornuta alba	Lupines	Iris aurea	Linum narbonnense	Dianthus, Mule vars.	Centaurea dealbata
Dianthus Napoleon III	Iris ochroleuca; Japanese	Campanula latifolia macrantha	Iris Monnieri	Veronica incana	Armerias	Sidalcea malvaeflora
Heuchera Pluie de Feu	Lupines	Geranium ibericum	Papaver rupifragum	Veronica spicata	Saponaria ocymoides	Lychnis coronaria
Gaillardia	Tradescantia virginica alba	Pentstemon diffusus	Corydalis lutea	Salvia pratensis	Saponaria officinalis fl. pl.	Centranthus ruber
Lychnis chalcedonica	Heuchera	Pentstemon ovatus	Achillea sericea	Tradescantia virginica	Heucheras	Epilobium angustifolium
Lychnis Haageana	Salvia pratensis alba	Veronica amethystina	Alyssum rostratum	Lupines	Tunica saxifraga	Geranium sanguineum
Lilium tenuifolium	Silene alpestris	Viola cornuta	Hemerocallis Queen of May; Sovereign; fulva; aurantiaca; Thunbergii; luteola; citrina; ochroleuca	Centaurea montana	Campanula Medium	Lythrum Salicaria
Lilium elegans, vars. fulgens and grandiflorum	Centaurea montana alba	Iris, Japanese		Anchusas	Potentilla formosa	Phlox suffruticosa
Potentilla, many vars.	Campanula persicifolia alba	Campanula Medium		Campanula persicifolia	Phlox Nettie Stewart and Enchantress	Erodium Manescavi
Clematis coccinea	Campanula carpatica alba	Erigeron speciosus		Campanula carpatica		Lychnis Flos-cuculi
Pentstemon barbatus	Campanula Medium album	Stachys Lanata	Helianthemum vulgare	Campanula rotundifolia	Coronilla varia	Veronica spicata rosea
Lilium canadense	Campanula latifolia flore albo	Scabiosa japonica	Cystisus scoparius	Campanula pusilla	Robinia hispida	Spiraea Peach Blossom
Asclepias tuberosa	Campanula rotundifolia alba	Lavendula	Linum flavum	Delphinium grandiflorum	Calystegia pubescens	Filipendula purpurea
	Campanula pusilla alba	Salvia Sclarea	Asphodelus luteus	Delphinium, all vars.	Sidalcea Lysteri	Callirhoe involucrata
	Dianthus deltoides	Salvia turkestanica	Gaillardia	Iris monspur	Lathyrus Pink Pearl	
	Dianthus Mrs. Sinkins	Salvia virgata (nemorosa)	Digitalis ambigua	Aconitum tauricum	Lilium Krameri	
	Gypsophila repens	Galega officinalis	Linaria dalmatica	Hyssopus officinalis	Malva moschata	
	Lychnis chalcedonica alba	Galega Hartlandi	Coreopsis grandiflora	Catananche coerulea		
		Prunella grandiflora	Lilium elegans vars. aureum citrinum Prince of Orange		Dianthus superbus	
		Stokesia cyanea (S. laevis)	Scabiosa ochroleuca			
		Prunella grandiflora				

RED AND SCARLET	WHITE AND CREAM	LAVENDER AND PURPLE	YELLOW AND ORANGE	DARK BLUE AND LIGHT BLUE	PINK AND ROSE	MAGENTA AND CRIMSON

JULY 1ST—*Continued*

	WHITE AND CREAM		YELLOW AND ORANGE			
	Aruncus sylvester		Cephalaria alpina			
	Filipendula hexapetala fl. pl.		Potentilla, many vars.			
	Geranium sanguineum album		Oenothera fruticosa			
	Lychnis coronaria alba		Thermopsis caroliniana			
	Scabiosa caucasica alba		Verbascum phlomoides			
	Clematis recta		Verbascum densiflorum			
	Saxifraga umbrosa		Aconitum pyrenaicum			
	Delphinium grandiflorum album		Lilium Hansoni			
	Delphinium cashmerianum album		Lilium canadense			
	Delphinium, hybrids		Helenium Hoopesii			
	Centranthus ruber alba		Sedum acre			
	Anthemis tinctoria alba		Anthemis tinctoria			
	Phlox Miss Lingard		Thalictrum glaucum			
	Veronica spicata alba		Oenothera missouriensis			
	Lilium candidum		Cassia marilandica			
	Sidalcea candida		Lilium Humboldti			
	Gillenia trifoliata		Hieracium aurantiacum			
	Filipendula Ulmaria		Hypericum Moserianum			
	Galega officinalis alba		Genista tinctoria			
	Lathyrus White Pearl		Achillea filipendulina			
	Lilium Browni					
	Sedum album					
	Malva moschata alba					
	Stokesia cyanea alba					

COLOUR IN MY GARDEN

RED AND SCARLET	WHITE AND CREAM	LAVENDER AND PURPLE	YELLOW AND ORANGE	DARK BLUE AND LIGHT BLUE	PINK AND ROSE	MAGENTA AND CRIMSON
			JULY 8TH			
Papaver nudicaule	Linum perenne album	Viola tricolor	Aquilegia chrysantha	Linum perenne	Dicentra eximia	Salvia pratensis rosea
Geum coccineum	Viola cornuta alba	Viola cornuta	Papaver rupifragum	Linum narbonnense	Dianthus, Mule vars.	Centaurea dealbata
Dianthus Napoleon III	Iris, Japanese	Nepeta Mussini	Corydalis lutea	Veronica incana	Armeria	Sidalcea malvaeflora
Heuchera Pluie de Feu	Tradescantia virginica alba	Campanula latifolia macrantha	Hemerocallis Queen of May, Sovereign, luteola, citrinum, aurantiaca, fulva, Thunbergii, ochroleuca	Veronica spicata	Saponaria ocymoides	
Gaillardia	Heuchera	Geranium ibericum		Salvia pratensis	Saponaria officinalis fl. pl.	Lychnis coronaria
Lychnis Haageana	Salvia pratensis alba	Iris, Japanese		Tradescantia virginica	Heucheras	Centranthus ruber
Potentilla, many vars.	Silene alpestris	Campanula Medium		Centaurea montana	Tunica saxifraga	Epilobium angustifolium
Clematis coccinea	Centaurea montana alba	Erigeron speciosus		Anchusa	Campanula Medium	Geranium sanguineum
Pentstemon barbatus	Campanula persicifolia alba	Stachys lanata	Helianthemum vulgare	Campanula persicifolia	Potentilla formosa	Lythrum Salicaria
Lilium canadense	Campanula carpatica alba	Scabiosa caucasica	Cytisus scoparius	Campanula carpatica	Phlox Nettie Stuart	Phlox suffruticosa, many vars.
Asclepias tuberosa		Scabiosa japonica	Linum flavum	Campanula rotundifolia	Phlox Enchantress	
Kniphofia Express	Campanula Medium album	Lavendula	Gaillardia	Campanula pusilla	Coronilla varia	Erodium Manescavi
Kniphofia Saundersii	Campanula latifolia flore albo	Salvia Sclarea	Digitalis ambigua	Delphinium grandiflorum	Robinia hispida	Lychnis Flos-cuculi
Kniphofia Torchlight	Campanula rotundifolia alba	Salvia turkestanica	Linaria dalmatica	Delphinium, all vars.	Calystegia pubescens	Veronica spicata rosea
Hollyhocks	Campanula pusilla alba	Salvia virgata (nemorosa)	Coreopsis grandiflora	Iris monspur	Sidalcea Lysteri	Spiraea Peach Blossom
	Gypsophila repens	Galega officinalis	Scabiosa ochroleuca	Aconitum tauricum	Lathyrus latifolius Pink Pearl	Filipendula purpurea
	Aruncus sylvester	Galega Hartlandii	Potentilla, many vars.	Hyssopus officinalis	Lilium Krameri	Callirhoe involucrata
	Filipendula hexapetala fl. pl.	Prunella grandiflora	Oenothera fruticosa	Catananche caerulea	Malva moschata	Physostegia virginica
	Filipendula Ulmaria	Stokesia cyanea	Thermopsis caroliniana	Platycodon grandiflorum	Dianthus superbus	Lathyrus tuberosus
	Geranium panguineum album	Hollyhocks	Verbascum phlomoides	Platycodon Mariesi	Hollyhocks	Hollyhocks
	Lychnis Coronaria alba	Campanula turbinata	Aconitum pyrenaicum	Eryngium amethystinum		
	Scabiosa caucasica alba	Scutellaria baicalensis	Lilium Hansoni	Eryngium giganteum		
	Clematis recta	Funkia Sieboldiana	Lilium Humboldti	Eryngium Oliverianum		
	Saxifraga umbrosa		Lilium canadense	Eryngium maritimum		
	Delphinium grandiflorum album		Helenium Hoopesii	Eryngium planum		
	Delphinium, hybrid vars.		Sedum acre			
			Anthemis tinctoria			
			Thalictrum glaucum			
			Oenothera missouriensis			
			Cassia marilandica			
			Hieracium aurantiacum			
			Genista tinctoria			

276

RED AND SCARLET	WHITE AND CREAM	LAVENDER AND PURPLE	YELLOW AND ORANGE	DARK BLUE AND LIGHT BLUE	PINK AND ROSE	MAGENTA AND CRIMSON

JULY 8TH—*Continued*

RED AND SCARLET	WHITE AND CREAM	LAVENDER AND PURPLE	YELLOW AND ORANGE	DARK BLUE AND LIGHT BLUE	PINK AND ROSE	MAGENTA AND CRIMSON
	Centranthus ruber alba		Hypericum Moserianum			
	Anthemis tinctoria alba		Achillea filipendulina			
	Phlox Miss Lingard		Verbascum olympicum			
	Veronica spicata alba		Hollyhocks			
	Lilium candidum		Althaea ficifolia			
	Sidalcea candida					
	Gillenia trifoliata					
	Galega offi-cinalis alba					
	Lathyrus latifolius White Pearl					
	Lilium Browni					
	Sedum album					
	Malva mos-chata alba					
	Stokesia cyanea alba					
	Physostegia virginica alba					
	Chrysanthe-mum Par-theneum album					
	Bocconia cordata					
	Campanula turbinata alba					
	Clethra alnifolia					
	Platycodon grandi-florum al-bum					
	Veronica virginica					
	Cimicifuga racemosa					
	Gypsophila paniculata					
	Hollyhocks					
	Verbascum Miss Will-mott					

JULY 16TH

RED AND SCARLET	WHITE AND CREAM	LAVENDER AND PURPLE	YELLOW AND ORANGE	DARK BLUE AND LIGHT BLUE	PINK AND ROSE	MAGENTA AND CRIMSON
Papaver nudicaule	Linum perenne album	Viola tricolor	Aquilegia chrysantha	Linum perenne	Dicentra eximia	Salvia pra-tensis rosea
Geum coccineum		Viola cornuta	Papaver rupifragum	Linum nar-bonnense	Dianthus, Mule vars.	Centaurea dealbata

RED AND SCARLET	WHITE AND CREAM	LAVENDER AND PURPLE	YELLOW AND ORANGE	DARK BLUE AND LIGHT BLUE	PINK AND ROSE	MAGENTA AND CRIMSON

JULY 16TH—*Continued*

RED AND SCARLET	WHITE AND CREAM	LAVENDER AND PURPLE	YELLOW AND ORANGE	DARK BLUE AND LIGHT BLUE	PINK AND ROSE	MAGENTA AND CRIMSON
Dianthus Napoleon III	Viola cornuta alba	Nepeta Mussini	Corydalis lutea	Centaurea montana	Dianthus superbus	Sidalcea malvae-flora
Heuchera Pluie de Feu	Tradescantia virginica alba	Geranium ibericum	Hemerocallis luteola, citrinum, aurantiaca, fulva, Thunbergii, ochroleuca	Veronica spicata	Armerias	Lychnis coronaria
Gaillardia	Heuchera	Erigeron speciosus		Salvia pratensis	Saponaria officinalis fl. pl.	Geranium sanguineum
Lychnis Haageana	Salvia pratensis alba	Scabiosa caucasica		Tradescantia virginica	Heucheras	Lythrum Salicaria
Potentilla, many vars.	Centaurea montana alba	Scabiosa japonica	Linum flavum	Campanula carpatica	Tunica saxifraga	Phlox suffruticosa
Clematis coccinea	Campanula carpatica alba	Salvia Sclarea	Gaillardia	Campanula rotundifolia	Potentilla formosa	Erodium Manescavi
Pentstemon barbatus	Campanula rotundifolia alba	Salvia turkestanica	Digitalis ambigua	Campanula pusilla	Phlox Nettie Stewart and Enchantress	Lychnis Flos-cuculi
Lilium canadense	Campanula pusilla alba	Salvia virgata (nemorosa)	Linaria dalmatica	Delphinium grandiflorum	Coronilla varia	Veronica spicata rosea
Asclepias tuberosa	Gypsophila repens	Galega officinalis	Coreopsis grandiflorum	Delphinium, hybrid vars.	Calystegia pubescens	Spiraea Peach Blossom
Kniphofia Express	Gypsophila paniculata	Galega Hartlandi	Scabiosa ochroleuca	Aconitum tauricum	Sidalcea Lysteri	Filipendula purpurea
Kniphofia Saundersii	Geranium sanguineum album	Prunella grandiflora	Potentilla, many vars.	Aconitum Napellus	Lathyrus latifolius Pink Pearl	Callirhoe involucrata
Kniphofia Torchlight Hollyhocks	Lychnis coronaria alba	Stokesia cyanea	Oenothera fruticosa	Aconitum Napellus bicolor	Lilium Krameri	Physostegia virginica
Montbretias, many vars.	Scabiosa caucasica alba	Hollyhocks	Oenothera missouriensis	Hyssopus officinalis	Malva moschata	Lathyrus tuberosus
	Delphinium, grandiflorum album	Campanula turbinata	Thermopsis caroliniana	Catananche caerulea	Hollyhocks	Hollyhocks
	Delphinium, hybrid vars.	Campanula trachelium	Verbascum phlomoides	Platycodon grandiflorum		Echinacea purpurea
	Anthemis tinctoria alba	Scutellaria baicalensis	Verbascum olympicum	Platycodon Mariesi		
	Phlox Miss Lingard	Funkia Sieboldiana	Verbascum densiflorum	Eryngium amethystinum		
	Veronica spicata alba	Funkia variegata	Aconitum pyrenaicum	Eryngium giganteum		
	Veronica virginica		Lilium Humboldti	Eryngium Olivarianum		
	Sidalcea candida		Lilium canadense	Eryngium maritimum		
	Galega officinalis alba		Helenium Hoopesii	Eryngium planum		
	Lathyrus latifolius White Pearl		Sedum acre			
	Sedum album		Anthemis tinctoria			
	Malva moschata alba		Thalictrum glaucum			
	Stokesia cyanea alba		Hieracium aurantiacum			
			Genista tinctoria flore pleno			
			Hypericum Moserianum			
			Achillea filipendulina			
			Hollyhocks			
			Althaea ficifolia			
			Helenium pumilum			

278

RED AND SCARLET	WHITE AND CREAM	LAVENDER AND PURPLE	YELLOW AND ORANGE	DARK BLUE AND LIGHT BLUE	PINK AND ROSE	MAGENTA AND CRIMSON

JULY 16TH—*Continued*

RED AND SCARLET	WHITE AND CREAM	LAVENDER AND PURPLE	YELLOW AND ORANGE	DARK BLUE AND LIGHT BLUE	PINK AND ROSE	MAGENTA AND CRIMSON
	Physostegia virginica alba		Helianthus multiflorus flore pleno			
	Chrysanthemum Parthenium					
	Chrysanthemum Leucanthemum, many vars.					
	Bocconia cordata					
	Campanula turbinata alba					
	Clethra alnifolia					
	Platycodon grandiflorumalbum					
	Cimicifuga racemosa					
	Hollyhocks					
	Verbascum Miss Willmott					
	Aconitum Napellus album					
	Lysimachia clethroides					

JULY 24TH

RED AND SCARLET	WHITE AND CREAM	LAVENDER AND PURPLE	YELLOW AND ORANGE	DARK BLUE AND LIGHT BLUE	PINK AND ROSE	MAGENTA AND CRIMSON
Dianthus Napoleon III	Tradescantia virginica alba	Viola cornuta	Papaver rupifragum	Linum perenne	Dicentra eximia	Salvia pratensis rosea
Heucheras	Heucheras	Nepeta Mussini	Corydalis lutea	Linum narbonnense	Dianthus, Mule vars.	Centaurea dealbata
Gaillardia	Campanula carpatica	Erigeron speciosus	Hemerocallis citrinum, ochroleuca, Kwanso, Sir Michael Foster	Centaurea montana	Dianthus superbus	Sidalcea malvaeflora
Lychnis Haageana	Campanula lactiflora alba	Scabiosa caucasica		Veronica spicata	Armeria	Lychnis Coronaria
Potentilla, many vars.	Campanula rotundifolia alba	Scabiosa japonica		Veronica longifolia subsessilis	Saponaria officinalis fl. pl.	Geranium sanguineum
Pentstemon barbatus	Campanula pusilla alba	Salvia Sclarea	Linum flavum		Heuchera	Lythrum Salicaria
Lilium canadense	Gypsophila repens	Salvia turkestanica	Gaillardia	Salvia pratensis]	Tunica saxifraga	Phlox suffruticosa
Kniphofia Express	Gypsophila paniculata	Salvia virgata (nemorosa)	Digitalis ambigua	Tradescantia virginica	Potentilla formosa	Erodium Manescavi
Kniphofia Saundersii	Geranium sanguineum album	Galega officinalis	Linaria dalmatica	Campanula carpatica	Phlox Nettie Stewart and Enchantress	Lychnis Flos-cuculi
Kniphofia Torchlight	Lychnis coronaria alba	Galega Hartlandii	Coreopsis grandiflora	Campanula pusilla	Coronilla varia	Veronica spicata rosea
Hollyhocks	Scabiosa caucasica alba	Prunella grandiflorum	Potentilla, many vars.	Aconitum Napellus	Calystegia pubescens	Spirea Peach Blossom
Montbretia, many vars.		Stokesia cyanea	Oenothera fruticosa	Aconitum Napellus bicolor	Sidalcea Lysteri	Filipendula purpurea
Geums		Hollyhocks	Oenothera missouriensis	Hyssopus officinalis	Lathyrus latifolius Pink Pearl	Callirhoe involucrata
Phlox decussata, many vars.		Campanula Trachelium	Thermopsis caroliniana	Catananche caerulea		
			Verbascum phlomoides			

279

RED AND SCARLET	WHITE AND CREAM	LAVENDER AND PURPLE	YELLOW AND ORANGE	DARK BLUE AND LIGHT BLUE	PINK AND ROSE	MAGENTA AND CRIMSON

JULY 24TH—*Continued*

RED AND SCARLET	WHITE AND CREAM	LAVENDER AND PURPLE	YELLOW AND ORANGE	DARK BLUE AND LIGHT BLUE	PINK AND ROSE	MAGENTA AND CRIMSON
	Anthemis tinctoria alba	Campanula lactiflora coerulea	Verbascum densiflorum	Platycodon grandiflorum	Lilium Krameri	Physostegia virginica
	Phlox decussata, many vars.	Campanula lactiflora E. Molineux	Verbascum olympicum	Platycodon Mariesii	Malva moschata	Lathyrus tuberosus
	Veronica virginica	Scutillaria baicalensis	Aconitum pyrenaicum	Eryngium amethystinum	Hollyhocks	Hollyhocks
	Veronica longifolia alba	Funkia Sieboldiana	Helenium Hoopesii	Eryngium giganteum		Echinacea purpurea
	Sidalcea candida	Funkia variegata	Sedum acre	Eryngium Olivarianum		Phlox decussata, many vars.
	Galega officinalis alba	Thalictrum dipterocarpum	Anthemis tinctoria	Eryngium planum		
	Lathyrus latifolius White Pearl	Clematis Davidi and many vars.	Thalictrum glaucum			
	Sedum album	Phlox decussata, many vars.	Genista tinctoria flore pleno			
	Malva moschata alba	Statice latifolia	Hypericum Moserianum			
	Stokesia cyanea alba		Achillea filipendulina			
	Physostegia virginica alba		Hollyhocks			
	Chrysanthemum Parthenium		Althaea ficifolia			
	Chrysanthemum Leucanthemum many vars.		Helenium pumilum			
	Bocconia cordata		Helianthus multiflorus flore pleno			
	Platycodon grandiflorum album		Helianthus rigidus			
	Cimicifuga racemosa		Montbretias, many vars.			
	Hollyhocks		Rudbeckia Newmani			
	Verbascum Miss Willmott		Centaurea macrocephala			
	Aconitum Napellus album					
	Lysimachia clethroides					
	Lilium auratum					

AUGUST 1ST

RED AND SCARLET	WHITE AND CREAM	LAVENDER AND PURPLE	YELLOW AND ORANGE	DARK BLUE AND LIGHT BLUE	PINK AND ROSE	MAGENTA AND CRIMSON
Gaillardia	Tradescantia virginica alba	Viola cornuta	Papaver rupifragum	Veronica longifolia subsessilis	Dicentra eximia	Lychnis coronaria
Potentilla, many vars.	Heucheras	Erigeron speciosus	Corydalis lutea	Tradescantia virginica	Saponaria officinalis flore pleno	Geranium sanguineum
Geums	Campanula carpatica	Scabiosa japonica	Hemerocallis Kwanso			Lythrum Salicaria
Pentstemon barbatus						

RED AND SCARLET	WHITE AND CREAM	LAVENDER AND PURPLE	YELLOW AND ORANGE	DARK BLUE AND LIGHT BLUE	PINK AND ROSE	MAGENTA AND CRIMSON

AUGUST 1st—*Continued*

RED AND SCARLET	WHITE AND CREAM	LAVENDER AND PURPLE	YELLOW AND ORANGE	DARK BLUE AND LIGHT BLUE	PINK AND ROSE	MAGENTA AND CRIMSON
Kniphofia Uvaria	Campanula lactiflora alba	Salvia Sclarea	Hemerocallis Sir Michael Foster	Campanula carpatica	Tunica saxifraga	Callirhoe involucrata
Kniphofia Pfitzeri	Campanula pusilla	Salvia turkestanica	Linum flavum	Campanula pusilla	Potentilla formosa	Physostegia virginica
Kniphofia Saundersii	Campanula pyramidalis alba	Salvia virgata (nemorosa)	Gaillardia	Aconitum Napellus	Phlox decussata, many vars.	Lathyrus tuberosa
Kniphofia Torchlight	Gypsophila repens	Galega officinalis	Linaria dalmatica	Aconitum Napellus bicolor	Calystegia pubescens	Hollyhocks
Hollyhocks	Gypsophila paniculata	Galega Hartlandii	Coreopsis grandiflora	Hyssopus officinalis	Sidalcea Lysteri	Echinacea purpurea
Montbretia, many vars.	Lychnis coronaria alba	Prunella grandiflora	Potentilla, many vars.	Platycodon grandiflorum	Lathyrus latifolius Pink Pearl	Phlox decussata, many vars.
Phlox decussata	Phlox decussata, many vars.	Stokesia cyanea	Oenothera fruticosa	Platycodon Mariesi	Malva Moschata	Monarda didyma
	Veronica virginica	Hollyhocks	Oenothera missouriensis	Eryngium amethystinum	Hollyhocks	Monarda didyma atro-violacea
	Veronica longifolia alba	Campanula trachelium	Verbascum phlomoides	Eryngium giganteum	Statice incana	Cedronella cana
	Sidalcea candida	Campanula lactiflora coerulea	Verbascum densiflorum	Eryngium Olivarianum	Boltonia latisquama	Chelone Lyoni
	Galega officinalis	Campanula lactiflora E.Molineux	Verbascum olympicum	Eryngium planum	Boltonia latisquama nana	Lyatris pychnostachia
	Lathyrus latifolius White Pearl	Scutellaria baicalensis	Helenium Hoopesii	Echinops Ritro	Silene Schafta	
	Malva moschata alba	Funkia Sieboldiana	Anthemis tinctoria	Echinops bannaticus	Origanum vulgare	
	Stokesia cyanea alba	Funkia variegata	Hypericum Moserianum	Gentiana Andrewsii		
	Physostegia virginica alba	Thalictrum dipterocarpum	Achillea filipendulina	Lobelia syphilitica		
	Chrysanthemum Partheneum	Clematis Davidi, many vars.	Hollyhocks			
	Chrysanthemum Leucanthemum, many vars.	Phlox decussata, many vars.	Althaea ficifolia			
	Bocconia cordata	Statice latifolia	Helenium pumilum			
	Platycodon grandiflorum alba	Statice eximia	Helianthus multiflorus flore pleno			
	Hollyhocks		Helianthus rigidus			
	Verbascum Miss Willmott		Helianthus Miss Mellish			
	Aconitum Napellus album		Montbretias, many vars.			
	Lysimachia clethroides		Rudbeckia speciosa			
	Lilium auratum		Kniphofia Lachesis			
	Cimicifuga simplex		Lilium tigrinum			
			Hypericum calycinum			
			Centaurea macrocephala			

281

RED AND SCARLET	WHITE AND CREAM	LAVENDER AND PURPLE	YELLOW AND ORANGE	DARK BLUE AND LIGHT BLUE	PINK AND ROSE	MAGENTA AND CRIMSON
			AUGUST 1ST—*Continued*			
	Oenothera speciosa					
	Chelone glabra					
	Monarda didyma alba					
	Boltonia asteroides					
	Statice eximia alba					
			AUGUST 8TH			
Gaillardia	Campanula carpatica	Viola cornuta	Papaver rupifragum	Veronica longifolia subsessilis	Dicentra eximia	Lychnis Coronaria
Potentilla	Campanula lactiflora alba	Scabiosa japonica	Corydalis lutea	Tradescantia virginica	Saponaria officinalis flore pleno	Lythrum Salicaria
Pentstemon barbatus	Campanula pyramidalis	Salvia Sclarea	Hemerocallis Kwanso	Campanula carpatica; pyramidalis	Tunica saxifraga	Callirhoe involucrata
Kniphofia Uvaria	Phlox decussata, many vars.	Salvia turkestanica	Hemerocallis Sir Michael Foster	Aconitum Napellus	Phlox decussata, many vars.	Physostegia virginica
Kniphofia Pfitzeri	Veronica virginica	Salvia virgata (nemorosa)	Linum flavum	Aconitum Napellus bicolor	Calystegia pubescens	Lathyrus tuberosa
Hollyhocks	Veronica longifolia alba	Stokesia cyanea	Gaillardia	Hyssopus officinalis	Hollyhocks	Hollyhocks
Montbretia	Sidalcea candida	Campanula lactiflora coerulea	Linaria dalmatica	Platycodon grandiflorum	Malva moschata	Echinacea purpurea
Phlox decussata	Stokesia cyanea alba	Campanula lactiflora E. Molineux	Coreopsis grandiflora	Platycodon Mariesi	Statice incana	Phlox decussata, many vars.
	Malva moschata alba	Funkia Sieboldiana	Oenothera missourien- sis	Eryngium, many vars.	Boltonia latisquama	Monarda didyma
	Chrysanthe- mum Leu- canthe- mum, many vars.	Funkia variegata	Verbascum phlomoides	Echinops Ritro	Boltonia latisquama nana	Monarda didyma atro- violacea
	Boconia cordata	Thalictrum dipterocar- pum	Verbascum densiflorum	Echinops bannaticus	Silene Schafta	Cedronella cana
	Physostegia virginica	Clematis Davidi, many vars.	Verbascum olympicum	Gentiana Andrewsii	Origanum vulgare	Chelone Lyoni
	Platycodon grandi- florum al- bum	Phlox decussata, many vars.	Helenium Hoopesii	Lobelia syphilitica		Lyatris pych nostachia
	Hollyhocks	Statice latifolia	Anthemis tinctoria	Salvia azurea		
	Verbascum Miss Will- mott	Statice eximia	Centaurea macroce- phala	Salvia uliginosa		
	Aconitum Napellus album	Caryopteris incana	Hypericum Moserianum	Plumbago Larpentae		
	Cimicifuga simplex	Eupatorium coelestinum	Hypericum calycinum			
	Lilium auratum	Aster Thompsoni	Hollyhocks			
	Oenothera speciosa	Aster amellus, many vars.	Althaea ficifolia			
	Chelone glabra		Helenium pumilum			
			Achillea filipendulina			
			Helianthus multiflorus flore pleno			
			Helianthus rigidus			

COLOUR IN MY GARDEN

RED AND SCARLET	WHITE AND CREAM	LAVENDER AND PURPLE	YELLOW AND ORANGE	DARK BLUE AND LIGHT BLUE	PINK AND ROSE	MAGENTA AND CRIMSON

AUGUST 8TH—*Continued*

RED AND SCARLET	WHITE AND CREAM	LAVENDER AND PURPLE	YELLOW AND ORANGE	DARK BLUE AND LIGHT BLUE	PINK AND ROSE	MAGENTA AND CRIMSON
	Boltonia asteroides		Helianthus Miss Mellish			
	Statice eximia alba		Montbretia, many vars.			
	Salvia azurea alba		Rudbeckia speciosa			
	Monarda didyma alba		Rudbeckia nitida			
	Echinops sphaerocephalus		Kniphofia Lachesis			
	Artemisia lactiflora		Lilium tigrinum			
	Funkia subcordata					

AUGUST 16TH

RED AND SCARLET	WHITE AND CREAM	LAVENDER AND PURPLE	YELLOW AND ORANGE	DARK BLUE AND LIGHT BLUE	PINK AND ROSE	MAGENTA AND CRIMSON
Gaillardia	Campanula carpatica	Viola cornuta	Papaver rupifragum	Veronica longifolia subsessilis	Dicentra eximia	Lythrum Salicaria
Pentstemon barbatus	Campanula lactiflora alba	Scabiosa japonica	Corydalis lutea	Tradescantia virginica	Saponaria officinalis flore pleno	Callirhoe involucrata
Kniphofia Pfitzeri	Campanula pyramidalis	Salvia Sclarea	Hemerocallis Kwanso	Campanula carpatica	Tunica saxifraga	Physostegia virginica
Kniphofia Uvaria	Campanula alliariaefolia	Salvia virgata nemorosa	Hemerocallis Sir Michael Foster	Campanula pyramidalis	Phlox decussata, many vars.	Lathyrus tuberosa
Montbretia	Phlox decussata, many vars.	Stokesia cyanea	Linum flavum	Aconitum Napellus	Calystegia pubescens	Phlox decussata, many vars.
Phlox decussata	Physostegia virginica alba	Campanula lactiflora coerulea	Gaillardia	Aconitum Napellus bicolor	Statice incana	Monarda didyma
	Veronica virginica	Campanula lactiflora E. Molineux	Linaria dalmatica	Platycodon grandiflorum	Boltonia latisquama	Monarda didyma atro-violacea
	Veronica longifolia alba	Funkia Sieboldiana	Coreopsis grandiflora	Platycodon Mariesi	Boltonia latisquama nana	Echinacea purpurea
	Stokesia cyanea alba	Funkia variegata	Oenothera missouriensis	Hyssopus officinalis	Silene Schafta	Cedronella cana
	Chrysanthemum leucanthemum, many vars.	Thalictrum dipterocarpum	Verbascum olympicum	Eryngium, many vars.	Origanum vulgare	Chelone Lyoni
	Platycodon grandiflorum album	Clematis Davidi, many vars.	Anthemis tinctoria	Echinops, many vars.		Lyatris pychnostachia
	Verbascum Miss Willmott	Phlox decussata, many vars.	Centaurea macrocephala	Lobelia syphilitica		
	Aconitum Napellus album	Statice latifolia	Hypericum Moserianum	Gentiana Andrewsii		
	Cimicifuga simplex	Statice eximia	Hypericum calycinum	Salvia azurea		
	Lilium auratum	Caryopteris incana	Althaea ficifolia	Salvia uliginosa		
	Oenothera speciosa	Eupatorium coelestinum	Helenium pumilum	Salvia Pitcheri		
		Aster Thompsoni	Helianthus multiflorus flore pleno	Plumbago Larpentae		
		Aster amellus many vars.	Helianthus rigidus			
			Helianthus Miss Mellish			
			Montbretia, many vars.			

283

RED AND SCARLET	WHITE AND CREAM	LAVENDER AND PURPLE	YELLOW AND ORANGE	DARK BLUE AND LIGHT BLUE	PINK AND ROSE	MAGENTA AND CRIMSON
			AUGUST 16TH—Continued			
	Chelone glabra		Rudbeckia speciosa			
	Boltonia asteroides		Rudbeckia nitida			
	Statice eximia alba		Kniphofia Lachesis			
	Statice incana alba		Lilium tigrinum			
	Salvia azurea alba		Lilium Henryi			
	Monarda didyma alba					
	Echinops sphaerocephalus					
	Artemisia lactiflora					
	Funkia subcordata					
			AUGUST 24TH			
Gaillardia	Campanula carpatica	Salvia virgata (nemorosa)	Papaver rupifragum	Veronica longifolia subsessilis	Saponaria officinalis flore pleno	Lythrum Salicaria
Kniphofia Pfitzeri	Campanula lactiflora alba	Stokesia cyanea	Corydalis lutea	Tradescantia virginica	Tunica saxifraga	Callirhoe involucrata
Kniphofia Uvaria	Campanula pyramidalis alba	Campanula lactiflora coerulea	Hemerocallis Kwanso	Campanula carpatica	Phlox decussata, many vars.	Physostegia virginica
Montbretias	Campanula alliariaefolia	Campanula lactiflora E. Molineux	Hemerocallis Sir Michael Foster	Campanula pyramidalis	Calystegia pubescens	Lathyrus tuberosus
Phlox decussata, many vars,	Physostegia virginica alba	Campanula lactiflora	Gaillardia	Aconitum Napellus	Statice incana	Phlox decussata, many vars.
Lobelia cardinalis	Veronica longifolia alba	Thalictrum dipterocarpum	Centaurea macrocephala	Aconitum Fischeri	Boltonia latisquama	Monarda didyma
	Stokesia cyanea alba	Clematis Davidi, many vars.	Hypericum Moserianum	Aconitum Wilsoni	Boltonia latisquama nana	Monarda didyma atroviolacea
	Chrysanthemum leucanthemum	Phlox decussata, many vars.	Hypericum calycinum	Eryngiums, many vars.	Silene Schafta	Echinacea purpurea
	Aconitum Napellus alba	Statice latifolia	Helenium pumilum	Echinops, many vars.	Origanum vulgare	Cedronella cana
	Cimicifuga simplex	Statice eximia incana	Helianthus rigidus	Lobelia syphilitica	Lilium speciosum roseum	Chelone Lyoni
	Oenothera speciosa	Caryopteris incana	Helianthus multiflorus flore pleno	Gentiana Andrewsi	Lilium speciosum Melpomene	Lyatris pychonstachia
	Chelone glabra	Eupatorium coelestinum	Helianthus orgyalis	Salvia azurea	Hibiscus Moscheutos	Veronia arkansana
	Boltonia asteroides	Aster Thompsoni	Montbretias, many vars.	Salvia uliginosa	Aster ericoides Enchantress	Desmodium penduliflorum
	Statice eximia alba	Aster amellus, many vars.	Rudbeckia nitida and speciosa	Salvia Pitcheri		
	Statice incana alba	Aster acris	Kniphofia Lachesis	Plumbago Larpentae		
	Salvia azurea alba	Aster amethystinus	Lilium Henryi			
	Monarda didyma alba					

RED AND SCARLET	WHITE AND CREAM	LAVENDER AND PURPLE	YELLOW AND ORANGE	DARK BLUE AND LIGHT BLUE	PINK AND ROSE	MAGENTA AND CRIMSON

AUGUST 24TH—*Continued*

RED AND SCARLET	WHITE AND CREAM	LAVENDER AND PURPLE	YELLOW AND ORANGE	DARK BLUE AND LIGHT BLUE	PINK AND ROSE	MAGENTA AND CRIMSON
	Echinops sphaerocephalus					
	Artemisia lactiflora					
	Funkia subcordata alba					
	Lilium speciosum album					
	Chrysanthemum uliginosum					
	Hibiscus Moscheutos alba					

SEPTEMBER 1ST

RED AND SCARLET	WHITE AND CREAM	LAVENDER AND PURPLE	YELLOW AND ORANGE	DARK BLUE AND LIGHT BLUE	PINK AND ROSE	MAGENTA AND CRIMSON
Gaillardia	Campanula carpatica	Stokesia cyanea	Papaver rupifragum	Campanula carpatica	Saponaria officinalis flore pleno	Callirhoe involucrata
Kniphofia Pfitzeri	Campanula lactiflora alba	Clematis Davidi, many vars.	Corydalis lutea	Campanula pyramidalis	Tunica saxifraga	Lathyrus tuberosus
Kniphofia Uvaria	Campanula alliariaefolia	Phlox decussata	Gaillardia	Aconitum Fischeri	Calystegia pubescens	Echinacea purpurea
Montbretia	Campanula pyramidalis	Statice latifolia	Hypericum Moserianum	Aconitum Wilsoni	Boltonia latisquama	Cedronella cana
Phlox decussata	Physostegia virginica alba	Caryopteris incana	Hypericum calycinum	Echinops	Boltonia latisquama nana	Veronica Arkansana
Lobelia cardinalis	Veronica longifolia alba	Eupatorium coelestinum	Helenium pumilum	Salvia azurea	Silene Schafta	Desmodium penduliflorum
	Stokesia cyanea alba	Aster Thompsoni	Helianthus multiflorus flore pleno	Salvia uliginosa	Origanum vulgare	Aster novae-belgii, many vars.
	Cimicifuga simplex	Aster amellus, many vars.	Helianthus rigidus	Salvia Pitcheri	Lilium speciosum roseum	Aster novae-angliae, many vars.
	Oenothera speciosa	Aster acris	Helianthus orgyalis	Plumbago Larpentae	Lilium speciosum Melpomene	Aster Colwall Pink
	Boltonia asteroides	Aster amethystinus	Montbretia, many vars.		Hibiscus Moscheutos	Aster vimineus, many vars.
	Statice eximia alba	Aster novae-belgii, many vars.	Rudbeckia nitida		Aster ericoides Enchantress	
	Statice incana alba	Aster novae-angliae, many vars.	Rudbeckia speciosa		Aster cordifolius giganteus	
	Salvia azurea alba	Aster cordifolius, many vars.	Kniphofia Lachesis		Anemone japonica, many vars.	
	Artemisia lactiflora	Aster Beauty of Colwell	Kniphofia Chloris			
	Funkia subcordata	Aster Climax	Kniphofia Lemon Queen			
	Lilium speciosum album	Aster Eileen	Lilium Henryi			
	Chrysanthemum uliginosum	Aster Saturn				
	Hibiscus Moscheutos alba	Aster laevis harvardi				
	Eupatorium ageratoides					

RED AND SCARLET	WHITE AND CREAM	LAVENDER AND PURPLE	YELLOW AND ORANGE	DARK BLUE AND LIGHT BLUE	PINK AND ROSE	MAGENTA AND CRIMSON

SEPTEMBER 1ST—Continued

RED AND SCARLET	WHITE AND CREAM	LAVENDER AND PURPLE	YELLOW AND ORANGE	DARK BLUE AND LIGHT BLUE	PINK AND ROSE	MAGENTA AND CRIMSON
	Aster Peter's White					
	Phlox Jeanne d'Arc					
	Polygonum compactum					
	Anemone japonica, many vars.					
	Aster ericoides					

SEPTEMBER 8TH

RED AND SCARLET	WHITE AND CREAM	LAVENDER AND PURPLE	YELLOW AND ORANGE	DARK BLUE AND LIGHT BLUE	PINK AND ROSE	MAGENTA AND CRIMSON
Gaillardia	Campanula carpatica	Stokesia cyanea	Papaver rupifragum	Campanula carpatica	Boltonia latisquama	Callirhoe involucrata
Kniphofia Pfitzeri	Campanula pyramidalis alba	Clematis Davidi, many vars.	Corydalis lutea	Campanula pyramidalis	Latisquama nana	Echinacea purpurea
Kniphofia Uvaria	Oenothera speciosa	Statice latifolia	Gaillardia	Aconitum Fischeri	Origanum vulgare	Cedronella cana
Montbretias	Boltonia asteroides	Caryopteris incana	Hypericum Moserianum	Aconitum Wilsoni	Lilium speciosum roseum	Veronica arkansana
Lobelia cardinalis	Phlox Jeanne d'Arc	Eupatorium coelestinum	Hypericum calycinum	Echinops	Lilium speciosum Melpomene	Desmodium penduliflorum
Helenium autumnale rubrum	Chrysanthemum uliginosum	Aster acris	Helenium autumnale	Salvia azurea	Hibiscus Moscheutos	Aster novae-belgi, many vars.
	Statice incana alba	Aster amethystinus	Helenium pumilum	Salvia uliginosa	Aster vimineus, several vars.	Aster novae-angliae, many vars.
	Stokesia cyanea	Aster novae-belgi, many vars.	Helianthus multiflorus flore pleno	Salvia Pitcheri	Aster cordifolius giganteus	Anemone japonica
	Artemisia lactiflora	Aster novae-angliae, many vars.	Helianthus orgyalis	Plumbago Larpentae	Anemone japonica, many vars.	Sedum spectabilis
	Salvia azurea alba	Aster cordifolius, many vars.	Montbretia	Gentiana crinita	Tunica saxifraga	
	Lilium speciosum album	Aster Climax	Kniphofia Chloris			
	Hibiscus Moscheutos albus	Aster Feltham Blue	Kniphofia Lemon Queen			
	Eupatorium ageratoides	Aster Saturn	Lilium Henryi			
	Aster Peter's White	Aster Eileen	Rudbeckia nitida			
	Aster ericoides	Aster laevis harvardi	Rudbeckia speciosa			
	Polygonum compactum					
	Anemone japonica					
	Aster vimineus, several vars.					

COLOUR IN MY GARDEN

RED AND SCARLET	WHITE AND CREAM	LAVENDER AND PURPLE	YELLOW AND ORANGE	DARK BLUE AND LIGHT BLUE	PINK AND ROSE	MAGENTA AND CRIMSON

SEPTEMBER 16TH

RED AND SCARLET	WHITE AND CREAM	LAVENDER AND PURPLE	YELLOW AND ORANGE	DARK BLUE AND LIGHT BLUE	PINK AND ROSE	MAGENTA AND CRIMSON
Gaillardia Kniphofia Pfitzeri Kniphofia Uvaria Montbretia Helenium autumnale rubrum	Campanula carpatica Campanula pyramidalis Phlox Jeanne d'Arc Artemisia lactiflora Hibiscus Moscheutos Eupatorium agera-toides Aster Peter's White Aster ericoides Aster vimineus, several vars. Anemone japonica Colchicum autumnale album Chrysanthemum nipponicum	Statice latifolia Caryopteris incana Eupatorium coelestinum Aster novae-belgi, many vars. Aster novae-angliae, many vars. Aster cordifolius, many vars. Aster laevis, several vars. Aster Climax Aster Eileen Aster Saturn Crocus speciosus Colchicum autumnale	Papaver rupifragum Corydalis lutea Gaillardia Hypericum calycimum Helianthus multiflorus flore pleno Helenium autumnale Helenium pumilum Kniphofia Chloris Rudbeckia nitida Rudbeckia speciosa Helianthus Maximilianii	Campanula carpatica Aconitum Fischeri Aconitum Wilsoni Aconitum autumnale Plumbago Larpentae Gentiana crenata	Origanum vulgare Aster vimineus, several vars. Aster cordifolius giganteus Anemone japonica, many vars. Tunica saxifraga	Callirhoe involucrata Cedronella cana Vernonia arkansana Desmodium penduliflorum Aster novae-belgi, many vars. Aster novae-angliae, many vars. Anemone japonica Sedum spectabile

SEPTEMBER 24TH

RED AND SCARLET	WHITE AND CREAM	LAVENDER AND PURPLE	YELLOW AND ORANGE	DARK BLUE AND LIGHT BLUE	PINK AND ROSE	MAGENTA AND CRIMSON
Gaillardia Kniphofia Pfitzeri Kniphofia Uvaria Helenium autumnale rubrum	Campanula carpatica alba Phlox Jeanne d'Arc Artemisia lactiflora Eupatorium ageratoides Aster Peter's White Aster ericoides Aster vimineus, several vars. Anemone japonica Colchicum autumnale album Chrysanthemum nipponicum Aster gracillimus	Statice latifolia Caryopteris incana Eupatorium coelestinum Aster novae-belgi, many vars. Aster novae-angliae, many vars. Aster Climax Aster Eileen Aster Saturn Crocus speciosus Crocus zonatus Colchicum autumnale Aster cordifolius Ideal Aster grandiflorus Aster tataricus	Gaillardia Corydalis lutea Helianthus multiflorus flore pleno Helenium autumnale Helenium pumilum Rudbeckia speciosa Kniphofia Chloris Helianthus Maximiliani	Campanula carpatica Aconitum Fischeri Aconitum Wilsoni Aconitum autumnale Plumbago Larpentae Gentiana crinata	Origanum vulgare Aster vimineus, several vars. Aster cordifolius gigantea Anemone japonica, several vars. Tunica saxifraga	Callirhoe involucrata Cedronella cana Vernonia arkansana Desmodium penduliflorum Aster novae-belgi, many vars. Aster novae-angliae, many vars. Anemone japonica Aster Novelty

LATIN AND ENGLISH PLANT NAMES

LATIN AND ENGLISH PLANT NAMES

The flower names marked * have originated with my children and are in common use in our garden. (Plant names frequently encountered in books, trade catalogues, etc., with their popular or "English" equivalents.)

N.B. Plant names enclosed by square brackets are the current (as of 1990) botanical names of the plants Mrs. Wilder describes. These modern names should be used when searching for actual plants.

Abronia umbellata—Sand Verbena.
Abutilon—Flowering Maple.
Acaena microphylla—New Zealand Burr.
Acantholimon venustum—Prickly Thrift.
Acanthus—Bear's-breech.
Acer pennsylvanicum—Moosewood, Stripe-bark Maple.
    pseudoplantanus—Sycamore Maple.
    rubrum—Swamp Maple, Soft Maple.
    saccharinum—Silver or White Maple.
    saccharum—Sugar Maple, Rock Maple.
Achillea Ageratum—Sweet Maudlin.
    Eupatorium or fillipendulina—Fern-leaved Yarrow, Noble Yarrow. [*A. filipendulina*]
    Millefolium—Milfoil, Old-man's Pepper, Nose-bleed, Sanguinary, Carpenter's Grass.
    Ptarmica—Sneezewort, White Tansy, Bastard Pellitory, Seven-years-love.
    sericea—Compact Milfoil. [*A. coarctata*]
    tomentosa—Downy Milfoil.
Aconitum autumnale—Autumn Monkshood. [*A. Henryi*]
    Lycoctonum—Yellow Wolfsbane, Yellow Helmet-flower.
    Napellus—Common Monkshood, Wolfsbane, Friar's-cowl, Blue Rocket, Pharaoh's Chariot.
Acorus Calamus—Sweet Flag, Myrtle-grass, Cinnamon Sedge.
Actaea rubra—Red Baneberry, Coral and Pearl, Red Cohosh, Poison-berry, Redberry-Snake-root.
    spicata—Herb Christopher, Baneberry, Necklace-weed, White Beads, White Grapewort, Rattlesnake-weed.
Actinidia arguta—Silver Vine.
Adenophora—Gland Bellflower.
Adlumia cirrhosa—Alleghany Vine, Mountain Fringe, Fairy Creeper, Climbing Fumatory. [*A. fungosa*]
Adonis autumnalis—Red Camomile, Rosaruby. [*A. annua*]
    vernalis—Spring Adonis, Bird's Eye, Pheasant's Eye, Ox-eye, Flos Adonis.
Aegopodium Podograria—Goutweed, Soapsuds, Masterwort, Jack-jump-a-bout, Ash-weed, Herb Gerald.
Aethionema cordifolium—Lebanon Candytuft.
    grandiflorum—Persian Candytuft.
Agathaea coelestis—Blue Daisy. [*Felicia amelloides*]
Ageratum mexicanum—Floss-flower. [*A. Houstonianum*]
Agrostemma Coronaria—Mullein Pink, Rose-of-Heaven, Rose Campion, Crown-of-the-field, Old-maid's-Pink, Popille. *See* Lychnis coronaria. [*Lychnis coronaria*]
Ajuga reptans—Creeping Bugle, Middle-consound, Dead-men's-elbows, Carpenter's-Herb.
Akebia quinata—Tricorne Vine.*
Alchemilla—Lady's Mantle, Great-Sanicle, Breakstone.
Allium Moly—Moly, Golden Garlic.

LATIN AND ENGLISH PLANT NAMES

Alnus incana—Speckled or Hoary Alder.
    rugosa—Tag or Green Alder.
    viridis—Mountain Alder.
Alonsoa linifolia—Mask-flower. [*A. linearis*]
Aloysia citriodora—Sweet Verbena, Lemon Verbena. [*A. triphylla*]
Alstroemeria—Peruvian Lily.
Alternanthera Telanthera—Joy-weed.
Althaea officinalis—Marsh Mallow, Mortification Root, Sweat-weed.
    rosea—Hollyhock, Hock, Holy Oak, Althea Rose. [*Alcea rosea*]
Alyssum argenteum—Silver Alyssum. [*A. murale*]
    maritimum—Sweet Alyssum, Sweet Alison, Madwort. [*Lobularia maritima*]
    montanum—Mountain Madwort.
    saxatile—Golden Madwort, Basket-of-gold, Gold-dust. [*Aurinia saxatile*]
    spinosum—Spiny Madwort.
Amaranthus caudatus—Love-lies-bleeding, Amaranth, Nun's Whipping-post, Flower-gentle.
    tricolor—Joseph's coat.
Ambrosia mexicana—Ambrosia. [*Chenopodium Botrys*]
Amelanchier canadensis—Juneberry, Shad-bush, Shad-blow, Indian Cherry, Snowy Mespilus.
Ammobium alatum—Winged Everlasting.
Amorpha canescens—Bastard Indigo, Lead-plant, Shoe-strings.
Ampelopsis quinquefolia—Virginia Creeper, Woodbine. [*Parthenocissus quinquefolia*]
    tricuspidata Veitchii—Boston Ivy. [*Parthenocissus tricuspidata*]
Anagallis arvense—Scarlet Pimpernel, Poor-man's-weather-glass, Burnet Rose, Red Chick-weed, John-go-to-bed-at-noon, Shepherd's Warning, Wink-a-peep.
    indica—Italian Pimpernel. [*A. arvensis*]
    linifolia—Blue Pimpernel. [*A. Monelli*]
Anchusa capensis—Cape Forget-me-not.
    italica—Italian Alkanet. [*A. azurea*]
    myosotidiflora—Forget-me-not Anchusa. [*Brunnera macrophylla*]
Andromeda Polifolia—Moorwort, Wild Rosemary, Marsh Holy-rose.
Androsace—Rock Jasmine.
Anemone alpina—Alpine Windflower, Devil's Beard.
    angulosa—Great Hepatica. [*Hepatica transsilvanica*]
    apennina—Apennine Windflower.
    blanda—Blue Winter Windflower.
    coronaria—Poppy Anemone.
    fulgens—Scarlet Windflower. [*A. x fulgens*]
    japonica—Japanese Windflower. [*A. x hybrida*]
    nemorosa—Windflower, Bow-bells, Granny's Night-cap.
    Pulsatilla—Pasque-flower.
    stellata—Star Anemone. [*A. hortensis*]
    sylvestris—Wood Anemone, Snowdrop Anemone.
Anetheum graveolens—Dill, Dilly. [*Anethum graveolens*]
Angelica—Archangel, Holy-ghost, Belly-ache-root.
Antennaria dioica—Mountain Cudweed, Cat's-ears, Petty-mountain, Petty-cotton, Cudweed.
    tomentosa—Silver Everlasting, Mountain Everlasting. [*A. dioica 'Tomentosa'*]
Anthemis arabica—Rock Camomile. [*Cladanthus arabicus*]
    tinctoria—German Camomile, Ox-eye or Yellow Camomile, Golden Marguerite.
Antirrhinum—Snapdragon, Lion-snap.
Aponogeton angustifolium—Cape Pond-flower. [*A. distachyus*]
Aquilegia alpina—Alpine Columbine.
    caerulea—Rocky Mountain Columbine.
    californica—California Columbine. [*A. formosa var. truncata*]
    canadensis—Wild Columbine, Boots-and-shoes, Rock-lily, Chuckies, Honeysuckle, Jack-in-trousers, Meeting Houses.
    chrysantha—Golden Columbine.
    glandulosa—Altaian Columbine.
    vulgaris—Culverwort, Blue-starry, Dove's-foot, Capon's-feather, Common Columbine.
Arabis albida [*A. caucasica*] and **alpina**—Rock Cress, Wall Cress, Alpine Molewort, Dusty Husband, Bishop's-hat, March-and-May, Sweet Alice, White Alison, Snowdrift.

LATIN AND ENGLISH PLANT NAMES

Aralia spinosa—Angelica tree.
Arenaria balearica—Balearic Sandwort.
    montana—Mountain Sandwort.
Arethusa bulbosa—Arethusa, Wild Pink, Dragon's-mouth, Rose-lip.
Argemone alba—White Poppy-thistle.
    mexicana—Devil's-fig, Yellow Mexican Poppy, Thorn Poppy.
Aristolochia Sipho (syn. **macrophylla**)—Dutchman's Pipe, Heartwort, Pipe-vine. [*A. durior*]
Armeria cephalotes (syn. **formosa**)—Great Thrift.
    maritima—Sea Pink, Cushion Pink, Thrift, Lady's Cushion.
Artemisia Abrotanum—Southernwood, Old Man, Smelling-wood, Maiden's-ruin, Lad's-love,
    Lad's-savour, Kiss-me-quick-and-go, Sweet Benjamin, Sloven-wood.
    Absinthium—Wormwood, Warmot, Old Women, Madder-wort.
    Dracunculus—Tarragon, Biting-dragon.
    vulgaris—Mugwort, Smotherwood, Apple-pie, Green Ginger, Sailor's Tobacco.
Arum maculatum—Lords-and-ladies, School-masters, Kings-and-queens, Nightingales,
    Cuckoo-pint, Starch-root.
Arundo Donax—Province Reed.
Asclepias tuberosa—Butterfly-weed, Pleurisy-root, Indian Posy.
Asperula azurea—Blue Woodruff. [*A. orientalis*]
    odorata—Sweet Woodruff, Master-of-the-wood, Hay-plant, Wood-rowel, Sweet-hair-
    hoof, Mug-wet.
Asphodelus luteus—Yellow Asphodel. [*Asphodeline lutea*]
    racemosus—King's-spear. [*A. cerasiferus*]
Aster, Hardy—Starwort, Michaelmas Daisy, Good-bye-summer. [*Selections and hybrids of A.
    novae-angliae and A. novi-belgii*]
    alpinus—Alpine Daisy.
    Amellus—Italian Starwort.
    cordifolius—Heart-leaved Aster, Frost Flower,* Blue Wood Aster, Bee-tongue.
    diffusus—Calico Aster. [*A. lateriflorus*]
    ericoides—White Heath Aster, White Rosemary, Scrub-brush.
    grandiflorus—Christmas Daisy.
    laevis—Smooth Aster.
    novae-angliae—New England Starwort.
    novi-belgii—New York Aster, Willow Aster.
    puniceus—Red-stalk Starwort, Cocash, Swanweed, Meadow Scabish.
    Tradescanti—Blue Camomile, Blue Daisy.
Astilbe—False Goat's-beard.
Astragalus—Milk Vetch.
Astrantia major—Masterwort, Black Sanicle.
Aubrietia—False or Purple Wall Cress.
Azalea nudiflora—Wild Honeysuckle, Election Pink, Swamp Pink, Pinxter-flower, Swamp
    Apple-blossom, Spice-flower, May-apple. [*A. periclymenoides*]
    viscosa—Swamp Pink, Swamp Honeysuckle, Clammy Azalea, Springbloom. [*Rhododen-
    dron viscosum*]
Babiana—Baboon-root.
Baptisia australis—False Indigo, Blue Rattle-bush.
    tinctoria—American Indigo, Indigo or Clover Broom, Dyer's-broom.
Bartonia aurea—Golden Bartonia. [*Mentzelia Lindleyi*]
Begonia—Elephant's ear.
Bellis perennis—English Daisy, Bruise-wort, Cockilorie, Hen-and-chickens, Margaret, Gowan.
Benzoin aestivale—Spice-bush, Benjamin-bush, Wild Alspice. [*Lindera benzoin*]
Berberis vulgaris—Barberry, Pepperidge, Jaundice Berry.
Betula alba—White Birch, Make-peace, Ribbon-tree. [*B. pendula*]
    lenta—Sweet Birch, Cherry Birch, Mountain Mahogany.
    nigra—Black Birch.
    papyrifera—Canoe Birch, Silver or Paper Birch, Spool-wood.
Bignonia—(*See* Campsis).
Bocconia cordata—Plume Poppy, Tree Celandine. [*Macleaya cordata*]
Boltonia asteroides—False Starwort, Cloud Daisy,* False Camomile.
Borago officinalis—Burrage, Borage, Bee's-bread, Cool-tankard, Lang-de-beef.

LATIN AND ENGLISH PLANT NAMES

Brachycome—Swan River Daisy.
Bravoa—Scarlet Twin-flower. [*Polinathes*]
Brodiaea congesta—Ookow. [*Dichelostemma congestum*]
    grandiflora—California Hyacinth. [*B. coronaria*]
    laxa—Ithuriel's Spear. [*Tritelaria laxa*]
    minor—Harvest Hyacinth.
Buddleia Davidii (Veitchii, magnifica, etc.)—Summer Lilac, Butterfly bush.
    globosa—Orange-ball Tree.
Bulbocodium vernum—Spring Meadow Saffron.
Butomus umbellatus—Flowering Rush.
Buxus—Box, Dudgeon.
Caladium esculentum—Elephant's Ear. [*Colocasia esculenta*]
Calandrinea umbellata—Rock Purslane.
Calceolaria—Slipperwort.
Calendula officinalis—Pot Marigold, Goldings, Gold-bloom, Holy-gold, Gools.
Calla palustris—Bog Arum.
Callirhoe involucrata—Poppy Mallow.
Callistephus hortensis—China Aster. [*C. chinensis*]
Calochortus albus—Satin Bell, White Globe Tulip.
    Benthami—Yellow Pussy-ears. [*C. monophyllus*]
    Kennedyi—Orange Mariposa Tulip.
    luteus—Butterfly Tulip, Mariposa Lily.
    Maweanus—White Pussy-ears. [*C. Tolmiei*]
    Nuttalli—Sego Lily.
Calopogon pulchellus—Grass Pink. [*C. tuberosus*]
Caltha palustris—March Marigold.
Calycanthus floridus—Sweet Shrub, Allspice, Strawberry-shrub.
Calystegia pubescens—Bearbind. [*C. hederacea 'Flore Pleno'*]
Camassia esculenta—Quamash, Camash. [*C. Quamash*]
    Leichtlini—White Quamash.
Campanula caespitosa—Tufted Hairbell, Dane's-blood.
    carpatica—Carpathian Hairbell.
    glomerata—Cluster Hairbell.
    lactiflora—Milky Bellflower.
    latifolia—Great Bellflower, Coventry Bells.
    macrostyla—Candelabra Bellflower.
    Medium—Canterbury Bells, Marian, Mercury's Violet, Night Caps.
    persicifolia—Peach-leaved Bellflower, Peach-bells.
    Portenschlagiana—Rock Hairbell.
    pulla—Austrian Hairbell.
    pyramidalis—Chimney Bellflower.
    rapunculoides—Rampion, Creeping Bellflower.
    rotundifolia—English Hairbell, Blue-bell, Blaewort, Heath-bell, Gowk's-thimble.
    Trachelium—Throatwort, Haskwort.
    turbinata (syn. **carpatica turbinata**)—Turban Hairbell. [*C. carpatica*]
Campsis radicans—Trumpet Vine, Cross-vine.
Canna indica—Indian Shot, Indian Reed, China Shot.
Cannabis sativa—Hemp Plant.
Carum Carvi—Caraway, Carvies.
Caryopteris Mastacanthus—Blue Spiraea, Verbena Shrub. [*C. incana*]
Cassiope fastigiata—Himalayan Heath.
Catananche caerulea—Cupid's-dart, Blue Cupidone.
Ceanothus americanus—New Jersey Tea.
    azureus—Mountain Sweet. [*C. caeruleus*]
Celastrus scandens—Bitter-sweet, Staff-vine, Waxwork, Fever-twig, Roxbury Waxwork,
    Orange-root.
Celosia—Cockscomb.
Celsia cretica—Cretan Mullein.
Centaurea Cyanus—Blue Cornflower, Blue-bottle, Ragged-Robin, Bachelor's-buttons, Break-
    your-spectacles, Blue-buttons, Corn Binks, Corn Centaury, Ragged Sailors.

LATIN AND ENGLISH PLANT NAMES

Centaurea dealbata—Mealy Centaury.
  macrocephala—Great Knapweed.
  montana—Hardy Cornflower, Mountain Knapweed.
  moschatus—Sweet Sultan. [*C. moschata*]
Centranthus ruber—Red or Spur Valerian.
Cephalanthus occidentalis—Button-bush, Crane-willow, Honey-balls, Mountain Globeflower, Swamp-wood.
Cerastium tomentosum—Snow-in-summer, Mouse-ear chickweed.
Cercis canadensis—Red-bud, Judas-tree, Salad-bud, Wild Lilac.
  Siliquastrum—Love Tree.
Cerintha retorta—Purple-leaved Honeywort. [*Cerinthe retorta*]
Chamaepeuce diacantha—Fish-bone Thistle. [*Cersium diacantha*]
Cheiranthus Cheiri—Wallflower, Bloody Warrior, Stock Jillofer, Cherisaunce.
Chelone glabra—Turtle-head, Balmony, Cod-head, Salt-rheum.
Chenomales—(*See* Cydonia).
Chimaphila maculata—Pipsissewa, Spotted Wintergreen.
Chimonanthus fragrans—Winter-sweet. [*C. praecox*]
Chionanthus—Fringe Tree.
Chionodoxa—Glory-of-the-snow, Snow Glory.
Chrysanthemum arcticum—Arctic Daisy.
  Balsamita—Costmary, Ale-cost, Bible-leaf, Sweet Mary Ann, Sweet Maudlin.
  carinatum—Tricolor Daisy.
  coronarium—Crown Daisy, Garland Daisy.
  frutescens—Paris Daisy, Yellow Marguerite.
  inodorum—Double Mayweed. [*Tripleurospermum maritimum*]
  Leucanthemum—Moon-penny Daisy, Ox-eye Daisy, Dutch Curse, Dog-blow, Poor-land-Daisy, Poverty-weed, Herb-Marguerite.
  nipponicum—Nippon Daisy, Shrubby Ox-eye.
  Parthenium—Fever-few, Feather-few, Pellitory, Wild Camomile, Flirtwort, Bunchelory Vetter-voo.
  segetum—Corn Marigold, Gools, Yellowby, Yellow Ox-eye.
Cichorium Intybus—Chicory, Succory, Blue Sailors, Bunk.
Cimicifuga japonica—Japanese Snakeroot.
  racemosa—Black Cohosh, Black Snakeroot, Bugbane, Richweed, Squawroot, Rattleroot.
Cineraria maritima—Dusty Miller. [*Senecia maritima*]
Cistus—Rockrose.
Clarkia—Pink Fairies.
Claytonia virginica—Spring Beauty, May-flower, Good-morning-Spring, Grass-flower, Wild Potato, Miscodeed.
Clematis coccinea—Scarlet Clematis, Urn-flowered Clematis.
  crispa—Blue Jasmine, Bluebell Vine, Frill-flower.
  Flammula—Sweet-scented Virgin's-bower.
  japonica—Japanese Virgin's-bower.
  montana—Mountain Clematis.
  virginiana—Virgin's Bower, Traveller's Joy, Bind-with-love, Woodbine, Love-vine, Devil's-hair.
  Vitalba—Old-man's-beard, Grey-beard, Crocodile, Love-bind, Robin Hood's-fetter, Devil's-hair, Maiden's Honesty, Smoke-wood, Withy-wind, Snow-in-harvest.
  Viticella—Vine-bower.
Cleome—Spider-flower.
Clethra alnifolia—Sweet Pepper Bush, Honey Sweet, White Bush, Spiked Alder.
Clianthus—Glory Pea.
Cobaea scandens—Cup-and-saucer-vine.
Colchicum autumnale—Autumn Crocus, Fog or Michaelmas Crocus, Son-before-the-father, Naked Ladies, Orphans.
Collinsea bicolor—Blue-eyed-Mary, Innocence, Chinese Houses, Blue-lips. [*Collinsia heterophylla*]
Collomia grandiflora (syn. **Gilia grandiflora**)—Wild Bouvardia.
Commelina coelestis—Day flower, Blue Spider-flower.
Convallaria majalis—Lily-of-the-valley, Ladders-to-heaven, Lily-convally, Valleys, Mugget, Our Lady's Tears, Little Dandies, Constancy, Liriconfancy.

LATIN AND ENGLISH PLANT NAMES

Convolvulus japonicus—California Rose. [*Calystegia hederacea*]
    mauritanicus—Blue Rock Bindweed.
    pubescens—Double Bindweed. [*Calystegia hederacea 'Flore Pleno'*]
    Soldanella—Sea Bindweed. [*Calystegia Soldanella*]
    tricolor—Dwarf Morning Glory, Blue Eyes.
Coreopsis—Tickweed.
Cornus alba—Siberian Dogwood.
    alternifolia—Purple Dogwood, Green Osier.
    Amomum—Silky Cornel, Red Osier, Swamp Dogwood, Female Dogwood, Kinnikinic.
    canadensis—White Dogwood, Bunchberry, Bunch Plum, Low Dogwood, Crackerberry.
    florida—White Cornel, Flowering Dogwood, Indian Arrowwood, Nature's Mistake, False Boxwood.
    mas—Cornelian Cherry, Male Cornel, Redwood-of-Turkey.
    sanguinea—Catteridge Tree, Gaiterberry, Red-twigged Dogwood.
    stolonifera—Red Osier, Gutter Tree, Red Brush, Waxberry. [*C. sericea*]
Coronilla varia—Scorpion Scenna.
Corydalis cheilanthifolia—Fern-leaved Fumatory.
    lutea—Yellow Fumatory, Yellow Corydal, Mother-of-thousands.
    nobilis—Noble Fumatory.
Cotoneaster—Rock-spray.
    Pyracantha (syn. **Pyracantha coccinea**)—Fire-thorn, Christ's Thorn. [*Pyracantha coccinea*]
Crambe cordifolia—Heart-leaved Seakale.
Crataegus coccinea—Scarlet Thorn. [*C. biltmoreana or C. pedicellata*]
    crus-galli—Cockspur Thorn, New Castle Thorn, Pin Thorn.
    oxyacantha—Common Hawthorn, May, Haythorn, Quickset, May Tree. [*C. laevigata*]
    praecox—Glastonbury Thorn. [*C. monogyna 'Biflora'*]
    Pyracantha—(*See* Cotoneaster). [*Pyracantha coccinea*]
Crocus biflorus—Scotch or Cloth-of-silver Crocus.
    chrysanthus—Yellow Spring Crocus.
    sativus—Saffron, Saff Flower.
    susianus—Cloth-of-gold Crocus. [*C. angustifolius*]
Crucianella stylosa—Crosswort, Skunk-plant.
Cyclamen europaeum—Sowbread, Bleeding Nuns. [*C. purpurascens*]
Cydonia japonica—Japanese Quince, Fire Bush. [*Chaenomeles speciosa*]
Cyperus longus—Galingale.
Cypripedium acaule—Pink or purple Lady's Slipper, Camel's-foot, Whip-poor-wills-shoes, Moccasin-flower, American Valerian, Nerveroot, Noah's Arks, Two-lips, Venus Shoe, Old Goose.
    hirsutum—Yellow Lady's Slipper or Moccasin Plant, Yellows, Male Nervine. [*C. Calceolus*]
    spectabile—Showy Moccasin Flower. [*C. reginae*]
Cytisus albus—White Spanish Broom.
    scoparius—Bonny or Scotch Broom, Besom, Hagweed, Golden Willow.
Daphne alpina—Alpine Mezereon.
    Blagayana—King's Garland-flower.
    Cneorum—Garland Flower.
    Genkwa—Lilac Garland Flower.
    Mezereum—Mezereon, Dwarf Bay, Spurge Olive, Paradise Plant, Magell.
    odora—Sweet Daphne.
    rupestris (syn. **D. petraea**)—Rock Garland Flower. [*D. petraea*]
    striata—Fairy Garland-flower.
Datura—Thorn Apple.
Delphinium—Larkspur, Knightspur, King's Consound.
    belladonna—Belladonna Larkspur. [*x Belladonna*]
    cardinale—Christmas Horns, Scarlet Larkspur.
    formosum—Bee Larkspur.
    grandiflorum—Chinese Larkspur.
Desmodium penduliflorum—Tick-trefoil. [*Lespedeza Thunbergii*]
Dianthus alpinus—Alpine Pink.
    arenarius—Sand Pink.
    Armeria—Deptford Pink.

LATIN AND ENGLISH PLANT NAMES

Dianthus barbatus—Sweet William, Sweet John, London Tufts, None-so-pretty, Bunch Pink, French Pink, Blooming Down, Painted Ladies, Tolmeiner.
    caesius—Cheddar Pink. [*D. gratianopolitanus*]
    Caryophyllus—Clove Carnation, Crown Pink, Sops-in-wine, Gillyflower, Grenadine.
    chinensis—China Pink.
    deltoides—Maiden Pink.
    dentosus—Amoor Pink.
    fimbriatus—Fringed Pink. [*D. orientalis*]
    graniticus—Granite Pink.
    neglectus—Glacier Pink. [*D. pavonius*]
    petraeus—Rock Pink.
    plumarius—Grass Pink, Scotch Pink, Clove Pink.
    superbus—Ragged Pink, Fringed Pink.
    sylvestris—Wood Pink.
Dicentra Cucularria—Dutchman's-breeches, Indian-boys-and-girls, White-hearts, Kitten's-breeches.
    eximia—Wild Bleeding Heart, Turkey- or Squirrel-corn.
    spectabilis—Bleeding Heart, Lyre-flower, Clocks-and-watches.
Dictamnus fraxinella—Fraxinella, Gas-plant, Dittany. [*D. albus*]
Digitalis ambigua—Yellow Foxglove. [*D. grandiflora*]
    purpurea—Foxglove, Fairy Petticoats, Thimbles, Ladies' Fingers, Fairy Cap, Scotch Mercury, Folk's Glove, Dead-men's-fingers.
Dimorphotheca aurantiaca—African Daisy, Cape Marigold. [*D. sinuata*]
Dodecatheon Media—American Shooting Star, Mosquito Bells, Mad Violet, Wild Cyclamen, Prairie Pointer, Indian Chief, American Cowslip, Pride-of-Ohio. [*D. Meadia*]
Doronicum—Leopards'-bane.
Draba azoides—Whitlow-grass. [*D. aizoides*]
Dracocephalum—Dragon's-head.
Drosera filiformis—Sundew.
Dryas—Mountain Avens.
Echinacea purpurea—Purple Cone-flower.
Echinops—Globe Thistle.
    sphaerocephalus—Silver Thistle.*
Echium vulgare—Viper's Bugloss.
Elaeagnus—Oleaster, Silver Thorn, Silverberry.
Elymus arenarius—Sea Lyme Grass, Gray Ribbons.*
Epilobium angustifolium—French Willow.
    hirsutum—Willow-herb, Codlins-and-cream, Apple-pie, Rose-bay.
    palustris—Swamp Willow-herb, Wickup. [*E. palustre*]
Epigaea repens—Arbutus, Mayflower, Trailing Arbutus, Gravel-plant, Shad-flower, Winter or Mountain Pink, Crocus, Ground Laurel.
Epimedium—Barrenwort.
Eragrostis—Love Grass.
Eranthus hyemalis—Winter Aconite, Winter Wolfsbane.
Erica—Heath, Heather, Ling, Honey-bottle.
Erigeron aurantiacus—Orange Daisy.
    speciosus—Purple Fleabane.
Eritrichium nanum—Fairy Forget-me-not.
Erodium—Stork's-bill, Clocks, Red-stemmed Filaree.
Eryngium—Sea Holly, Blue Thistle, Sea Hulver.
Erysimum arkansanum—Western Wallflower. [*E. asperum*]
    ochroleucum—Alpine Wallflower. [*E. decumbens*]
    pulchellum—Hedge-mustard, Treacle-mustard, Fairy Wallflower.
Erythraea diffusa—Centaury. [*Centaurium scilloides*]
Erythronium americanum—Dog-tooth Violet, Yellow Adder's tongue, Trout Lily, Scrofula-root, Snake-leaf.
    grandiflorum—Fawn Lily, Chamase Lily, Adam-and-Eve.
Eschscholtzia californica—California Poppy.
Euonymus atropurpurea—Strawberry-tree, Waahoo, Burning-bush, Bursting-heart, American Spindle-tree.

LATIN AND ENGLISH PLANT NAMES

Eupatorium ageratoides—White Snake-root, White Sanicle, Deerwort, Squaw-weed, Rich-weed, Stevia. [*E. rugosum*]
    coelestinum—Mist-flower, Blue Boneset.
    purpureum—Joe-Pye weed, Queen-of-the-meadow, Purple Boneset, Nigger-weed, Gravel-root.
Euphorbia corollata—Flowering Spurge, Milkwort.
    Cyparissias—Cypress Spurge, Kiss-me-quick, Bonapart's Crown, Graveyard-weed, Welcome-to-our-house.
    Lathyrus—Caper Spurge.
    marginata—Snow-on-the mountain, Mountain Spurge.
Exochorda grandiflora—Pearl Bush. [*E. racemosa*]
Ferula—Giant Fennel.
Festuca glauca—Blue Fescue Grass. [*F. ovina var. glauca*]
Forsythia—Golden Bell.
Fragaria—Strawberry.
Francoa ramosa—Maiden's Wreath.
Fritillaria imperialis—Crown Imperial.
    Meleagris—Guinea-hen-flower, Checker Lily, Widow's Wail, Weeping Widow, Snake's-head.
Fumaria officinalis—Fumatory, Beggary, Delicacy, Earth-smoke.
Funkia (Hosta) coerulea—Blue Day Lily. [*Hosta ventricosa*]
    grandiflora—Corfu Lily, Plantain Lily, White Day Lily. [*Hosta plantaginea 'Grandiflora'*]
    lanceolata variagata—Striped Lily. [*Hosta lancifolia var. variegata*]
Galax—Wand Plant.
Galega officinalis—Goat's-rue.
Galtonia candicans—Summer Hyacinth, Cape Hyacinth.
Gaultheria procumbens—Winter Green, Deer-, Ground-, Spice-, or Partridgeberry, Mountain Tea, Ivory Plums, Pippins, Rapper-dandies.
Gaura Lindheimeri—Butterfly-flower.
Gazania nivea—Treasure-flower.
Genista tinctoria—Dyer's Green-weed, Wood-waxen, Alleluia, Dyer's Whin, Widow-wisse.
Gentiana acaulis—Gentianella.
    Andrewsii—Closed or Bottle Gentian, Cloister-heart, Barrel Gentian, Dumb Foxglove.
    asclepiadea—Willow Gentian.
    bavarica—Bavarian Gentian.
    crinita—Fringed Gentian, French Gentian. [*Gentianopsis crinita*]
    septemfida—Crested Gentian.
    verna—Spring Gentian.
Geranium maculatum—Wild Geranium, Granesbill, Chocolate-flower.
    Robertianum—Herb-Robert, Mountain Geranium, Death-come-quickly, Jenny Wren, Wren's-flower.
Gerardia tenuifolia—Purple Geradia, Gerade's Flower. [*Agalinis tenuifolia*]
Gerbera Jamesoni—Transvaal Daisy.
Geum—Avens.
Gilia californica—Prickly Phlox. [*Leptodactylon californicum*]
    tricolor—Bird's-eye.
Gladiolus—Corn Flag, Sword Flag.
Glaucium luteum—Horned Poppy, Yellow Sea Poppy, Squatmore, Bruise-root. [*G. flavum*]
Globularia—Globe Daisy.
Godetia—Fare-well-to-spring, Satin Flower. [*Clarkia*]
Goodyera pubescens—Rattle-snake Plantain.
Gunnera—Prickly Rhubarb.
Gypsophila paniculata—Baby's-breath, Lace Shawls*, Chalk Plant, Summer Mist.
    repens—Creeping Chalk Plant.
Habenaria—Fringed Orchis, Tatter-fringe, Meadow Pink, Soldier's Plume.
Halesia tetraptera—Snowdrop Tree. [*H. carolina*]
Hamamelis japonica—Japanese Witch Hazel.
    virginica—Witch Hazel, Winter Bloom, Striped Alder. [*H. virginiana*]
Hedera Helix—English Ivy, Bentwood, Woodbine, Bindwood.
Hedysarum—French Honeysuckle.

298

LATIN AND ENGLISH PLANT NAMES

Helenium—Sneezeweed.
Helianthemum—Sunrose, Frost-weed, Scrofula Plant.
Helianthus—Sunflower, Comb-flower, Golden, Gold, Turnsol, Larrabell.
Helichrysum bracteatum—Everlasting Flower, Sun Gold, Immortelle, Yellow Flower-gentle.
Heliopsis—False Sunflower, Orange Sunflower.
Heliotropum peruvianum—Heliotrope, Cherry-pie, Turnsole. [*H. arborescens*]
Helleborus niger—Christmas Rose, Christmas Flower, Clove-tongue, Felon-grass, Christ's-herb.
Helonius bullata—Stud-flower.
Helxine Soleirolii—Pellitory-of-the-wall. [*Soleirolla Soleirolii*]
Hemerocallis—Day Lily, Brass-and-copper Lilies.*
    flava—Lemon Lily, Custard Lily, Yellow Day Lily. [*H. Lilioasphodelus*]
    fulva—Orange Day Lily, Tawny Lily, False Tiger Lily, Eve's Thread.
Hepatica triloba—Liver-leaf, Kidneywort, Mayflower, Herb-Trinity, Squirrel-cup, Ivy-flower.
    [*H. americana*]
Heracleum lanatum—Cow-parsnip, Madness, Masterwort, Youthwort.
Herniaria glabra—Rupturewort, Pearlwort.
Hesperis matronalis—Sweet Rocket, Dames Violet, Damask Violet, Queen's Gillyflower,
    Rogue's Gillyflower, Night-scented Gillyflower.
Heuchera sanguinea—Coral Bells, Alum-root, Rock Geranium.
Hibiscus africanus—Black-eyed-beauty,* African Rose. [*H. Trionum*]
    Moschatus—Swamp Rose Mallow, Sea Hollyhock, Marsh Mallow, Mallow Rose.
    syriacus—Althaea, Syrian Mallow, Rose of Sharon.
    Trionum—Flower-of-an-hour, Venice Mallow, Good-night-at-nine, Bladder Ketmia, Modesty, Devil's-head-in-a-bush.
Hieracium aurantiacus—Orange or Tawny Hawk-weed, Hawk-bit, Devil's Paint Brush, Grim-the-colliar, Painter's Brush. [*H. aurantiacum*]
Hottonia palustris—Water Violet.
Houstonia caerulea—Bluets, Angel's-tears, Little-washer-women, Bright-eyes, Quaker Ladies,
    Quaker-bonnets, Nuns, Wild Forget-me-not. [*Hedyotis caerulea*]
Humulus—Hop.
Hyacinthus orientalis—Hyacinth, Jacinth.
Hypericum calycinum—St. John's-wort, Aaron's-beard, Rose-of-Sharon.
Hyssopus officinalis—Hyssop.
Iberis coronaria (I. amara coronaria)—Crown Candytuft. [*I. coronaria*]
    odorata—Fragrant Candytuft.
    sempervirens—Hardy Candytuft, Evergreen Candytuft.
Ilex Aquifolium—European Holly, Aunt Mary's Tree, He-holly, Crocodile, Prick-hollen.
    opaca—American Holly, White Holly, Winterberry.
    verticillata—Black or False Alder, Fever-bush, Winterberry.
Impatiens Balsamina—Balsam, Lady's-slipper.
Inula Helenium—Elecampane, Heal-all, Elf-dock, Horse-heal, Velvet-dock, Scabwort.
Ionopsidium acaule—Violet Cress.
Ipomoea grandiflora alba—Moonflower, Star-glory. [*I. alba*]
    imperialis (I. hederacea vars.)—Imperial Japanese Morning-glory. [*I. nil*]
Iris alata—Scorpion Iris. [*I. planifolia*]
    albicans—White Florentine. [*I. x albicans*]
    arenaria (I. flavissima)—Sand Iris.
    asiatica (I. pallida)—Asiatic Flag. [*I. pallida*]
    aurea—Golden Flag, Frilled Flag. [*I. crocea*]
    cristata—Crested Iris.
    florentina—Florentine Iris, White Flag, Sweet Flower-de-luce. [*I. x germanica var. florentina*]
    foetidissima—Gladwyn.
    fulva—Tawny Flag.
    germanica—German Flag. [*I. x germanica*]
    gigantea (I. orientalis)—Gold-banded Flag. [*I. orientalis*]
    graminea—Grass-leaved Flag.
    iberica—Iberian Flag.
    juncea—Rush-leaved Iris.

LATIN AND ENGLISH PLANT NAMES

Iris lacustis—Lake Iris.
    laevigata (syn. **Kaempferi**)—Japan Iris.
    lupina (**I. Saari**)—Wolf's-ear Iris. [*I. sari*]
    lurida—Mahogany Iris.
    missouriensis—Western Blue Flag.
    pallida—Great Blue Flag.
    pavonia—Peacock Iris. [*Moraea neopavonia*]
    persica—Persian Iris.
    Pseudacorus—Yellow Water Flag, Bastard Flag, Daggers, Jacob's Sword, Flagons, Yellow Water-skegs.
    pumila—Dwarf Iris.
    reticulata—Netted Iris.
    sambucina—Elder-scented Iris.
    sibirica—Siberian Iris.
    stylosa (**I. unguicularis**)—Algerian Iris. [*I. unguicularis*]
    susiana—Mourning Iris.
    tectorum—Japan Roof Iris.
    tuberosa—Snake's-head Iris. [*Hermodactylus tuberosus*]
    verna—Spring Iris.
    versicolor—Blue Flag, Wild Iris, Flag-lily, American Fleur-de-lis, Snake Flag.
    xiphioides—Spanish Iris.
    Xiphium—English Iris.
Itea virginica—Virginia Willow.
Jasione—Sheep Scabius.
Jasminum grandiflorum—Jasmine or Jessamy.
    nudiflorum—Naked Jasmine, Winter Stars.
    officinale—Common Sweet White Jasmine.
Jeffersonia diphylla—Twin-leaf.
Juniperus communis—Juniper Tree, Fairy Circle, Horse-savin.
    Sabina—Savin, Saving-tree, Cover-shame.
    virginiana—Red Cedar, Pencilwood.
Kalmia latifolia—Rose Laurel, Calico Bush, Broad-leaved Laurel, Spoonwood, Sheep-poison.
Kerria japonica—Jew's-mallow.
Kniphofia (syn. **Tritoma**)—Red-hot-poker, Devil's-poker, Torch Lily.
Kochia trichophylla—Summer Cypress, Belvedere, Mexican Fire-plant, Mock Cypress, Sunset Plant, Burning Bush. [*K. scoparia*]
Laburnum vulgare—Laburnum, Golden Chain or Rain, He-broom, False Ebony. [*L. anagyroides*]
Lamium maculatum—Dead or Blind Nettle, Babe-in-the-cradle, Suckie-Sue.
Lapageria—Napoleon's-bell.
Lathryus latifolius—Everlasting-pea.
    odoratus—Sweet Pea, Painted Lady.
    tuberosa—Garnet-flower,* Tuber Pea. [*L. tuberosus*]
Lavandula Spica—Spiked Lavender, Lavender-spike, French Lavender, Male-lavender. [*L. dentata*]
    Stoechas—Arabian Lavender, Sticadose, Cast-me-down, Lavender-gentle.
    vera—True Lavender. [*L. angustifolia var. angustifolia*]
Lavatera—Tree Mallow.
Layia elegans—Tidy-tips. [*L. platyglossa*]
Leiophyllum buxifolium—Sand Myrtle.
Leontopodium alpinum—Edelweiss.
Leptosiphon—(*See* Gilia).
Leptosyne maritima—Sea Dahlia, False Tidy-tips. [*Coreopsis maritima*]
Leucojum—Snowflake.
Leucothoë Catesbaei—Swamp Leucothe, White Osier, White Pepper, Dog Laurel, Branch Ivy. [*L. Fontanesiana*]
Levisticum—Lovage, Smellage, Smelling-root, Levorce.
Liatris pychnostachya—Kansas Gay-feather, Blazing Star, Sky-rockets.*
Ligustrum—Privet, Prim, Print, Skedge.
Lilium auratum—Gold-banded Lily.

LATIN AND ENGLISH PLANT NAMES

Lilium Brownii—Brown's Lily.
    canadense—Canada Lily, Nodding Lily, Meadow Lily.
    candidum—Madonna Lily, Juno's-rose, June Lily, Bourbon Lily.
    chalcedonicum—Scarlet Martagon.
    croceum—Herring Lily, Saffron Lily. [*L. bulbiferum var. croceum*]
    Martagon—Turk's-cap Lily.
    pardalinum—Panther Lily.
    Parryi—Lemon Lily.
    parvum—Small Tiger Lily.
    philadelphicum—Wood Lily, Huckleberry Lily, Flame Lily.
    pomponium—Scarlet Pompone.
    rubescens—Ruby Lily, Chaparral Lily.
    superbum—Turk's-cap Lily, Swamp Lily.
    tenuifolium—Coral Lily, Red Wax Lily.* [*L. pumilum*]
    testaceum—Nankeen Lily. [*L. x testaceum*]
    tigrinum—Tiger Lily.
    umbellatum—Nodding Lily, Western Red Lily. [*L. philadelphicum var. andinum*]
    Washingtonianum—Shasta Lily.
Limnanthes Douglasi—Marsh-flower, Pool-flower, Meadow Foam. [*L. Douglasii*]
    Douglasi alba—Evening Snow.
Linaria alpina—Alpine Toadflax.
    bipartita—Annual Heather.
    Cymbalaria—Ivy-leaved Toadflax, Kennelworth Ivy. [*Cymbalaria muralis*]
    dalmatica—Dalmatian Toadflax. [*L. genistifolia dalmatica*]
    vulgaris—Butter-and-eggs, Bread and Butter, Haycock, Impudent-lawyer, Dead-men's-bones, Bride-weed, Devil's-flax.
Linnaea borealis—Twin flower.
Linum alpinum—Mountain Flax. [*L. perenne alpinum*]
    flavum—Yellow Flax.
    grandiflorum—Wine-flower.*
    monogynum—New Zealand Flax.
    narbonense—Narbonne Flax.
    perenne—Blue Flax, Fairy Flax.
    salsoloides—White Rock Flax. [*L. suffruticosum salsoloides*]
    viscosum—Clammy Flax.
Liquidamber—Sweet-gum, Red-gum, Alligator Tree, Opossum Tree, Satin Walnut.
Liriodendron Tulipifera—Tulip Tree, Whitewood, Canoe-wood, Saddle-leaf, Blue Poplar, Yellow Poplar.
Lithospermum prostratum (L. fruticosum)—Creeping Gromwell. [*Lithodora diffusa*]
Loasia hispida—Chili Nettle. [*Loasa urens*]
Lobelia Cardinalis—Cardinal-flower, Red Lobelia, Red Betty, Slinkweed, Hog-physic.
    syphilitica—Great Lobelia, High-belia, Blue Lobelia. [*L. siphilitica*]
Lonicera fragrantissima—Twin-flowered Honeysuckle, Winter Honeysuckle.
    japonica—Japanese Honeysuckle, Silver-and-gold-vine.
    Periclymenum—Woodbine, English Honeysuckle, Twisted Eglantine, Suckling.
    sempervirens—Trumpet Honeysuckle, Coral Honeysuckle.
    tatarica—Tartarian, Garden, or Fly Honeysuckle.
Lotus corniculatus—Bird's-foot-trefoil, Crow-toe, Ground-Honeysuckle, Cat-in-clover, Jack-jump-about, Lady's-shoes-and-stockings.
Lunaria biennis—Honesty, Money-in-both-pockets, White Satin, Satin-pod, Monkey-flower, Penny-flower, Lunary, Gold-and-silver, Matrimony. [*L. annua*]
Lupinus—Lupine, Old-maid's-sunbonnets, Quaker-bonnets, Sundial plant.
Lychnis alba—White Campion, Thunder-flower, White Cuckoo-flower, White Robin. [*Silene alba*]
    alpina—Alpine Campion, Rock Lychnis.
    chalcedonica—Scarlet Lightning, Campion-of-Constantinople, Jerusalem Cross, Nonesuch, Fire-balls, Mock–Sweet William, Flower of Bristol.
    Coronaria—Rose Campion or Champion, Crowned Campion, Gardener's Eye, Pink Mullein, Dusty Miller. (*See* Agrostemma).
    Flos-cuculi—Cuckoo flower, Indian Pink, Cuckoo Gillyflower, Meadow Campion, Ragged Jack, Ragged Robin, Wild Williams.

LATIN AND ENGLISH PLANT NAMES

Lychnis Flos-Jovis—Flower-of-Jove, Jove's Campion.
  Viscaria—Clammy Lychnis, German Catchfly.
Lycium chinense—Matrimony Vine, Bastard Jasmine, Boxthorn, Duke-of-Argyll's-tea-tree.
Lysimachia Nummularia—Moneywort, Creeping Loosestrife, Creeping Jenny, Down-hill-of-life, Herb Twopence, Meadow-runnegates, Strings-of-sovereigns, Wandering-sailor, Creeping Charlie, Yellow Myrtle.
  vulgaris—Common Loosestrife, Yellow Willow-herb, Yellow Myrtle.
Lythrum Salicaria—Rose Loosestrife, Red Sally, Long-purples, Rainbow-weed, Purple-grass, Milk Willow-herb, Sage Willow, Trooper's Feather.
Magnolia conspicua—Yulan magnolia. [*M. heptapeta*]
  glauca—Swamp Bay, Sweet Magnolia, Beaver Tree, Holly Bay, Elk-bark. [*M. virginiana*]
  stellata (M. Halleana)—Star magnolia.
Malcomia elegans—Virginia Stock. [*M. maritima*]
Malva moschata—Musk Mallow.
Malvastrum—False Mallow, Rock Mallow.
Marrubium vulgare—Horehound.
Matricaria—Balderbrae, Corn Feverfew.
Matthiola annua—Ten-weeks'-stock, Stock Gillyflower. [*M. incanna 'annua'*]
  bicornis—Night-scented Stock. [*M. longipetala bicornis*]
  incana—Brompton Stock, Queen's Stock.
Meconopsis cambrica—Welsh Poppy.
  heterophylla—Flaming Poppy, Blood-drops, Wind Poppy. [*Stylomecon heterophylla*]
  Wallichii—Satin Poppywort, Blue Poppy. [*M. napaulensis*]
Melilotus alba—White Meliot, Honey Lotus, Sweet Lucern.
Melissa officinalis—Balm, Sweet Mary, Lemon Balm, Cure-all, Honey-plant, Lemon Lobelia.
Mentha piperita—Peppermint, Brandy Mint, Lamb Mint. [*M. x piperita*]
  Requini—Corsican Mint. [*M. Requienii*]
  rotundifolia—Round-leaved or Apple Mint, Patagonia Mint. [*M. x rotundifolia*]
  spicata—Spearmint, Heart Mint, Mackerel Mint, Our Lady's Mint.
  viridis—Spearmint. [*M. spicata*]
Mentzelia Lindleyi—Evening Star.
Mertensia virginica—Virginia Cowslip, Roanoke Bells, Virginia Lungwort.
Mesembryanthemum—Fig-Marigold, Ice-plant.
Michauxia campanuloides—Michaux's Bellflowers. [*Mindium campanuloides*]
Mimulus moschatus—Musk, Vegetable Musk, Monkey-flower.
Mina lobata—Mexican Morning Glory.
Mirabilis Jalapa—Marvel-of-Peru, Four-o'clock, Jalap, Belle de nuit, World's Wonder, Good-afternoon-Ladies.
Mitchella repens—Partridge Berry, Twin-berry, Squaw-vine, Wild running-box, Checker-berry, Winter-Clover, Squaw-plum.
Monarda didyma—Bergamot, Bee-balm, Crown-flower,* Sweet Mary, Indian's-plume.
Morina longifolia—Whorl-flower.
Muscari botryoides—Grape Hyacinth, Jacinth, Pearls of Spain (White variety).
  comosum—Feathered Hyacinth, Purple Tassels, Purse-tassels, Tuzzie-muzzie.
  moschatum—Musk Hyacinth. [*M. racemosum*]
  racemosum—Starch Hyacinth.
Myosotidium nobile—Chatham Island Forget-me-not, Antarctic Forget-me-not. [*M. Hortensia*]
Myosotis alpestris—Alpine Forget-me-not.
  palustris—Common Forget-me-not, Mouse-ear, Love-me, Scorpion-grass. [*M. scorpioides*]
  sylvatica—Wood Forget-me-not.
Myrica cerifera—Bay-berry, Candle-berry, Wax-berry, Tallow Shrub.
  Gale—Sweet Gale, Burren Myrtle, Devonshire Myrtle.
Myrrhis odorata—Sweet Cicily, Sweet Angelica, Spanish Chervil.
Narcissus—Daffodil, Daffy-down-dilly, Lent Lily, Chalice flower, Easter Lily, Yellow Crow-bells, Queen Ann's Daffodil, Saffron Lily, Affodil, Glen.
  albicans moschatus (N. Pseudo-Narcissus var.)—White Musk Daffodil. [*N. Pseudonarcissus abscissus*]
  biflorus—Primrose Peerless. [*N. x medioluteus*]
  Bulbocodium—Hoop-petticoat Daffodil.

LATIN AND ENGLISH PLANT NAMES

Narcissus Burbidgei—Dolly-cup Narcissus. [*N. x Barrii*]
    Campernelli (N. odorus)—Campernelle. [*N. x odorus*]
    cyclamineus—Cyclamen Daffodil.
    incomparabilis albus plenus—Orange Phoenix. [*N. x incomparabilis 'Orange Phoenix'*]
    incomparabilis aurantius plenus—Butter and Eggs. [*N. x incomparabilis var. plenus*]
    incomparabilis aurantius plenus luteus—Eggs and Bacon. [*N. x incomparabilis aurantius 'Eggs and Bacon'*]
    incomparabilis plenus sulphureus—Codlins and Cream, Sulphur Phoenix.
    Jonquilla—Jonquil, Yellow Jack.
    juncifolius—Rush-leaved Daffodil.
    Leedsii—Silver-winged or Star Daffodils, Eucharis-flowered. [*N. x incomparabilis*]
    moschatus—Musk Daffodil.
    obvallaris (N. Pseudo-Narcissus var.)—Tenby Daffodil.
    odorus—Sweet Campernel. [*N. x odorus*]
    odorus minor plenus—Queen Ann's Double Daffodil. [*N. eystettensis*]
    odorus plenus—Double Campernel. [*N. o. 'Plenus'*]
    poeticus—Poet's Daffodil, Sweet Nancy, Rose-of-May.
    poeticus albus plenus odoratus—Gardenia-flowered. [*N. poeticus 'Albus Plenus Odoratus'*]
    poeticus recurvus—Pheasant's Eye.
    Pseudo-Narcissus—English Daffodil, Lent Lily. [*N. Pseudonarcissus*]
    Pseudo-Narcissus plenissimus—Parkinson's Rose-flowered Daffodil. [*N. P. 'Major Plenissimus'*]
    Pseudo-Narcissus scotius plenus—Double Scotch Garland Lily. [*N. P. 'Scoticus Plenus'*]
    Tazetta—Bunch-flowered or Polyanthus Narcissus.
    triandus albus—Angel's Tears, Gannymede's Cap.
Nemophila insignis—Love-grove, Baby-blue-eyes, California Bluebell, Baby's Eyes. [*N. Menziesii*]
Nepeta Mussini—Cat-mint.
Nicotiana affinis—Sweet White Tobacco. [*N. alata*]
Nierembergia rivularis—Cup-flower, White Cup. [*N. repens*]
Nigella damascena—Love-in-a-mist, Devil-in-a-bush, St. Katherine's Wheel, Fennel-flower, Jack-in-prison, Lady-in-a-bower, Ragged Lady, Bishop's-wort, Love-in-a-puzzle, Prick-my-nose.
    sativa—Black Cumin, Roman Coriander, Nutmeg-flower, Fitch.
Nolana—Chilian Bellflower.
Notospartium—New Zealand Pine Broom.
Nymphaea alba—Water Lily, Pond Lily.
Nyssa sylvatica—Pepperidge, Sour-gum, Tupelo, Hornpipe, Swamp Hornbeam.
Ocimum Basilicum—Basil.
Oenothera biennis—Common Evening primrose, Sun-cups.
    Youngii—California Primrose. [*O. tetragona*]
Omphalodes linifolia—Venus' Navelwort.
    verna—Spring, Navelwort, Creeping Forget-me-not.
Ononis arvensis—Rest-harrow, Cammock-whin, Ground-furze, Steadfast, Sit-fast, Stay-plow. [*O. spinosa*]
Onopordon—Cotton Thistle.
Onosma taurica—Golden-drop. [*O. tauricum*]
Opuntia vulgaris—Prickly Pear, Indian Fig, Barbary Fig.
Orchis mascula—Adam-and-Eve, Male-orchis, Bloody-butcher, Dead-men's-fingers, Kettle-case, Dog-stones, Gander-goose, Gramfer-gray-legs, Soldier's Jacket, Spree-springle.
    morio—Goose-and-Goslins, Meadow Orchis.
Origanum vulgare—Sweet Marjoram, Mountain Mint, Wind Marjoram.
Ornithogalum umbellatum—Star-of-Bethlehem, Eleven-o'clock-lady, Ten-o'clock, Sleepy Dick, Nap-at-noon, John-go-to-bed-at-noon.
Orobus vernus—Spring Bitter-veitch. [*Lathyrus vernus*]
Orontium aquaticum—Golden Club, Tuckahoe, Water-dock.
Osmunda cinnamomea—Cinnamon Fern, Fiddle-heads, Swamp-brake, Bread-root.
    regalis—Royal Fern, Ditch Fern, Regal Fern.
Oxalis—Wood Sorrel, Sleeping Clover, Cuckoo-sour, Alleluia, Wood-sour, Gowk's Clover, Green-sauce, Sleeping-beauty.

LATIN AND ENGLISH PLANT NAMES

Pachysandra terminalis—Mountain Spurge.
Paeonia—Peony, Piny, Cheeses, Vinegar Rose.
Papaver alpinum—Alpine Poppy.
    glaucum—Tulip Poppy.
    nudicaule—Iceland Poppy.
    orientale—Oriental Poppy.
    pavonia—Peacock Poppy.
    Rhoeas—Corn Poppy, Field Poppy, Corn or Copper Rose, Cheese-bowl, Headaches, Thunder-flower.
    rupifragum—Apricot Poppy, Spanish Poppy.*
    somniferum—Opium Poppy, Joan-silver-pin, Marble-flower.
Parnassia palustris—Grass of Parnassus, White Butter-cup.
Parthenacissus (*See* Ampelopsis).
Passiflora—Passion Flower.
Pedicularis—Lousewort, Beefsteak Plant, Wood Betony.
Pentstemon barbatus—Scarlet Beard-tongue, Scarlet Bugler.
    Digitalis—False Fox-glove.
Periploca—Silk-vine, Climbing Dogbane.
Perovskia atriplicifolia—Silver Sage.
Persica—Peach. [*Prunus Persica*]
Petasites fragrans—Winter Heliotrope, Butterfly-dock, Pestilence Weed, Oxwort, Butter-burr.
Petrocallis pyrenaica—Rock Beauty.
Phacelia campanularia—Wild Canterbury Bell, Wild Heliotrope.
Phalaris arundinacea—Ribbon Grass, Gardener's Garters, Striped Grass, Daggers, Ladies' Laces, Brides'-laces, London Lace.
Philadelphus—Mock-orange.
Phlomis fruticosa—Jerusalem Sage, Sage-leaf Mullein.
    lychnitis—Lamp-wick.
Phlox bryoides—Moss Phlox.
    divaricata—Wild Sweet William.
    Douglasii—Alpine Phlox.
    Drummondii—Drummond's Phlox.
    maculata—Wild Sweet William.
    subulata—Moss Pink, Flowering Moss, Wild or Ground Pink, Creeping Phlox, Grave-yard plant.*
Phormium tenax—Flax Lily, New Zealand Flax.
Physalis peruvianum—Chinese-lantern Plant, Strawberry-Tomato, Cape Gooseberry. [*P. peruviana*]
Physostegia virginiana—False-dragon's-head, Obedient-plant.
Picea (Abies)—Spruce-fir, Gallipot Tree, Mast Tree. [*P. Abies*]
    canadensis—White Spruce, Pine, Cat, or Skunk Spruce. [*P. glauca*]
    mariana—Blue Spruce, Spruce-gum Tree, He-balsam.
Pieris mariana—Stagger-bush. [*Lyonia mariana*]
Pimpinella Anisum—Garden Anise, Sweet Anny.
    Saxifraga—Bennet, Burnet Saxifrage, Break-stone, Old-man's Plaything. [*S. major*]
Pinus Cembra—Swiss Stone Pine.
    palustris—Georgia Pine, Long-leaved Pine, Yellow Pine, Yellow Jack.
    rigida—Pitch Pine, Sap-pine, Candlewood, Torch-pine, Light-wood.
    Strobus—White Pine, Deal Pine, Weymouth Pine.
    sylvestris—Scotch Pine, Red Deal.
    Taeda—Loblolly Pine, Old Field Pine, Longshucks and Bastard, Foxtail, Virginia, Swamp, Indian, and Rosemary Pine.
Platanus acerifolia—London Plane Tree. [*P. x acerifolia*]
    occidentalis—Button Ball, Button Wood, False Sycamore, American Plane Tree.
Platycodon grandiflorum—Chinese Bellflower, Balloon-flower. [*P. grandiflorus*]
Platystemon californica—Cream-cups. [*P. californicus*]
Plumbago Larpentae—Leadwort. [*Ceratostigma plumbaginoides*]
Podophyllum—Duck's Foot, Wild Mandrake, May-apple.
Pogonia ophioglossoides—Rose Pogonia, Snake-mouth.
Polemonium caeruleum—Greek Valerian, Jacob's Ladder, Charity, Ladders-to-heaven, Makebale.

LATIN AND ENGLISH PLANT NAMES

Polemonium reptans—Creeping Valerian, Abscess-root, Sweet-root, Blue-eyed Susan.
Polianthes tuberosa—Tuberose, Funeral Flower.
Polygala paucifolia—Milkwort, Gay-wings, Babies' Slippers, Indian Pink, Flowering Winter-green.
    polygama—Bitter Milkwort.
Polygonatum biflorum—Solomon's Seal.
Polygonum—Knotweed.
    cuspidatum—Japanese Knotweed.
    orientale—Persicary.
Polypodium vulgare—Polypody, Fever Fern, Ever Fern, Moss Fern, Golden-locks, Wall Fern.
Pontederia cordata—Pickerel Weed.
Populus alba—White or Silver Poplar, Dutch Beech.
    deltoides—Cottonwood, Necklace Poplar, Alamo.
    tremuloides—American Aspen, Mountain Ash, Quiver-leaf, Auld-Wive's Tongues.
Portulaca grandiflora—Sunplant, French or Garden Purslane, Wax Pink, Mexican Rose, Kentucky Moss.
Potentilla fruticosa—Hardhack, Prairie-weed, Shrubby Potentilla.
    Other names applied to various species—Cinquefoil, Barren Strawberry, Silverweed, Silver-feather, Tormintilla, Running Buttercup, Five-finger.
Poterium Sanguisorba—Salad Burnet.
Primula acaulis—Stemless Primrose. [*P. vulgaris*]
    amoena—Caucasian Primrose.
    Auricula—Auricula, Bear's Ear, French Cowslip, Tanner's Apron.
    denticulata—Toothed Primrose.
    elatior—Oxlip, Great Cowslip, Paigles.
    farinosa—Mealy Primrose, Bird's-eye, Scotch Primrose, Bonny-bird-een, Powdered-beau.
    japonica—Japanese Primrose.
    officinalis—Cowslip, Petty-mullen, Culverkeys, Herb Peter, Palsey-wort, Key-flower. [*P. veris*]
Prunus americana—Wild Red Plum.
    Amygdalus (syn. **Amygdalus communis**)—Almond. [*P. dulcis*]
    angustifolia—Chicksaw Plum.
    avium—Mazzard, Gean.
    Cerasus—Morello Cherry.
    domestica—Green Gage.
    japonica—Japanese Cherry.
    maritima—Beach Plum.
    Mume—Japanese Apricot.
    nigra—Canada Plum.
    Padus—Bird Cherry.
    pendula—Rose-bud Cherry. [*a listed name of no botanical standing*]
    persica fl. pl.—Rose-flowered Peach. [*one of many double-flowered cultivars*]
    Pissardi—Purple-leaved Plum. [*P. cerasifera 'Atropurpurea'*]
    serotina—Rum Cherry, Wild Black Cherry.
    spinosa—Sloe, Black-thorn.
    triloba—Rosette Plum.
    virginiana—Choke Cherry, Wild Cherry.
Pulmonaria angustifolia—Blue Cowslip.
    officinalis—Lungwort, Jerusalem Cowslip, Spotted-Mary, Beggar's-basket, Joseph-and-Mary, Bedlam Cowslip, Spotted Comfrey, Virgin Mary's Honeysuckle, Sage-of-Bethlehem.
Puschkinia scilloides—Striped Squill.
Pyracantha coecinea or Lolaude—Fire-thorn, Evergreen Thorn. [*P. coccinea*]
Pyrethrum aureum—Golden Feather. [*Chrysanthemum Parthenium 'Aureum'*]
    hybridum—Painted Feverfew, Painted Daisies. [*Chrysanthemum coccineum*]
    Tchihatchewii—Turfing Daisy. [*Tripleurospermum Tchihatchewii*]
    uliginosum—Great Daisy. [*Chrysanthemum serotinum*]
Pyrola rotundifolia—Shin-leaf, False Wintergreen, Consumption-weed, Canker Lettuce.
Pyrus Aucuparia—Mountain Ash, Rowan. [*Sorbus Aucuparia*]
    baccata—Siberian Crab. [*Malus baccata*]

LATIN AND ENGLISH PLANT NAMES

Pyrus coronaria—Garland Crab, American Sweet-scented Crab. [*Malus coronaria*]
    floribunda—Japanese Crab-apple. [*Malus floribunda*]
    Malus—Crab-apple, Hedgeapple, Scrog. [*Malus sylvestris*]
    Malus praecox—Paradise Crab. [*Malus pumila paradisiaca*]
    Malus sempervirens—Evergreen Crab. [*Malus angustifolia*]
Pyxidanthera barbulata—Pine-barren-beauty, Flowering Moss, Pyxie Moss.
Quercus acuminata—Chestnut Oak, Chinquapin. [*Q. Muehlenbergii*]
    alba—White or Turkey Oak.
    robur—English Oak, Gospel Tree, Female Oak.
    virginiana—Live Oak.
Ramondia pyrenaica—Rosette Mullein. [*Ramonda Myconi*]
Ranunculus aconitifolius—Fair-maids-of-France.
    aconitifolius alba—White Bachelor's-buttons.
    acris—Meadow Buttercup, Crazies, Gold-knops, Locket-gowan, Guilty-cup, Meadow-gowans.
    alpestris—Alpine Buttercup.
    amplexicaulis—White Buttercup.
    arvensis—Devil's Claws, Goldweed, Corn-crowfoot.
    bulbosus—St. Anthony's Turnip, Bulbous Buttercup, Frogwort, Gill-cup, Meadow-bloom.
    Ficaria—Pilewort.
    Lyalli—Rockwood Lily.
    monspeliacus—Montpelier Buttercup.
    repens—Creeping Crowfoot, Granny-threads, Meg-many-feet, Hod-the-rake, Lantern-leaves, Devil's Guts, Tether-toad.
Reseda odorata—Mignonette, Frenchman's Darling.
Rhamnus—Buckthorn.
Rhexia virginica—Deer-grass, Meadow Beauty, Handsome-Harry.
Rhodanthe—Swan-river Everlasting. [*Helipterum*]
Rhododendron catawbiense—Rose Bay, Catawba Rhododendron.
    chrysanthemum—Siberian Rhododendron, Siberian Rose, Snow Rose, Yellow Rhododendron. [*R. chrysanthum*]
    indicum—Indian Azalea.
    maximum—Wild Rose Bay, Great Laurel, Spoon-hutch.
Rhodora canadensis—May Pink, Lamb-kill. [*Rhododendron canadense*]
Rhodotypus kerrioides—White Jew's Mallow. [*R. scandens*]
Rhus aromatica—Fragrant Sumach, Squaw-berry.
    coriaria—European Sumach, Tanner's-bush.
    cotinoides (Cotinus americanus)—American Smoke Tree, Chittam Wood. [*Cotinus obovatus*]
    Cotinus (Cotinus Coggygria)—Smoke Tree, Wild Olive, Venetian Sumach. [*Cotinus Coggygria*]
    hirta—Stag-horn Sumach. [*Rhus typhina*]
    Toxicodendron—Poison Ivy, Black Mercury, Poison Oak.
    typhina—Stag-horn Sumach.
Ribes aureum—Buffalo Currant, Flowering or Clove Currant.
    nigrum—Black Currant, Squinancy-berry, Quinsy-berry.
    rubrum—Northern Red Currant, Garnet-berry, Gazle-berry.
Ricinus communis—Castor Oil Plant, Palma-Christi, Man's Motherwort, Stedfast, Oil Nut.
Robinia hispida—Rose acacia, Moss Locust.
    Pseudacacia—Honey Locust, Bastard acacia, Silver-chain, Yellow or Black Locust.
Roemeria hybrida—Purple Horned Poppy, Wind Rose.
Romneya Coulteri—California Tree Poppy, Mitilija Poppy, Mission Poppy.
Rosa alba—Single White Rose, Blush Rose. [*R. x alba*]
    alpina—Alpine Rose. [*R. pendulina*]
    arvensis—Field Rose, Ayrshire Rose.
    Banksiae—Banksian Rose.
    blanda—Smooth Rose, Swamp Rose.
    bourbonica—Bourbon Rose. [*R. x borboniana*]
    bracteata—McKartney Rose.
    Brunonii—White Indian Rose.

LATIN AND ENGLISH PLANT NAMES

Rosa canina—Dog Rose, Canker-bloom, Cat-whin, Hip-brier, Brier-rose, Soldier's or Lawyer's Rose, Wild-brier.
carolina—Carolina Swamp Rose or Hip Tree.
centifolia—Hundred-leaved Rose, Cabbage Rose, Provence Rose, Provins Rose.
cinnamomea—Cinnamon Rose.
damascena—Damask Rose, Patience Rose. [*R. x damascena*]
damascena variagata—York and Lancaster Rose. [*R x damascena versicolor*]
Eglanteria (R. rubiginosa)—Eglantine, Sweet Brier, Kitchen Rose.
Fortuneana—Fortune's Yellow Rose, Yellow Wreath Rose. [*R. chinensis 'Fortune's Double Yellow'*]
gallica—French Rose, Provins Rose, Red Rose, Dutch Rose.
gallica muscosa—Moss Rose. [*R. x centrifolia 'Moscosa'*]
gallica pomponia—Pompon or Miniature Rose. [*R. x centrifolia 'Pomponia'*]
humilis—Pastures Rose, Low Wild Rose. [*R. carolina*]
indica—China or Monthly Rose, Indian Rose.
indica fragrans—Tea Rose.
indica minima—Fairy Rose.
indica sanguinea—Crimson China Rose.
laevigata—Cherokee Rose, Jamaica Buckthorn.
Lawrenceana—Miss Lawrence's Rose. [*R. chinensis minima*]
lucida—Dwarf Wild Rose. [*R. virginiana*]
lutea (R. foetida)—Austrian Yellow Brier. [*R. foetida*]
lutea bicolor—Austrian Copper Rose. [*R. foetida 'bicolor'*]
moschata—Musk Rose.
multiflora—Chinese Many-flowered Rose.
multiflora Grevillei—Seven-sisters Rose.
nitida—Shining Rose, North-western Rose.
Noisettiana—Noisette Rose. [*R. x Noisettiana*]
rugosa—Japanese Rose.
setegera—Prairie Rose, Michigan Rose. [*R. setigera*]
spinossissima—Scotch Rose, Burnet Rose. [*R. spinossissima*]
spinossissima Harrisonii—Harrison's Yellow Rose. [*R. x harisonii*]
spinossissima lutea—Persian Yellow Rose.
Wichuraiana—Japanese Trailing Rose.
Rosmarinus officinalis—Rosemary.
Rubus caesius—Dew-berry, Black-berry-token, Blue Bramble.
canadensis—Low Black-berry, Dew-berry.
chamoemorus—Cloud Berry, Ground Mulberry, Averine, Noops, Baked-apple-berry. [*R. Chamaemorus*]
deliciosus—Rocky Mountain Bramble.
idaeus—European Raspberry, Sivven, Hain or Hind-berry.
laciniatus—Cat-leaved Bramble.
odoratus—Flowering Raspberry, Purple- or Rose-flowering Raspberry.
parviflorus—Small-leaved Thimble-berry.
spectabilis—Salmon Berry.
Rudbeckia—Cone-flower.
Ruta graveolens—Rue, Herb-o'-grace, Herb Repentance, Countryman's Treacle.
Sabbatia angularis—New England Pink, Bitter-bloom, American Centaury, Pink Bloom, The Rose of Plymouth. [*Sabatia angularis*]
Sagina glabra—Pearlwort, Make-beggar.
Sagittaria—Arrow-head.
Salix alba—Common European Willow, Duck Willow.
alba argentea—Silver Willow.
alba vitellina—Golden Willow, Golden Osier.
babylonica—Weeping Willow, Ring Willow.
discolor—Pussy Willow.
Salpiglossis sinuata—Painted Tongue.
Salvia fulgens—Scarlet Sage.
Greggii—Rosemary Sage.
Horminum—Horminum Clary Red-top, Purple-top. [*S. viridis*]

LATIN AND ENGLISH PLANT NAMES

Salvia officinalis—Garden Sage, Save.
   pratensis—Meadow Sage.
   Sclarea—Clary, Oculus Christi, See-bright, Godes-eie.
Sambucus canadensis—American Elder, Sweet Elder.
   nigra—European Elder, Aldern, Hilder Bore-tree.
   racemosa—Red-berried Elder, Scarlet Elder.
Sanguinaria canadensis—Blood-root, Red Puccoon, Sweet Slumber, Coon-root.
Santolina incana—Lavender Cotton, Yellow-buttons.* [*S. Chamaecyparissus*]
Sanvitalia procumbens—Thirst-plant.
Saponaria Ocymoides—Prostrate Soapwort.
   officinalis—Bouncing Bet, Bruisewort, Soapwort, Chimney Pink, Boston Pink, Old-maid's
      Pink, Fuller's Herb, Latherwort, Sweet Betty, Mock Gilliflower, Lady-by-the-Gate,
      World's Wonder, Crow-soap, Dusty Lady.
   vaccaria—Cow-herb. [*Vaccaria pyramidata*]
Sassafras—Sassafras Tree, Ague Tree.
Satureia montana—Winter Savory. [*Satureja montana*]
   hortensis—Summer Savory. [*Satureja hortensis*]
Saxifraga granulata—Meadow Saxifrage.
   hypnoides—Dovedale Moss.
   pellata—Umbrella Plant. [*Peltiphyllum peltatum*]
   sarmentosa—Beefsteak or Strawberry Geranium, Aaron's Beard, Creeping Sailor, Humil-
      ity, Mother-of-thousands, Old-man's-beard, Pedler's Basket, Poor-man's-geranium,
      Roving Jenny, Thread-of-life. [*S. stolonifera*]
   umbrosa—London Pride, St. Patrick's Cabbage, None-so-pretty, Sweet Nancy, Pratling
      Parnell, Prince's Feather.
   virginiensis—Early Saxifrage, Sweet Wilson, Mountain Lettuce.
Scabiosa atropurpurea—Sweet Scabious, Pincushion Flower, Mournful Widow, Egyptian Rose,
   Mourning Bride.
Schizanthus—Butterfly Flower, Fringe Flower.
Scilla amoena—Star Hyacinth, Star Squill.
   bifolia—Two-leaved Squill.
   festalis—Bluebell, Hair-bell, Bell-bottle, Crow-leek, Crow-bell, Wild Hyacinth, Wood
      Hyacinth. [*Endymion non-scriptus*]
   hispanica—Spanish Squill. [*Endymion hispanicus*]
   nutans—Nodding Hyacinth. [*Endymion non-scriptus*]
   siberica—Star Hyacinth.
   verna—Sea Onion.
Scutellaria baicalensis—Skull-cap, Blue Pimpernel, Mad-dog.
Sedum acre—Biting Stonecrop, Bird's Bread, Creeping Charlie, Gold-chain, Wall-pepper, Gold
      Moss or Dust, Creeping Jack, Jack-o'-the-buttery, Love-entangle, Poor-man's-pepper,
      Prick-madam, Kit-o'-the-wall, Stonnard, Treasure-of-love, Tangletail, Trip-madam.
   album—Wormgrass, White Stonecrop.
   Anacampseros—Herb-of-friendship, Evergreen Orpine.
   coeruleum—Blue Stonecrop or Wall Pepper. [*S. caeruleum*]
   kamtschaticum—Orange Stonecrop.
   pulchellum—Widow's-cross, Rock Moss, Bird's-foot Stonecrop.
   reflexum—Stone Orpine.
   roseum—Rose Root, Snowdon Rose. [*S. Rosea*]
   rupestre—Jealousy-root, Rock Stonecrop.
   Sieboldii—Japanese Stonecrop, Constancy, Lover's Wreath.
   spectabile—Showy Stonecrop.
   stoloniferum—Crimson Stonecrop.
   Telephium—Orpine, Orphan-John, Bag-leaves, Midsummer-men, Witches-Money-bags,
      Life-of-man, Solomon's Puzzles, Live-forever, Frog's Bladder.
   telephoides—Wild Live-forever, American Orpine, Sweetheart. [*S. telephioides*]
Sempervivum arachnoideum—Cobweb Houseleek.
   globiferum—Hen-and-chickens. [*S. montanum*]
   tectorum—Houseleek, Homewort, Hockerie-top-ner, Jupiter's Beard, Thunder plant.
   triste—Red-leaved Stonecrop. [*S. tectorum*]
Senecio clivorum—Groundsel. [*Ligularia dentata*]

LATIN AND ENGLISH PLANT NAMES

Senecio elegans—Flower of St. James, Jacobea.
Silene acaulis—Moss Campion, Cushion Pink.
    alba—White Campion.
    alpestris—Alpine Catchfly. [*S. quadrifida*]
    Armeria—Sweet-William, Catch-fly, Dwarf or French Pink, Mice-pink, Sweet Susan,
        Pretty Pink, Wax-plant, Old Maid's Pink, Pretty Nancy, None-so-pretty.
    californica—Indian Pink.
    Hookeri—Hooker's Catchfly.
    laciniata—The Indian Pink.
    latifolia (syn. **Cucubalus**)—Bladder Campion. [*S. vulgaris*]
    maritima—Witches Thimbles, Sea Catchfly, Cliff Rose. [*S. vulgaris maritima*]
    pennsylvanica—Wild Pink. [*S. carolina pennsylvanica*]
    stellata—Starry Campion.
    virginica—Fire Pink, Wild Pink.
    vulgaris—Bladder Campion, Maiden's Tears, Frothy Poppy.
Sisyrinchium grandiflorum—Satin Flower. [*S. Douglassii*]
Solanum—Nightshade.
Soldanella alpina—Blue Moonwort.
Solidago—Golden Rod.
Sparaxis—African Harlequin Flower.
Spartium junceum—Spanish Broom.
Spigelia marilandica—Pink-root, Indian Pink, Star Bloom, Worm-grass, Maryland Pink.
Spiraea Aruncus (Aruncus sylvester)—Goat's-beard. [*Aruncus sylvester*]
    Filipendula (Filipendula hexapetala)—Dropwort. [*Filipendula vulgaris*]
    prunifolia—Bridal-wreath, May-wreath, St. Peter's-Wreath, Italian May.
    salicifolia—Queen-of-the-meadow.
    tomentosa—Steeple Bush, Hard-hack, Rosy-bush, Poor-man's-Soap, Queen's Needlework.
    Ulmaria (Filipendula Ulmaria)—Meadow-sweet. [*Filipendula Ulmaria*]
Stachys corsica—Corsican Woundwort.
    lanata—Woundwort, Lamb's-tongue, Hedge Nettle, Savior's Blanket. [*S. byzantina*]
Staphylea—Bladder Nut.
Statice incana—Sea-lavender. [*Gonolium callicomum*]
    latifolia—Great Sea Lavender. [*Limonium latifolia*]
Stellaria Holostea—Stitchwort, Star Flower, Easter Bell.
Sternbergia lutea—Lily-of-the-field, Autumn Daffodil.
Stipa pennata—Feather Grass.
Stokesia cyanea (syn. **S. laevis**)—Stokes' Aster. [*S. laevis*]
Styrax—Storax.
Symphoricarpos orbiculatus (S. vulgaris)—Indian Currant, Coral Berry.
    racemosus—Snowberry. [*S. albus*]
Symphytum officinale—Comfrey, Knit-back, Backwort, Ass-ear, Consound, Slippery-root.
Syringa chinensis (S. rothamagensis)—Rouen Lilac. [*S. x chinensis*]
    Josikaea—Hungarian Lilac.
    persica—Persian Lilac. [*S. x persica*]
    vulgaris—Common Lilac, Laylock, Blue-pipe Tree.
Tagetes erecta—African Marigold, Turkey Gilliflower, African Tansy, Flos Africanus.
    patula—French Marigold, Velvet Flower, Brown-buttons.
Tamarix—Tamarisk.
Tanacetum vulgare—Tansy, Bitter Buttons, Parsley-fern, English Cost.
Taxodium—Cypress.
Taxus baccata—English Yew, Chinwood, Wire-thorn.
    baccata fastigiata—Irish Yew.
Tecoma—(*See* Campsis).
Telanthera—Joy-weed. [*Alternanthera*]
Teucrium Botrys—Jerusalem Oak.
    Chamaedrys—Germander.
    Polium—Poly Germander.
    Scorodonia—Wood Sage.
Thalictrum adiantifolium—Fern-leaved Meadow-rue.
    anemonoides (Syndesmon)—Rue Anemone. [*Anemonella thalictroides*]

LATIN AND ENGLISH PLANT NAMES

Thalictrum aquilegifolium—Columbine-leaved Meadow-rue, Maid-of-the-Mist.
    dioicum—Early Meadow-rue, Feathered Columbine, Quick-silver-weed, Shining Grass.
    flavum—Fen-rue, Common Yellow Meadow-rue, Maiden-hair-rue, False or Monk's
      Rhubarb.
    glaucum—Spanish Tuft, Yellow Feathers.* [*T. speciosissimum*]
    minus—Dwarf Meadow Rue, Baby Meadow-rue.*
Thermopsis caroliniana—False Lupine.
Thuya occidentalis—Arbor-vitae, White Cedar, Feather-leaf, Indian Feather-leaf. [*Thuja occi-
    dentalis*]
    orientalis—Chinese Arbor-vitae. [*Platycladus orientalis*]
    plicata—Red or Canoe Cedar. [*Thuja plicata*]
Thymus Serpyllum—Wild Thyme, Creeping, Bank, or Running Thyme, Shepherd's Thyme,
    Mother-of-Thyme, Hill-Thyme, Brotherwort, Pellamountain, Pennymountain.
    Serpyllum albus—White-flowered Thyme. [*T. S. 'Albus'*]
    Serpyllum citriodorus—Lemon Thyme, Lemon-scented Thyme. [*T. x citriodorus*]
    Serpyllum citriodorus argentia-marginata—Silver Thyme. [*T. x c. 'Argenteus'*]
    Serpyllum citriodorus aurea-marginata—Golden Thyme. [*T. x c. 'Aureus'*]
    Serpyllum coccineus—Crimson Thyme. [*T. praecox arcticus coccineus*]
    Serpyllum lanuginosus—Woolly Thyme. [*T. pseudolanuginosus*]
    vulgaris—Garden Thyme, Common Thyme.
Tiarella cordifolia—Foam-flower, Coolwort, False-mitrewort, Gem-fruit.
Tigridia Pavonia—Peacock Tiger Iris, Tiger-flower, Shell-flower.
Tilia americana—American Linden, Bass-wood, White-wood, Black Lime-tree, Bast-tree, Bee-
    tree, Daddy-nut-tree, Monkey-nut-tree, Whistle-wood, Wickup.
    argentea (syn. **tomentosa**)—White Lime. [*T. tomentosa*]
    europaea (**T. vulgaris**) (**T. platyphyllos**)—European Linden, Lime Tree, Till-tree, Bast-
    tree. [*T. x europea*]
    vulgaris—Common Lime. [*T. x europea*]
Townsendia—Rocky Mountain Daisy.
Trachelium caeruleum—Blue Throatwort.
Tradescantia virginica—Flower-of-a-day, Spiderwort, Spider Lily, Widow's Tears. [*T. virgi-
    niana*]
Tragopogon pratensis—Goat's-beard.
Tricyrtis—Toad Lily.
Trientalis americana—Star-flower, May-star, Snake-flower. [*T. borealis*]
Trigonella coeruleum—Blue Meliot, Old-sow, Balm-of-Gilead. [*T. caerulea*]
Trillium cernuum—Nodding Wake-robin, White Benjamin, Cough-root, Ground Lily, Jews-
    harp-plant, Snake-bite.
    erectum—Birthwort, Bethroot, Red Benjamin, Bumble-bee root, Dish-cloth, Daffy-down-
    dilly, Indian Balm, Indian Shamrock, Wake-robin, Squaw-root, Nose-bleed, True-love,
    Orange-blossom, Painted Trillium.
    erythrocarpum—Painted Wood Lily, Sarah, Wild Pepper. [*T. undulatum*]
    grandiflorum—White Wake-robin, White Wood Lily, Bath-flower, White Birth-root.
Triteleia uniflora—Spring Starflower. [*Ipheion uniflora*]
Trollius asiaticus—Globe-flower.
    europaeus—Mountain Globe-flower, Troll-flower, Butter-basket, Cabbage-daisy, Lockin-
    gowan, Golden-ball.
Tropaeolum majus—Nasturtium, Indian Cress.
    peregrinum—Canary Creeper.
    speciosum—Flame Flower.
Tsuga canadensis—Hemlock, Hemlock-spruce, Tan-bark Tree, Spruce Pine.
    carolina—Carolina Spruce, Crag-tree. [*T. caroliniana*]
Tulip, old names Tulipase, Sacyrion, Dalmation, Turban-flower. [*Tulipa*]
Tulipa acuminata—Turkish Tulip.
    chrysantha—Golden Tulip.
    Clusiana—Lady Tulip.
    Didieri—Sweet Tulip.
    Gesneriana Dracontia—Parrot Tulip. [*T. Gesneriana*]
    Kaufmanniana—Water-lily Tulip.
    oculus-solis—Sun's-eye Tulip.

LATIN AND ENGLISH PLANT NAMES

Tulipa retroflexa—Lily Tulip.*
    sylvestris—Wild Tulip, Wood Tulip.
    vitellina—Orange-scented Tulip. [*T. 'Vitellina'*]
Tunica Saxifraga—Saxifrage Pink.
Tussilago Farfara—Colts-foot, Horse-, Ass-, or Bull-foot, Dove-dock, Ginger-root, Hoofs,
    Clayweed, British Tobacco.
Typha latifolia—Cat's-tail, Reed-mace, Black-a-moor, Bull-rush, Bull's-egg, Marsh-beetle,
    Pool-rush, Candle-wick, Cat-o-nine-tails, Water Torch, Asparagus-of-the-Cossacks.
Ulex europaeus—Gorse, Furse, Whin, Prickly Whin, Thorn-broom.
Ulmus americana—American Elm, White or Water Elm.
    campestris—European Elm, Horse-may. [*U. procera*]
    fulva—Slippery Elm, Moose or Red Elm, Sweet Elm. [*U. rubra*]
    montana—Wych-Elm, Scotch Elm. [*U. glabra*]
Uvularia grandiflora—Bellwort.
Vaccinium corymbosum—Common Blueberry, Giant Whortleberry, Huckleberry.
    Myrtillus—Whortleberry, Billberry, Blaeberry, Whinberry.
    Vitis-idaea—American Mountain Cranberry, Rock Cranberry, Wineberry, Cowberry,
    Cluster-berry, Flowering Box, Evergreen.
Valeriana celtica—Celtic-nard, Spikenard.
    officinalis—Cat-Valerian, Garden Heliotrope, All-heal, Setwall, Cut-heal, Herb-bennet,
    Vandle-root.
    Phu—Cretan Spikenard.
    Phu aurea—Golden Spikenard.
    pyrenaica—Capon's-tail Grass.
Valerianella—Lamb's Lettuce, Corn salad.
Veratrum album—False Hellebore, Lingwort, Sneezewort.
    viride—Indian Poke, American White Hellebore, Devil's-bit, Poor-Anna, Earth-gall, Tick-
    leweed.
Verbascum Blattaria—Moth Mullein.
    Chaixii—Nettle-leaved Mullein.
    olympicum—Greek Mullein.
    Thapsus—Torches, American Velvet Plant, Flannel-Plant, Witches' Candle, Aaron's Club,
    Hedge-taper, Feltwort, Clown's Lungwort, Candlewick, Jacob's-staff, Lady's Foxglove,
    Old-man's-flannel, Peter's Staff, Woollen.
Verbena—Vervain.
Vernonia arkansana—Ironweed. [*V. crinita*]
Veronica alpina—Alpine Speedwell.
    Beccabunga—Brooklime, Well-ink, Water-purple.
    Chamaedrys—Germander Speedwell, Angel's-eyes, Bird's Eyes, Blue-eye, God's Eye, For-
    get-me-not.
    gentianoides—Gentian-like Speedwell.
    incana—Hoary-leaf.
    longifolia subsessilis—Great Speedwell, Japanese Speedwell.
    officinalis—Fluellen.
    prostrata—Prostrate Speedwell.
    repens—Creeping Speedwell.
    rupestris (V. Teucrium prostrata)—Rock Speedwell. [*V. prostrata*]
    spicata—Spiked Speedwell.
    virginica—Virginia Speedwell, Culverwort. [*Veronicastrum virginicum*]
Vesicaria grandiflora—Bladder-pod. [*Lesquerellia grandiflora*]
Viburnum acerifolium—Maple-leaved Viburnum, Dock-mackie.
    alnifolium—Stagger-bush, Hobble-bush, Tangle-legs.
    cassinoides—Withe-rod, False Paraguay Tea.
    dentatum—Arrow-wood.
    Lantana—Wayfaring Tree, Giddy-berry.
    Lentago—Nanny-berry, Nanny-bush, Sweet-berry, Sheep-berry, Sweet Viburnum, Wild
    Raisin.
    Opulus—Guelder Rose, Cranberry Tree, High-bush Cranberry, Dog-rowan-tree.
    Opulus sterile—Snow-ball Tree, Summer Snowball.* [*V. O. 'Sterile'*]
    prunifolium—Black Haw, Boots.

LATIN AND ENGLISH PLANT NAMES

Vinca major—Large Periwinkle, Band Plant, Hundred-eyes.
minor—Periwinkle, Blue Myrtle, Blue Buttons, Sorcerer's Violet.
Viola blanda—Sweet White Violet, American Sweet Violet.
calcarata—Spurred Violet.
canadensis—Canada Violet, American Sweet Violet, June-flower, Hens.
canina—Dog Violet.
cornuta—Horned Violet, Bedding Pansy.
cucullata—Common Blue Violet, Meadow or Hooded Violet, Chicken-fighters and Roosters.
lanceolata—Lance-leaved Violet.
lutea—Yellow Violet.
odorata—Sweet English Violet.
odorata pallida—Neopolitan Violet. [*V. odorata 'Pallida Plena'*]
palustris—Marsh Violet.
pedata—Bird's-foot Violet, Crowfoot, Horse-shoe, or Wood Violet, American Pansy, Johnny-jump-up, Velvets.
pedunculata—Johnny-jump-up, Yellow Pansy.
reniformis—New Holland Violet. [*V. renifolia*]
rothamagensis—Rouen Violet. [*V. hispida*]
suavis—Sweet Violet.
tricolor—Pansy, Paunce, Fancy, Heart's-ease, Lady's-Delight, Trinity-flower, Battle-field-flower, Biddy's-eyes, Cupid's-delight, Five-faces-under-a-hood, Kiss-me-behind-the-garden-gate, Live-in-idleness, Johnny-jump-up, Kisses, Love-in-idleness, Monkey's-face, None-so-pretty, Step-mother.
villosa—Virginia, Wood Violet.
Viscaria—(*See* **Lychnis**). [*Lychnis*]
Walenbergia hederacea—Ivy-leaved Hairbell. [*Wahlenbergia hederacea*]
pumilio—Dalmation Blue-bell. [*Edraianthus pumilio*]
saxicola—New Zealand Blue-bell.
serpyllifolia—Thyme-leaved Blue-bell. [*Edraianthus serpyllifolius*]
Watsonia—Bush Lily.
Weigela (Diervilla)—Bush Honey.
Xeranthemum annuum—Immortelle, Straw-flower.
Yucca filamentosa—Silk Grass, Adam's Needle, Eve's Thread, Spanish Bayonet, Thread and Needle.
Zauschneria californica—California Fuchsia.
Zephyranthes—Flower-of-the-West-Wind, Zephyr Flower.
Zinnia—Youth-and-Old-Age.

INDEX

INDEX

INDEX